# SPIRAL GUIDES

*Trave* S0-BNQ-078

# NEW YORK

# Contents

## *the magazine* 5

## Finding Your Feet 33

## Midtown Manhattan 47

## Uptown and Central Park 77

Written by Danny Mangin

"Where to" sections by Lauren McGrath and Danny Mangin; updated by David Downing

Additional research by Richard Dworkin

Original copy edited by Julia Lisella and Janet Tabinski
Designed by Design 23
Indexed by Marie Lorimer

Edited, designed and produced by AA Publishing
© Automobile Association Developments Limited 2000, 2002
Maps © Automobile Association Developments Limited
2000, 2002

Published in the United States by AAA Publishing,
1000 AAA Drive, Heathrow, Florida 32746
Published in the United Kingdom by AA Publishing

ISBN 1-56251-674-4

Second edition

Color separation by Leo Reprographics
Printed and bound in China by Leo Paper Products

10 9 8 7 6 5 4 3 2 1

# new york

*the magazine*

# SKY HIGH
## The Race to be NUMBER 1

The race to build the world's tallest structure preoccupied U.S. developers and architects throughout the 20th century, and New Yorkers, always a competitive bunch, ranked among the fiercest contestants.

For most of the century, one Manhattan building or another reigned as the world's highest. How much did the record matter to real-estate titans? Enough that actual heights of buildings were concealed during construction and that plans were redrawn and redrawn again when developers got wind of rivals' taller designs. In the late 1920s, last-minute trickery vaulted the Chrysler Building past the Bank of the Manhattan Company's tower. This so angered one of the Manhattan Company's architects that he published an article accusing the winner of "cheating."

During the 1890s the headquarters of Joseph Pulitzer's *The World* newspaper and the Manhattan Life Building, both in Lower Manhattan, were the world's tallest. At the end of the 19th century, the 386-foot Park Row Building, near City Hall at 15 Park Row, held the honor (though at 986 feet the Eiffel Tower in Paris stretched skyward much farther). After its architect, R. H. Robertson, analyzed the effects of his building on downtown Manhattan – the Park Row

| They Were Number 1 |
| --- |
| **Park Row** (1899–1908) |
| **Singer Tower** (1908–09) |
| **Metropolitan Life** (1909–13) |
| **Woolworth Building** (1913–29) |
| **Bank of the Manhattan Company** (1929) |
| **Chrysler Building** (1929–31) |
| **Empire State Building** (1931–71) |
| **1 World Trade Center** (1971–74) |

created wind tunnels, blocked light and contributed to traffic congestion – he joined the opponents of skyscrapers and proposed laws limiting heights to a maximum of 150 feet.

New York architecture, however, was adamantly headed in the other direction. The Singer Tower, at 165 Broadway, completed in 1908 for the Singer Sewing Machine Company, topped out at 612 feet, only to be surpassed in 1909 by the 700-foot Metropolitan Life Insurance Tower (► 124). The glorious 792-foot Woolworth Building (► 153), at 233 Broadway, snatched the crown in 1913.

1 Chrysler Building – 1,048 feet
2 Bank of the Manhattan Company – 927 feet
3 Singer Tower – 612 feet
4 Metropolitan Life – 700 feet
5 Woolworth Building – 792 feet
6 Empire State Building – 1,250 feet
7 World Trade Center – 1,362 and 1,368 feet

(When the Singer Tower was taken down in 1968, it earned the dubious distinction of being the tallest building ever demolished.)

The Woolworth Building remained the world's highest for 16 years, but its next two successors – products of a nasty duel between former design partners – lasted only briefly in the top spot.

after his structure was completed in 1929, Van Alen's Chrysler Building sprouted a spire, which had been surreptitiously assembled inside it. Instead of being a few feet shorter than the 927-foot Manhattan Company skyscraper, the Chrysler soared to a whopping 1,048 feet, higher even than the Eiffel Tower. Severance's partner at

H. Craig Severance, architect of the Bank of the Manhattan Company Building, at 40 Wall Street, had once worked with William Van Alen, designer of the Chrysler Building (▶ 65), at 42nd Street and Lexington Avenue. Their rivalry, fueled by the quest of their respective developers for world architectural dominance, was not friendly. Each tried to outdo the other, scrapping one set of plans when the other's design was found to be taller.

Severance appeared to have won the battle, but he ended up losing the war. Shortly

the time, architect Yasuo Matsui, protested in the press that their structure was truly the tallest because the spire on the Chrysler Building was merely ornamentation, whereas the observation deck of the Manhattan was usable space.

The argument became superfluous in 1931 when the 1,250-foot Empire State Building (▶ 112–115), at 5th Avenue and 34th Street, topped out at 102 stories total – still taller than the Chrysler even if you only counted its 86 stories of usable floors. The Great Depression and

Construction workers take a lofty break

World War II, both of which put a damper on skyscraper construction, contributed to the Empire State's four-decade run as world leader. In the early 1970s, the twin towers of the World Trade Center, at Liberty and West streets, surpassed the Empire State, though the modernist skyscrapers, which stood 1,362 and 1,368 feet tall, never quite captured the public's imagination the way their predecessor did.

Trade Center architect Minoru Yamasaki's innovations included using the exteriors to resist the wind. Reinforcement in many older structures runs through to the core, a process that requires heavier materials. What looked like decorative latticework encasing the towers was actually steel bracing. No amount of fortification, however, could have withstood the assault that took place on September 11, 2001. Two hijacked commercial airliners crashed into the towers' upper floors, reducing both to rubble. The total energy released by the collision and subsequent collapse equaled about one twentieth of that released by the atom bomb dropped on Hiroshima in 1945.

"Building skyscapers is the nearest peace-time equivalent of war," wrote the developer William A. Starrett in his 1928 book *Skyscrapers and the Men Who Build Them*. Sadly for the World Trade Center towers, it took an act of war to destroy New York City's final two titleholders.

The view from the Empire State Building includes the skyscraper it succeeded as the world's tallest, the Chrysler Building

# THE BESTS, IFS AND MOSTS OF NEW YORK

## BEST BARS WITH A VIEW

The deco-tinged 26th-floor Top of the Tower (Beekman Hotel, 3 Mitchell Place, at 49th Street and 1st Avenue, tel: 212/355-7300), which opens at 4 daily, has splendid East River views. The bar, three blocks west of the 51st Street (6 subway) station, occasionally closes for private parties, so call ahead. For views of 5th Avenue and Central Park, join the beautiful people (daily after 5, except Sunday) at the Peninsula Hotel (2 West 55th Street, tel: 212/247-2200).

## BEST SPORTS EXPERIENCE

The New York Yankees (tel: 212/307-7171 for tickets) play baseball from April to October at Yankee Stadium. You can take a ferry (tel: 800/533-3779) from Manhattan's East Side or the 4 subway train to 161st Street.

Take time out to enjoy some greenery in Central Park

## BEST BUS RIDE

For a cheap tour of the city and a fine dose of local color, hop aboard Bus M5 along 5th Avenue in Midtown. You'll loop south to the Village and then north and west. Get off at Grant's Tomb (➤ 99).

## BEST WAY TO SIGHT A RARE BIRD

For the lowdown on sightings in Central Park and beyond, dial up the Rare Bird Alert (tel: 212/979-3070). With passages like "a greater white-fronted goose visited Hook Pond in East Hampton, then zipped away, perhaps to Connecticut," the hotline plays a bit like a society column.

## BEST WALKING TOURS

The Municipal Arts Society (tel: 212/439-1049) sponsors superb walking tours ($$ weekdays, $$$ weekends), including Central Park, 5th Avenue and Grand Central Terminal (this one, every Wednesday at 12:30, is free). The options at Big Onion Walking Tours (tel: 212/439-1090) include a delectable multiethnic eating tour ($$$) of Chinatown, Little Italy, and the Lower East Side.

## IF YOU ONLY GO TO ONE...

...**historic sight,** make it Ellis Island (➤ 143–144).
...**department store,** make it Bergdorf Goodman (➤ 74).

## IF YOU ONLY GO TO TWO...

...**museums,** make them the Guggenheim (➤ 92–93) and the Frick Collection (➤ 95).
...**skyscraper lobbies,** see the ones in the Chrysler (➤ 65) and the Woolworth (➤ 153) buildings.

...**neighborhoods,** make them the East Village (➤ 116–119) and SoHo (➤ 147–150).
...**restaurants,** make them Savoy (➤ 159) and Gramercy Tavern (➤ 129).

## MOST ROMANTIC PLACE TO WATCH THE SUN RISE

If you're an early riser, say hello to the morning sun as you walk east across the aesthetically pleasing Brooklyn Bridge (➤ 153–154).

## MOST ROMANTIC PLACE TO WATCH THE SUN SET

There's no more romantic time to soar to the top of the Empire State Building (➤ 112–115) than at sunset on a clear day, when the city views are something else.

## BEST PLACE TO CATCH UP ON THE NEWS FROM BACK HOME

**Universal News Cafe**
🔲 195 D1
✉ 484 Broome Street
☎ (212) 965-0730
carries American and international newspapers.

A weekend day game at Yankee Stadium always draws the crowds

# NEW YORKER STATE OF MIND

"*The New Yorker* will be the magazine that is not edited for the little old lady in Dubuque [Iowa]." So stated editor Harold W. Ross (1892–1951) in the prospectus for his now legendary publication. Sophistication, wit and an affectionately ironic stance toward its city have been hallmarks of *The New Yorker*, which upon its debut in 1925 quickly became an indispensable guide to New York and its psyche. It remains so to this day.

Ross had edited *Stars and Stripes* for the U.S. Army during World War I, and after the war he settled in New York. His cronies in the 1920s included Dorothy Parker and other members of what evolved into the Algonquin Round Table, creative types who met for much-publicized lunches at the Algonquin Hotel on West 44th Street.

During his 26 years editing the weekly *New Yorker*, Ross had a reputation for going on tirades and firing staffers wholesale. Even his detractors, though, acknowledged his zeal for perfection. Ross had a good nose for talent and nurtured his contributors.

Though

the magazine paid less than its competitors, writers tended to love working for *The New Yorker* because they were accorded such respect. E. B. White and James Thurber were among Ross's star performers.

One of the magazine's early triumphs was a 1936 profile by staff member Wolcott Gibbs about Henry Luce, the imperious publisher of *Time* magazine. Gibbs, a notorious wit, took a scalpel to the magazine's tortured, self-important prose of the 1930s: "Backward ran the sentences until reeled the mind." It's probably no coincidence that the type of writing Gibbs lampooned disappeared from *Time* shortly thereafter. Late in Ross's tenure *The New Yorker* devoted an entire issue to John Hersey's "Hiroshima," a powerful account of the first atom bomb dropped on a city.

William Shawn succeeded Ross as editor-in-chief in 1952. A shy man with phobias – he hated riding in elevators and subway trains – Shawn adhered to Ross's principles, mostly an obsession with clarity. Editors often sent writers lengthy queries about what

precisely they were trying to say, after which the fact-checking department submitted additional comments.

Shawn's many accomplishments included commissioning Truman Capote to write *In Cold Blood*, about the real-life murderers of a family on a Kansas ranch. Capote's "non-fiction novel" was serialized in four successive issues before the book became a best-seller. Earlier in the 1960s, James Baldwin challenged America to examine its racist ways in an essay that was later published in book form as part of *The Fire Next Time*. Interviewers often quizzed Shawn about the magazine's formula, but he insisted there wasn't one: "We run what we're interested in and assume the reader will be, too." For more than three generations, and under the leadership of subsequent editors, including Robert Gottlieb, and Tina Brown, that assumption has proved correct.

The magazine's covers and cartoons are as clever as the prose

Opposite: Eldon Dedini contributed many cartoons over the years

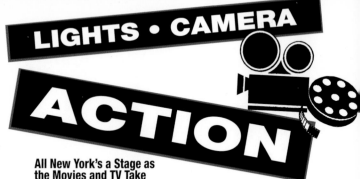

# LIGHTS • CAMERA
# ACTION

**All New York's a Stage as the Movies and TV Take (1, 2, 3...) Manhattan**

Wander through New York much and you're likely to stumble upon a movie or TV crew in action. You may even be asked to hold your stride so Woody Allen or Martin Scorsese can complete a scene from his next movie.

With more than $2.5 billion spent annually by film and television companies on 200-plus features and more than a dozen national series – not to mention commercials and documentaries – film and TV represent a major facet of New York's economy. The city in turn lends productions its glamour, grit and grandiosity. The "Seinfeld" show might

have been just as funny set in St. Louis, but then again angst and neurosis never pack quite the same punch outside the Big Apple.

The movie business here is as old as cinema itself. A plaque on Macy's flagship department store commemorates the former site of Koster and Bial's Music Hall, where the first public film screening took place in 1896. D. W. Griffith, who liked to shoot in Central Park and elsewhere around town, worked at the Biograph Co., at 11 East 14th Street, where he directed Mary Pickford's earliest pictures. The grungy Bowery provided texture for American cinema's

Robert De Niro, left, plays the psychotic Travis Bickle in "Taxi Driver," directed by Martin Scorsese, right

first feature-length gangster movie, "Regeneration" (1915). "There were enough bums and winos around to cut down on [paid] extras," recalled director Raoul Walsh in his autobiography.

As late as 1929, a quarter of all U.S. film production took place in New York. Among the notable movies from this period is the still vibrant "The Crowd" (1928), which contrasts the lives of the city's wealthy and the working class.

From the 1930s to the 1950s most visions of New York, including the invasion of King Kong in 1933, were created on Hollywood back lots. The 1949 musical "On the Town," whose opening number, "New York, New York," contains a montage of post-World War II sights, is credited with reviving interest in location shooting in the city. (Ironically, three-quarters of its sequences were shot in California.)

More of the real city shows up in "The Lost Weekend" (1945), about an alcoholic writer. Alfred Hitchcock, in

"It's a helluva town," sing Sinatra and pals in "On the Town"

Audrey Hepburn and George Peppard window shop in "Breakfast at Tiffany's"

### Famous New York Musicals

42nd Street (1933)
On the Town (1949)
The Band Wagon (1953)
Guys and Dolls (1955)
West Side Story (1961)
Saturday Night Fever (1977)
New York, New York (1977)
Fame (1980)

his wartime drama "Saboteur" (1942), used local props such as Radio City Music Hall, the Statue of Liberty and a navy ship sinking in New York Harbor (mobsters had destroyed it to encourage the U.S. government to pay for protection against the Nazis!).

By the 1970s, location shooting was more the norm, as movies such as "Cotton Comes to Harlem" (1970), "The French Connection" (1971), "Mean Streets" (1973), and "Serpico" (1973) took advantage of the city's now scruffy exteriors. Images of street crime and subway grime provided authenticity, though they probably didn't do much for the city's tourist trade.

Interrupted by a few brief lulls, the boom continued in the 1980s. Changes in city regulations during the 1990s made it easier than ever for productions to take to the streets. The citizenry occasionally grumbles about the inconvenience, but most accept the industry's integral role not only in New York's economy but also in disseminating the city's image throughout the world.

## Boroughing into the City's Psyche

### The Bronx
Robert De Niro directed and starred in "A Bronx Tale" (1993), about an Italian-American kid in the 1960s. Two police officers attempt to clean up the crime-ridden South Bronx in "Fort Apache, the Bronx" (1981). A young black Puerto Rican woman tries to make it as a model in "I Like It Like That" (1994). Four guys from a nowhere Bronx neighborhood get into no end of comedic scrapes during the one night portrayed in "Hangin' with the Homeboys" (1991).

### Brooklyn
A *New York* magazine article inspired the quintessential disco movie, "Saturday Night Fever" (1977), whose Brooklyn-based main character lives to dance. The title

Movie and TV producers have made stars out of many a city block

character of "Sophie's Choice" (1982), a survivor of Auschwitz, settles in post–World War II Brooklyn. The borough looks fabulous in "Moonstruck" (1987), in which Cher plays a widow who falls in love with the brother of her fiancé. To see more of Brooklyn, check out the excursion (► 164–167).

## Manhattan

Joan Micklin Silver's "Hester Street" (1975), a tale of Jewish immigrants living on the Lower East Side, was actually shot in Greenwich Village because the real-life street of the title had become too modern. Manhattan has never looked more gorgeous than it does in "Breakfast at Tiffany's" (1961), starring Audrey Hepburn. In "Midnight Cowboy" (1969), a dim-witted hustler discovers that the borough is tougher to conquer than he'd thought. As the title of "The Muppets Take Manhattan" (1984) indicates, Miss Piggy and friends find it less intimidating.

## Queens/Staten Island

Stars from Gloria Swanson in the 1920s to Bill Cosby in the 1980s and 1990s have shot movies and TV shows at the Kaufman–Astoria Studios in Queens. Adjacent to the studios is the American Museum of the Moving Image (35th Avenue and 36th Street, Astoria, tel: 718/784-4520; R subway train to Steinway Street), which displays a century's worth of props, costumes, photographs and equipment from cinema and TV. Many mobster types have called Staten Island home. Scenes from movies like "The Godfather Part 2" (1974), "Goodfellas" (1990) and "Donnie Brasco" (1997) were shot here. Comedian Rodney Dangerfield's "Easy Money" (1983) mildly satirizes life in the borough.

"Friends": amusing, if not realistic, slice of city life

## Nice Fantasy

"Friends," "Seinfeld," "Will and Grace," "NYPD Blue," and "Law & Order" are among the popular television shows set in New York. Viewers probably assume New Yorkers spend their days either nattering in coffee shops about nothing or committing violent crimes that are nearly always solved. Directors Woody Allen ("Manhattan," "Broadway Danny Rose," "Crimes and Misdemeanors"), Spike Lee ("She's Gotta Have It," "Do the Right Thing," "Summer of Sam") and Martin Scorsese ("Mean Streets," "Taxi Driver," "After Hours," "Goodfellas," "The Age of Innocence," "Bringing Out the Dead") have chronicled the city in multiple movies.

**New Yorkers can be cantankerous, but even today's surliest residents are pussycats compared to their forebears, who would take to the streets en masse to thwart injustice or avenge a mere insult.**

## NEW YORK

## Civil (and uncivil) Disturbances

### Can You Dig It?

Except on rare occasions, autopsies were prohibited during the 18th century. The news that New York Hospital students were digging up fresh graves and swiping cadavers prompted the Doctors' Riot of 1788. The mob was half right: To learn about the human body, students weren't digging – they were buying corpses from "resurrectionists." Physicians, who were aware of their students' practice, fled town until things quieted down.

### Shakespeare Worth Fighting For

Political agitators exploited class tensions on May 10, 1849, when America's premier Shakespearean actor, Edwin Forrest, and his British counterpart, William Macready, were performing in rival productions of *Macbeth*. New York's upper crust attended Macready's show at the Astor Place Opera House, where the Starbucks in Astor Place now stands. Told that the Brit had denigrated Forrest's acting abilities (there's no proof Macready actually did), a mob of 10,000 people tried to

break up his show. Thirty-one deaths were attributed to the Astor Place Riot.

### Officer, You're Under Arrest

During the Police Riots of June 16, 1857, two police forces – one state-sponsored and the other backed by a corrupt city administration – duked it out in front of City Hall for the right to bring law and order to New York. The squabbling squads skirmished for months – who had time to catch crooks? – before the state-backed set prevailed.

### Working-Class Antiheroes

The inequity of military conscription gave rise to the Civil War Draft Riots. For $300, a man could get out of service, leaving the poor more likely to fight and die (financier J. P. Morgan was among those who bought their way out of the war). The working class rebelled on July 13, 1863, the first of four days of violence. At least 105 of the 120 killed were African-Americans attacked by recent Irish immigrants unwill-

'S A RIOT

ing to fight for the emancipation of slaves in the South.

## Butchers Meat Their Match

When the price of kosher beef jumped 50 percent in 1902, previously law-abiding Jewish women went on the rampage, toppling pushcarts and smashing butcher-shop windows. On May 15, the most active day of the Kosher Beef Riots, 20,000 people participated. The mayhem continued for another month before cooler heads negotiated a price rollback.

## Green Was the Color of Their True Love's Eyes

Anarchist Abbie Hoffman's "zap" aimed at the New York Stock Exchange caused a major, though not violent, disturbance in the 1960s. To show Wall Streeters' true colors – actually one color, the seductive green of the American dollar – he and two dozen antiwar hippies snuck into the visitors gallery and hurled bills onto the trading floor, inciting a mad scramble for the cash.

## Harassment's a Drag

The modern gay-liberation movement dates from the Stonewall Rebellion, a weekend of rioting in late June 1969. At the time it was illegal to sell a drink to a homosexual or to wear the clothing of the opposite sex, and many drag queens were rounded up during a vice-squad raid at the Stonewall Inn, then at 51–53 Christopher Street (its successor now occupies 53 Christopher only). Instead of going quietly into the police wagons, the queens and other patrons fought back, sending the police into a temporary retreat. Many gays and lesbians were arrested, and the incident inspired future acts of resistance.

Abbie Hoffman threw money at the Wall Street problem

# A CENTURY IN
# TIMES
# SQUARE

A Broadway critic of the 1930s derided Times Square (▶ 63–64) as "a screeching amusement park without a roller coaster," a reference to the carnival-like diversions that opened when theater business dropped off during the Great Depression. The metaphor was apt in more ways than one, for New York's 24-hour playground has had its share of ups and downs during the past century.

Glamour was the order of the day in the 1910s and 1920s,

with vaudeville at its peak and the legitimate theater enjoying a golden age. In the 1927–28 season, 264 plays were produced. Colorful street life and white (and later neon) lights transformed Times Square into a dazzling entertainment center.

It hadn't always been that way, and it hadn't always been Times Square. The triangle formed by Broadway, 42nd Street and 7th Avenue was known as Longacre Square in the 19th century. In the 1880s, William K. Vanderbilt opened the American Horse Exchange Ltd., his era's version of Hertz Rent-a-Car, on Broadway a few blocks north of Longacre. Stables and carriage factories occupied much of the nearby land.

The triangle's current label came into use in 1904 when *The New York Times*, which had built a skyscraper (the shell of it is 1 Times Square) covering much of the wedge, requested that the city rename Longacre Square and christen the new subway station in honor of the newspaper.

Theatrical impresarios had already set up shop. Oscar Hammerstein I (grandfather of the famous songwriter) had built a huge theater on Broadway at 44th Street in 1895. Among the many that followed was the New Amsterdam Theatre, an art nouveau confection on 42nd Street, built in 1903. (Disney's "The Lion King" musical is presently settled in for a long run here.) By 1910, classy restaurants, cafés and cocktail lounges extended the merriment before and after performances.

With alcohol illegal during Prohibition (1920–33), gangster-run speakeasies supplied the nightlife with a risqué edge. The balance tipped more toward the risqué during the

Revelers fill Times Square to ring in 1937

pickpockets and swindlers worked the streets with near impunity. Some New Yorkers lament the passing of this licentious stage, which indeed had a certain decadent appeal.

That folks wax nostalgic over the grimy past is in part a tribute to the total makeover Times Square received in the 1990s, after Disney began refurbishing the New Amsterdam Theatre and a flood of investment followed. But period pieces like Paul Morrissey's 1982 movie "Forty Deuce" – whose title comes from one of 42nd Street's nicknames – tell the real story: The area had devolved into a sleazy, dangerous place.

Throughout its ups and downs, Times Square has been about entertainment. And this will continue, as E-Walk, the new virtual-reality arcade at 42nd Street and 8th Avenue, makes clear. Technologically, the complex's attractions may be light-years removed from those of the 1930s, but the effect – an amusement park without a roller coaster – remains the same.

*Sunset signs on the 24-hour playground that is Times Square*

Depression, when Billy Minsky introduced burlesque at the Republic Theatre (now the New Victory) on 42nd Street. "Naughty, bawdy, gaudy, sporty 42nd Street" went a line in the title number of the 1933 film musical "42nd Street." In addition to depicting the street's jollier aspects, the film featured gunshots, an attempted rape and a stabbing.

After a brief revival during World War II and immediately after it, Times Square declined into slime and crime. Porno houses proliferated and

## Notable Broadway Premieres

Angels in America – *Walter Kerr*
Born Yesterday – *Lyceum*
A Chorus Line – *Shubert*
Chicago – *Richard Rodgers (formerly "46th Street")*
Falsettos – *John Golden*
Porgy and Bess – *Neil Simon (formerly "Alvin")*
South Pacific – *Majestic*
Sweet Charity – *Palace*
Will Success Spoil Rock Hunter? – *Belasco*
Ziegfeld Follies – *New Amsterdam*

# Swell Digs
## and
# Crash Pads

**FAMOUS NEW YORK CITY ADDRESSES**

## EAST VILLAGE

### Emma Goldman
✉ **208 East 13th Street at 3rd Avenue**
🚇 **14th Street/Union Square (L, N, Q, R, W, 4, 5, 6)**

The feminist, anarchist and political agitator (1869–1940) lived in this tenement (its address was 210 back then) from 1903 to 1913. She began publishing the magazine *Mother Earth*, which rallied the anarchist troops, from her apartment here.

### Charlie Parker
✉ **151 Avenue B at East 10th Street**
🚇 **Astor Place (6)**

The alto saxophonist and bebop legend lived for five years in the basement of this brownstone in the early 1950s. The section of Avenue B between 7th and 10th streets bears the honorary name Charlie Parker Place.

### Leon Trotsky/W. H. Auden
✉ **77 St. Mark's Place at 1st Avenue**
🚇 **Astor Place (6)**

The English-born poet lived here on the second floor between 1953 and 1972. Earlier, in 1917, Trotsky published a socialist newspaper out of this building. Trotsky, who described New York as "the fullest expression of our modern age," actually lived in the Bronx. His local newspaper duly reported in 1917 that the "Bronx boy" was returning to Russia to join the Bolshevik Revolution.

## GREENWICH VILLAGE

### Jimi Hendrix
✉ **52 West 8th Street at 6th Avenue**
🚇 **West 4th Street (A, C, E, F)**
The guitar virtuoso established the still-extant Electric Lady Studios in the late 1960s. The site had been a rock venue (the Generation Club) and long before that a big-band dance joint. In August 1970 Hendrix left the studio's opening bash to catch a flight to England, where he died the next month. Hours of music he'd recorded before the official opening were later released on several albums.

## FLATIRON DISTRICT

### Edith Wharton
✉ **14 West 23rd Street west of Broadway**
🚇 **23rd Street (N, R)**
The action in several of Wharton's novels, including *The Age of Innocence*, takes place near the town house (long since converted into retail space) where she was born. Her neighborhood was the center of New York society in the middle to late 19th century.

### Stanford White
✉ **22 West 24th Street west of Broadway**
🚇 **23rd Street (N, R)**
Society architect Stanford White of the firm McKim, Mead and White, who designed many important New York buildings, was a notorious playboy. He seduced the underage showgirl Evelyn Nesbit at his apartment on the top two floors of this drab building. Nesbit later married Harry K. Thaw, who after she told him what had happened, murdered White in 1906.

## MIDTOWN

### Truman Capote
✉ **870 U. N. Plaza (1st Avenue north of 48th Street)**
🚇 **51st Street (6)**
The author of *Breakfast at Tiffany's* loved the East River views from his 22nd-floor apartment, especially when "the green lights on the bridges look like strings of emeralds."

EMMA GOLDMAN

NOEL COWARD

GRETA GARBO

JAMES DEAN

BARBRA STREISAND

### Greta Garbo/Noel Coward
✉ **450 East 52nd Street east of 1st Avenue**
🚇 **51st Street (6)**
"I'm lucky to be in my building. They don't like actresses there," said the great movie star about the Campanile, a 1930 brick structure that overlooks FDR Drive and the East River. Noel Coward was also a resident here.

## UPPER WEST SIDE

### James Dean
✉ **19 West 68th Street near Columbus Avenue**
🚇 **66th Street (1, 2)**
The 1950s icon lived in a cozy top-floor apartment strewn with records and books (like *Stanislavsky Directs*, about method acting) before leaving New York in 1954 to make "East of Eden."

## UPPER EAST SIDE

### Jacqueline Kennedy Onassis
✉ **1040 5th Avenue at East 85th Street**
🚇 **86th Street (6)**
The former First Lady and reclusive book editor lived her last years in a 14-room apartment overlooking Central Park. After she died, oil billionaire David Koch bought the place and had it decorated twice before he and his wife deemed it suitable to live in.

### The Marx Brothers
✉ **179 East 93rd Street east of Lexington Street**
🚇 **96th Street (6)**
The eccentric comedy team spent much of their boyhood in this tenement.

### Barbra Streisand
✉ **1153–1157 3rd Avenue at East 67th Street**
🚇 **68th Street (6)**
The diva's first Manhattan apartment had a view of a brick wall, and the smell of fish from the seafood restaurant below permeated the air. But "we were happy," said her first husband, Elliott Gould, who lived with her there.

### Andy Warhol
✉ **57 East 66th Street east of Madison Avenue**
🚇 **68th Street (6)**
From 1972 until his death in 1987, the pop artist and provocateur lived in this classic redbrick town house. Warhol turned out to be quite the pack rat – the entire place was jammed with things he'd collected.

For other famous addresses, see the listings for the **Hotel Chelsea** (► 126–127), the **Plaza Hotel** (► 67), the **Frick Collection** (► 95), the **Dakota Apartments** (► 98) and the **Morgan Library** (► 124).

TRUMAN CAPOTE

ANDY WARHOL

THE MARX BROS

# The **Backstory**

## The Tales Behind Famous People, Places and Events

### Flat Hills

By most accounts Manhattan means "island of the hills" in the Algonquin Indian language, so why's the place so flat? Hills were leveled, brooks and creeks drained, and valleys filled in during the 1800s for reasons that included making crosstown passage easier. Vestiges of the old contours can still be found in northern Central Park (➤ 82–86) and near The Cloisters (➤ 100).

### Banking on Burr

While serving as Vice President, Aaron Burr (1756–1836) killed political rival Alexander Hamilton (1755–1804) in a famous duel that took place in New Jersey (dueling had been outlawed in New York). One of Burr's less publicized endeavors lives on as the ubiquitous Chase Manhattan Bank. In a 1799 attempt to circumvent the banking monopoly of a bank Hamilton had founded, Burr started a water company and then used loopholes in its charter to divert capital to start the Bank of the Manhattan Company, which later merged with Chase.

### A Metropolitan Soap Opera

All Alva Smith Vanderbilt (1856–1933) wanted was a box at the Academy of Music opera house, a sign in her day that one had, socially speaking, arrived. Married to an heir to the Vanderbilt railroad fortune, she perceived herself more than qualified, but she and the wife of financier J. P. Morgan ran up against New York's social arbiter of the late 1800s, Caroline Webster Schermerhorn Astor (1830–1908). Mrs. Astor thought the Vanderbilts and Morgans were nouveau-riche vulgarians and told them the Academy hadn't a box to spare. Thus spurned, the parvenus built their own more fabulous Metropolitan Opera House, which opened in 1883 at 39th and Broadway. Within a few

His duel with Hamilton wasn't Burr's only nefarious act

years, the Academy's opera company had stopped performing and the Astors and their ilk were scrambling to buy boxes at the Met. There were plenty to spare – so many that after a few years a whole floor of boxes had to be removed because New York hadn't enough Verdi-loving millionaires. The Met moved in 1966 to Lincoln Center (▶ 105).

## Waldorf Hysteria
William Waldorf Astor (1848–1919) and his wife wanted to breathe some new life into New York society, but his Aunt Lina, the aforementioned Caroline Astor, consistently stymied them. Aunt

and nephew lived on adjoining lots on 5th Avenue at 33rd Street. To spite Mrs. Astor, he tore down his mansion and put up the Waldorf Hotel. In response, she allowed her son, John Jacob Astor IV, to rip down her mansion and have the Waldorf's (and later the Plaza Hotel's) architect, Henry J. Hardenbergh, design the Astoria Hotel. When the family feud died down, a hyphen and a connecting hallway transformed the place into the Waldorf-Astoria. The hotel was demolished in 1929 to make way for the Empire State Building. During the 1890s, William Waldorf Astor forsook America for England, where he later became the First Viscount Astor. John Jacob Astor IV perished on the *Titanic* in 1912. The current Waldorf-Astoria opened on Park Avenue at 49th Street in 1931.

New York was extensively developed by the late eighteenth century

## Taxi! Taxi!

With about 12,000 taxis operating in New York, you shouldn't have much trouble finding one.

## Frick Finagles

Stroll through the Frick Collection (▶ 95) on 5th Avenue, and you can't help but admire the man who shrewdly assembled the artworks and donated his mansion to house them. Truth be told, though, the philanthropy of industrialist Henry Clay Frick (1849–1919) was a late-in-life attempt to soften his reputation. The ruthless businessman's rabidly antiunion behavior included arranging, at the behest of Andrew Carnegie, his majority partner in Carnegie Steel, for the bloody putdown of the Pennsylvania's Homestead steelworkers' strike of 1892. New York's *The World* newspaper alleged that Lower East Side resident and anarchist Emma Goldman (▶ 23) masterminded a botched assassination attempt on Frick in retaliation, for which her lover, Alexander Berkman, served 14 years in prison.

## Alley Cats

Music aficionados often ask the way to Tin Pan Alley, but it's more a state of mind than an actual place. The name is usually associated with the stretch of 28th Street between Broadway and 6th Avenue where many songwriters, music publishers and arrangers had offices. It later came

Cole Porter was one of Tin Pan Alley's most sophisticated composers

Federal agents successfully raided many a bar, but not '21'

to refer to the dominant style of American popular music between 1890 and 1950. "Tin Pan Alley" came from a songwriter's observation that the cacophony of all those folks hawking their tunes sounded like the banging of tin pans. The culprits included the composers Lorenz Hart, Dorothy Fields, George and Ira Gershwin, Cole Porter, Irving Berlin and Johnny Mercer. Later the music-publishing scene shifted north of Times Square, to the Brill Building (1619 Broadway) and elsewhere.

## '21' Club Triumphs Over Law and Rockefeller

Most New Yorkers know that the famous '21' Club at 21 West 52nd Street was a speakeasy during Prohibition (1920–33), when the sale of alcohol was illegal. The bar's owners, Charles Berns and Jack Kriendler, eluded federal agents, partly because

the bartenders could activate a system that swept bottles and glasses from the bar and shelves and dumped them into the sewer. But Berns and Kriendler also triumphed over others who tried to put them out of business. John D. Rockefeller Jr., a tee-totaling Prohibition supporter who didn't appreciate all the illicit booze houses near his 54th Street mansion, intended that Rockefeller Plaza – the promenade in Rockefeller Center (► 56–59) between 47th and 50th streets – should extend to the Museum of Modern Art (► 60) at 53rd Street. When Berns and Kriendler refused to sell their property, he had to abandon his dream. Don't feel too sorry for John D., though. Instead, he built a skyscraper across 50th Street from the end of Rockefeller Plaza and collected a fortune in rent.

# VINTAGE

New York's 19th- and early 20th-century European immigrants brought their favorite recipes with them, adding zest and variety to the city's previously staid dining scene. Modern tastes and trendy haute cuisine have rendered some of these dishes – as well as some homegrown delicacies – mere memories, but at the delis, restaurants and shops listed below, you can still sample the flavors that tickled the citizenry's palates for decades.

## Chopped Liver at Barney Greengrass

- 198 B5
- 541 Amsterdam Avenue north of West 86th Street
- (212) 724-4707
- 86th Street (1, 2)

For a zesty, chunk-filled version of this quintessential New York nosh, head for this Upper West Side deli.

## Bagels from H&H Bagels

- 198 B4
- 2239 Broadway at West 80th Street
- (212) 595-8003
- 86th Street (1, 2)

When locals aren't squabbling about who chops the best liver, they often debate bagels. H&H wins many of the arguments.

## Borscht at Veselka

- 195 E3
- 144 2nd Avenue at East 9th Street
- (212) 228-9682
- Astor Place (6)

The borscht can't be beat (pardon that pun) at this Ukrainian restaurant in the East Village that's hopping all day, every day.

## Pizza at John's Pizzeria

- 194 B2
- 278 Bleecker Street east of 7th Avenue South
- (212) 243-1680
- West 4th Street (A, C, E, F)

You just may bite into the thin-crusted slice of your life at this Greenwich Village favorite, where you'll find the pies are still baked in brick ovens.

## Blintzes at Ratner's

- 195, off F1
- 138 Delancey Street near Suffolk Street
- (212) 677-5588
- Delancey Street (F)

The best place in town for that blintz blitz, Ratner's serves the pancakelike treats filled with cheese, fruit and a huge variety of other ingredients.

## Super Sours at Gus's Pickles

- 193 E5
- 35 Essex Street near Hester Street
- (212) 254-4477
- Delancey Street (F)

The super sours here are one pickle you'll like getting into. Tomatoes, onions, peppers – you name it, Gus's pickles it.

## Kosher Wine at Schapiro Wine Co.

- 195 F1
- 126 Rivington Street near Essex Street
- (212) 674-4404
- Delancey Street (F)

An early motto of this century-old family winery (the only winery in Manhattan) says it all: "Wine so thick you can almost cut it with a knife."

Opposite:
Bagels – a vintage flavor that remains a hit

## Pastrami on Rye at Katz's Delicatessen

✚ 195 F2
✉ 205 East Houston Street at Ludlow Street
☎ (212) 254-2246
Ⓜ Delancey Street (F)

Meg Ryan munched on a turkey sandwich here during the infamous scene in "When Harry Met Sally" in which she fakes orgasm, but New Yorkers in the know come here for the hand-sliced pastrami on rye bread. Past customers have included everyone from Harry Houdini to Jimmy Carter.

## Hot Dogs at F&B

✚ 194 B5
✉ 269 West 23rd Street at 8th Avenue
☎ (646) 486-4441
Ⓜ 23rd Street (C, E, 1, 2)

The humble hot dog was invented by a New Yorker a century ago, but F&B, a self-proclaimed purveyor of "great European street food," takes an international approach to the perennial favorite with wieners, bratwurst, and the Great Dane (with remoulade and Danish mustard). You can still go the traditional route, though, and get a chili dog or just a plain frankfurter with mustard.

## Cannoli at Veniero's

✚ 195 F3
✉ 342 East 11th Street at 1st Avenue
☎ (212) 674-7264
Ⓜ Astor Place (6)

The rush from a Veniero's cannoli – an éclairlike pastry made of lightly fried dough wrapped around a filling of ricotta cheese and sugar – may make you giddy as you savor its sweet perfection.

## Egg Cream at Gem Spa

✚ 195 E3
✉ 131 2nd Avenue at East 10th Street
☎ (212) 529-1146
Ⓜ Astor Place (6)

For a drink that's as sweet as a candy bar but as light as a soda, try one of this corner store's egg creams, made with half-frozen ice milk, Fox's U-Bet Chocolate Syrup and a spritzing of seltzer.

## Chocolate Malted at Lexington Candy Shop

✚ 199 F4
✉ 1226 Lexington Avenue at 83rd Street
☎ (212) 288-0057
Ⓜ 86th Street (4, 5, 6)

The last time anyone tweaked the decor at this soda fountain was 1948; the recipe for the chocolate malteds – chocolate syrup, chocolate ice cream, milk and malted-milk powder – hasn't changed since then either.

Hot dogs are a favorite New York snack

# Finding Your Feet

# First Two Hours

Kennedy (code JFK), La Guardia (LGA) and Newark (EWR) airports serve
New York City and all three have a variety of transportation alternatives.

**Ground Transportation Fees** (including tolls, if any, but excluding tip)
$ = under $12     $$ = $12–20     $$$ = $20–30     $$$$ = over $30

■ Public transportation from the airports costs less than $5.

## Best Bets for Airport Transfers

At the Ground Transportation Center booths near baggage claim, you can
make transportation reservations and get directions to public transit. Phone
(800) 247-7433 for transit and driving information.

■ **Taxis** are the foolproof method for getting from all three airports to Midtown
Manhattan. The rate is for the ride, making a taxi for two only marginally
more expensive than everything but public transportation.

■ **Shared-ride van services** load up with passengers heading for hotels,
residences and places of business in more or less the same part of town. The
vans serve Manhattan between Battery Park and 125th Street (96th Street
from Newark). Make reservations at the Ground Transportation Center.

■ **Public transportation** is a reasonably good option if you're on a budget and
traveling light (there are no luggage racks on public conveyances).

### John F. Kennedy International Airport
☎ (718) 244-4444
New York's main gateway is about a 40-minute drive from Midtown.

■ **Taxis** ($$$$) cost a flat fee, not including toll or tip. Taxis back to JFK are on
the meter. Avoid cabs that aren't yellow; drivers of private limousines who
solicit your business are breaking the law and aren't always trustworthy.

■ **Gray Line Air Shuttle** (6 am to 11 pm; tel: 212/315-3006 or 800/451-
0455) and **SuperShuttle Manhattan** (24 hours; tel: 212/258-3826) provide
shared-ride van service ($$).

■ **New York Airport Service** (tel: 212/875-8200) makes stops ($$) at
Pennsylvania (Penn) Station, the Port Authority Bus Terminal, Grand Central
Terminal and some Midtown hotels.

■ The **A subway train** ($) takes about 90 minutes to get to Midtown. Free
blue and yellow buses to the Howard Beach station stop on the arrivals
level.

■ If you're **driving**, head north on the Van Wyck Expressway (Interstate 678)
and west on the Long Island Expressway (I-495) to the Queens–Midtown
Tunnel.

### La Guardia Airport
☎ (718) 533-3400
La Guardia is about a 30-minute drive from Midtown.

- **Taxis** ($$$) charge regular metered rates from La Guardia.

- **Gray Line Air Shuttle** (6 am to 11 pm; tel: 212/315-3006 or 800/451-0455) and **SuperShuttle Manhattan** (24 hours; tel: 212/258-3826) provide shared-ride van service ($$).

- **New York Airport Service** (tel: 212/875-8200) makes stops ($) at Pennsylvania (Penn) Station, the Port Authority Bus Terminal, Grand Central Terminal and some Midtown hotels.

- **Buses** M60 and Q48 connect with various subways. The Q48 and the privately operated Q33 connect with the 7 subway train, which stops at Grand Central Terminal and Times Square ($).

- To **drive** from La Guardia, take Grand Central Parkway west. Follow signs to the Triborough Bridge. Take the Manhattan exit and follow signs to FDR Drive.

## Newark International Airport
☎ (973) 961-6000
The Newark, New Jersey, airport is a 25-minute drive from Midtown.

- **Taxis** ($$$$) charge more for trips to the Upper East Side than to Midtown.

- **Gray Line Air Shuttle** (6 am to 11 pm; tel: 212/315-3006 or 800/451-0455) and **SuperShuttle Manhattan** (24 hours; tel: 212/258-3826) provide shared-ride van service ($$).

- **Olympia Trails Airport Express Bus** (tel: 212/964-6233) serves Newark ($) and stops at Pennsylvania (Penn) Station, the Port Authority, and Grand Central Terminal.

- The public-transit **Airlink Bus 302** ($) links the airport with Newark's Pennsylvania Station, where you can catch the PATH commuter train ($) to New York.

- To **drive** from Newark, take Interstate 95 north and Route 495 east to the Lincoln Tunnel.

## Train and Bus Stations
Manhattan's long-distance train and bus terminals are on the West Side.

### Pennsylvania Station ✚ 196 B2
7th Avenue between 31st and 33rd streets, tel: (212) 630-6400
Amtrak, Long Island Railroad and New Jersey Transit trains stop at Penn Station, where you can connect with the subway or catch a taxi.

### Port Authority Bus Terminal ✚ 196 A3
8th Avenue between 40th and 42nd streets, tel: (212) 564-8484
Local buses from New Jersey and intercity buses from the United States and Canada serve the terminal, which is on several major subway lines.

### Grand Central Terminal ✚ 197 D3
**Metro North** (tel: 212/532-4900) commuter trains from Connecticut and suburban New York serve Grand Central, on the East Side.

## Orienting Yourself

Nearly all of New York's major attractions are within 4 miles of Midtown Manhattan.

### City Center Tourist Offices

Tourist offices can help with all types of information from tourist attraction opening hours to shopping advice.

**Times Square Visitor Center**
✚ 196 B4
✉ 1560 Broadway between 46th and 47th streets
☎ (212) 869-1890
🕐 Daily 8–8

**NYC & Company**
✚ 196 B5
✉ 810 7th Avenue between 52nd and 53rd streets
☎ (212) 484-1200
🕐 Mon–Fri 8:30–6; Sat–Sun 9–5

### Major Manhattan Neighborhoods

The names and boundaries of Manhattan neighborhoods are subject to interpretation, but the following is a rough outline of some of the major ones.

■ **Downtown** and **Uptown** refer to parts of town as well as to the direction in which you're traveling. You take a downtown subway train, for example, to get from the Upper East Side to Midtown, even though you never pass through Downtown (Lower Manhattan).

■ **Lower Manhattan** refers to the part of the island below Houston Street: this covers the areas of Chinatown, Little Italy, SoHo, TriBeCa, the Financial District, Civic Center, South Street Seaport and the Lower East Side.

■ **Greenwich Village** is north of Houston Street on the West Side to 14th Street.

■ The **East Village** is east of 4th Avenue above Houston Street to 14th Street.

■ **Midtown** refers to both sides of Manhattan between 42nd and 59th streets.

■ The **Upper West Side** encompasses the area west of Central Park to about 100th Street.

■ **Central Park** is bordered by 59th Street, Central Park West, 110th Street and 5th Avenue.

■ The **Upper East Side** is east of Central Park between 59th Street and about 100th Street.

---

## Admission Charges

The cost of admission for museums and places of interest mentioned in the text is indicated by the following:

**Inexpensive** under $7     **Moderate** $7–13     **Expensive** over $13

# Getting Around

## The Subway

The easiest way to get around Manhattan is by subway. It's reasonably safe, but you need to be sensible – don't wear flashy jewelry, keep valuables hidden, be aware of those around you. If you have to use the subway at night, travel in the center car where the conductor sits.

**Six Steps to Subway Success...**

Unless you're heading off the beaten path, you can make do riding a few lines whose routes are easy to figure out. Here's the short version:

- **Trains 1, 2, 3, A and C** head up and down Manhattan's west side. The 1, 2 and C are "locals" (stopping at all stations); the 3 and A trains provide express service (with stops only at major stations).

- **Trains 4, 5 and 6** head up and down the east side. The 6 is a local; the 4 and 5 make express stops.

- **Trains F, N, Q, R and W** travel between the east and west sides of Midtown and Downtown. The **E** train follows much the same route but terminates at Canal Street. (Note that **Q** and **W** trains, which run express, cease after 2004.)

- You use a **MetroCard** to enter the subway. You can purchase MetroCards at subway stations and at many hotels and shops. The fare includes free transfers to city buses within 2 hours. To use your MetroCard to enter the subway, swipe the MetroCard (fast, but not too fast) through the raised slot in the turnstile.

- If you aim to make several journeys during your stay in the city, you'll save money if you buy a weekly **MetroCard**, available at all stations and from machines, which allows unlimited rides. The one-day **Fun Pass** is sold at hotels and shops and in machines at many stations.

## Bus

Buses are helpful for crosstown travel but slower than the subway. The reconstruction of Lower Manhattan may cause route changes.

- **Crosstown** buses operate between the East and West sides on Houston, 14th, 23rd, 34th, 42nd, 57th, 66th, 72nd, 86th and 96th streets.

- Buses head **north** up 1st, 3rd, Madison, 6th and 8th avenues.

- Buses head **south** down Broadway and 2nd, Lexington, 5th, 7th and 9th avenues.

## Taxis

Contrary to legend, most Manhattan cabbies know the borough well.

- **To catch a cab** – you can't miss 'em, they're bright and yellow – stand just off the curb and extend your arm when you see one. Only during the weekday morning (7–9) and evening (5–8) rush hours is there a shortage of taxis.

- **On or off duty?** When only the four characters in the panel on a cab's roof are lit, the driver is seeking a rider. If the entire panel is lit, the driver is off duty. When the driver already has a rider the light in the panel will be off.

- Between 8 pm and 6 am taxi rides cost an additional 50 cents (shown on the "**Extras**" part of the meter).

## Walking

The addresses on the south and west sides of streets usually have even numbers; the addresses on the north and east sides usually have odd numbers. This is a general rule which doesn't always work south of Houston Street, but mostly does north of it.

- Numbered and named **avenues** run north–south through Manhattan. The numbered **streets** run east–west. Low numbered streets are downtown and high numbered streets are uptown. Above Washington Square Park, 5th Avenue separates the East Side from the West Side.

- Nearly everyone **jaywalks** in New York (the fine is $50, but it's rare that anyone is charged), but you always need to watch oncoming traffic. Never blindly follow someone into a crosswalk.

## Driving

The basic advice is don't drive.

- Traffic is often **gridlocked**, especially on crosstown routes; parking is tight in most neighborhoods below 70th Street; and garages are expensive ($16 or more for three hours in Midtown).

- If you do drive, **avoid commuting hours** in the morning and evening. New York drivers tend to be impatient – expect horns to blare if you don't move the second the light turns green.

- Unless otherwise indicated, the speed limit is **30mph**.

- **Seatbelts** must be worn at all times, and small children must be in child-safety seats.

## Car Services

Car services provide an alternative to driving or taking public transportation or taxis.

- You can hire a town car or limousine by the hour. The **rates** start at $25 per hour, with a 2-hour minimum. You can also arrange for transportation for a specific trip; the rate from a restaurant in East Village to your Midtown hotel, for example, would be about $13. Two companies that provide this type of service are **Allstate Car and Limousine Service** (tel: 212/741-7440) and **Carmel Car Service** (tel: 212/666-6666).

- The front desk staff or the **concierge** at your hotel can advise you about the car services available.

# Accommodations

In New York City, the sky's the limit for accommodations. Along with some of the world's finest, most well-established hotels, there is a new breed of sleek designer hot spots.

Some more moderately priced places are also fine alternatives. Overall, rates are quite high, as is the occupancy rate. Big price tags do usually mean pampering, so staying at a **top hotel** will surely be a treat. Lower-end establishments will be merely functional, though with pleasant touches if you're careful to choose the best. For a "small town in a big city" feeling, you could try a **small inn** or a **bed-and-breakfast**. Some of the latter come with hosts, for a truly personal (and more economical) experience, or you can get an **unhosted apartment** of your own and see what it feels like to live as a New Yorker. After you've considered which price level and ambience you prefer, you need to choose a **location**. Thanks to good public transportation, your location will not impede any pursuits, so consider instead which part of town you might like at your doorstep. **Midtown** is hotel central, but by choosing elsewhere you may become familiar with a wonderful neighborhood you might have missed otherwise.

## Booking Accommodations

Reserve your hotel room well before arriving, or even before purchasing airline tickets, because the top and even not-so-top places are often in great demand. You never know when a large convention might be in town. When reserving, always ask about special seasonal rates or promotions, or any corporate, weekend, senior-citizen or family discounts.

**For more information here are a few places to contact:**

■ AAA, Automobile Club of New York
   ✉ 1881 Broadway, New York, NY 10023
   ☎ (212) 757-2000
   Provides members with the New York TourBook®.

■ Hotel Association of New York City
   ✉ 437 Madison Avenue, New York, NY 10022
   ☎ (212) 754-6700; www.hanyc.org
   Can send you a list of participating hotels.

■ NYC & Company
   ✉ 810 7th Avenue, New York, NY 10019
   ☎ (800) NYC-VISIT or (212/397-8222); www.nycvisit.com
   Publishes a general booklet with guidelines for reserving accommodations.

## List of Places to Stay

Here is a selective list of some of the city's best lodgings grouped by neighborhood in alphabetical order. Rates may vary significantly if rooms are booked through an agent or if any discounts apply. Several newly reestablished, mid-priced "boutique" hotels (the Franklin, the Roger Williams, the Shoreham, Hotel Wales), operated by Unique Hotels and Resorts, have been included for their good value and nice style. Most standard names in the hotel industry (not listed here) also have branches in New York. Check with individual hotels about wheelchair access and the extent of their facilities for people with physical impairments.

Prices are for the least expensive double room, excluding 13.25 percent tax.
$ under $160   $$ $160–260   $$$ over $260

## Diamond Ratings

AAA field inspectors evaluate and rate each lodging establishment based on the overall quality and services. AAA's diamond rating criteria reflect the design and service standards set by the lodging industry, combined with the expectations of our members.

A one or two diamond rating (💎 or 💎💎) represents a clean and well-maintained property offering comfortable rooms, with the two diamond property showing enhancements in decor and furnishings. A three diamond property (💎💎💎) shows marked upgrades in physical attributes, services and comfort and may offer additional amenities. A four diamond rating (💎💎💎💎) signifies a property offering a high level of service and hospitality and a wide variety of amenities and upscale facilities. A five diamond rating (💎💎💎💎💎) represents a world-class facility, offering the highest level of luxurious accommodations and personalized guest services.

## Midtown

### 💎 Broadway Inn Bed and Breakfast $–$$

This well-run, impeccably clean and surprisingly charming spot is one of the best-kept secrets in New York for budget-conscious travelers. It's also one of the few respectable places in town that rent single rooms. Chrome and black-lacquer appointments add a little spice to the sedate room decor, but with the Theater district and Times Square so close by, you won't be in your room long enough to notice. There are no elevators, so ask for a room on a lower floor – you'll be closer to the free breakfast buffet, too.

➕ 164 B4  ✉ 264 West 46th Street, 10036
☎ (212) 997-9200 and (800) 826-6300;
fax (212) 768-2807; www.broadwayinn.com

### 💎💎💎 Royalton $$$

The interiors here are designed by Phillipe Starck, and the striking,

ultra-modern and white lobby is known as a chic place for a drink; the Vodka Bar is a cozy alternative. The rooms have attractive furnishings, with custom-made beds and window seats.

➕ 196 C4  ✉ 44 West 44th Street between 5th and 6th avenues, 10036  ☎ (212) 869-4400 and (800) 635-9013; fax (212) 869-8965

### 💎💎💎💎 St. Regis $$$

Explore the sumptuous Beaux Arts lobby with its many elegant parlors. There are 322 of New York's finest suites here, all with the expected amenities. Another perk is that the hotel can arrange reservations at Lespinasse, located off the lobby. Don't miss the King Cole Bar, a great setting for Midtown's finest cocktails.

➕ 197 D5  ✉ 2 East 55th Street between 5th and Madison avenues, 10022  ☎ (212) 753-4500; fax (212) 787-3447; www.sheraton.com

### 💎💎💎 Shoreham $$

This is a modern, convenient small hotel, with 47 rooms and 37 suites. Its art-deco interior has stylish aluminum furniture and other nice decorative touches. In the lobby is the acclaimed French restaurant, La Caravelle.

➕ 196 C5  ✉ 33 West 55th Street between 5th and 6th avenues, 10019  ☎ (212) 247-6700 and (800) 553-3347; fax (212) 765-9741; www.boutiquehg.com

### 💎💎💎 W New York $$

W is a sensation across Lexington Avenue from the Waldorf. Its New Age spa motif includes high-style rooms in pale earth tones and natural fibers, a healthy haute cuisine restaurant and a hot bar scene that attracts so many young professionals that the crowd spills out to the lobby on Thursday and Friday nights.

➕ 197 D4  ✉ 541 Lexington Avenue at 49th Street, 10022  ☎ (212) 755-1200; fax (212) 644-0951; www.whotels.com

# Uptown

### ♦♦♦♦ Carlyle $$$

The Carlyle is a bastion of discreet luxury and personalized service, with 180 apartment-style rooms and suites, some with terraces, dining rooms and views of Central Park. You need only go downstairs for some of New York's best nightlife at the Café Carlyle, which often features Bobby Short or Woody Allen, and Bemelmans Bar, with its famous murals and live entertainment.

🖿 199 F3 ⊠ 35 East 76th Street between and Park and Madison avenues, 10021 ☎ (212) 744-1600 and (800) 227-5737; fax (212) 717-4682

### ♦♦ Hotel Wales $$

This genteel haven has richly hued decor, fireplaces and a parlor where complimentary desserts and cappuccinos are served. There are 46 rooms and 41 spacious suites. A harpist plays during the complimentary breakfast.

🖿 200 C1 ⊠ 1295 Madison Avenue at 92nd Street, 10128 ☎ (212) 876-6000 and (800) 428-5252; fax (212) 860-7000

### ♦♦ Mayflower Hotel on the Park $$

The location by Central Park and Lincoln Center is lovely, and the decor traditional and inviting. If you pay a bit more you can have impressive views of the park. There are 165 rooms and 200 suites; request a renovated one.

🖿 198 C1 ⊠ 15 Central Park West between 61st and 62nd streets, 10023 ☎ (212) 265-0060 and (800) 233-4164; fax (212) 265-5098; www.mayflower.com

### ♦ Milburn Hotel $

This hotel in a prewar building is among town houses on a pretty, tree-lined Upper West Side block. The lobby has Persian rugs, and the large rooms are decorated simply. It's steps away from Central Park and in the heart of the bustling West Side residential neighborhood.

🖿 198 B3 ⊠ 242 West 76th Street, 10023 ☎ (212) 362-1006; fax (212) 721-5476; www.milburnhotel.com

# Empire State to Greenwich Village

### ♦♦ Abingdon Guest House $

Two 19th-century village town houses by tiny Abingdon Square Park form nine guest rooms, some with shared baths, others with private baths adjacent or enclosed. This venue provides a good opportunity to stay in the charming West Village.

🖿 194 A3 ⊠ 13 8th Avenue at 12th Street, 10014 ☎ (212) 243-5384; fax (212) 807-7473; www.abingdonguesthouse.com

### ♦♦♦♦ Roger Williams $$

The industrial-chic lobby contains original artworks. Rooms are small with shoji window screens and plenty of style. Rates include Continental breakfast as well as concerts accompanying a nightly dessert buffet.

🖿 197 D2 ⊠ 131 Madison Avenue at 31st Street, 10016 ☎ (212) 448-7000 and (888) 448-7788; fax (212) 448-7007; www.boutiquehg.com

# Lower Manhattan

### ♦ Larchmont $

In a converted Beaux Arts brownstone on a quiet residential street in Greenwich Village, you'll find 58 well-kept rooms. Thoughtful touches such as minilibraries, writing desks – even slippers for guests to wear – make the Spartan accommodations homey, and all the rooms have washbasins/sinks.

🖿 194 C3 ⊠ 27 West 11th Street, 10011 ☎ (212) 989-9333; fax (212) 989-9496; www.larchmonthotel.citysearch.com

### ♦♦♦ Mercer $$$

Trés chic in a completely SoHo way, the Mercer is understated and loft-like in its decor and layout. Most of the 75 rooms have floor-to-ceiling French windows and doors leading to small balconies. The lobby features Jean-Georges Vongrichten's latest restaurant, the Mercer Kitchen.

🖿 195 D1 ⊠ 147 Mercer Street at Prince Street, 10012 ☎ (212) 966-6060; fax (212) 965-3838

# Food and Drink

During your circuit of the city, you'll encounter an opportunity to eat or drink about every 10 seconds.

Mediocrity abounds, but excellence can easily be found at all price levels. In each neighborhood tour you will find a list of some truly exceptional dining destinations, some fancier and more expensive than others. To get a feel for the city's true makeup, sample a variety of dining experiences, from lunch counters and bars to formal restaurants.

## Ethnic Cuisine

The cuisine of most ethnic groups is well represented in New York, sometimes dominating entire neighborhoods. Classic New York eateries range from some well-established high-end spots to other fixtures, such as delis serving old-time Jewish food.

## Guide to Neighborhoods

If you prefer to wander and find your own restaurant, there are certain strips that are good bets for a decent meal.

- **Uptown** try Columbus and Amsterdam avenues from 86th Street to Lincoln Center (64th Street) on the West Side, and 2nd Avenue on the East Side for trendy, midrange neighborhood restaurants that thrive every night.

- In the **Theater district**, "Restaurant Row" – 46th Street between 8th and 9th avenues – has a block of unpretentious spots for the quick pre- or post-theater supper.

- "**Korea Town**" is in the low 30s between 5th Avenue and Broadway, and several spots are open 24 hours.

- In **Chelsea**, 8th Avenue between 14th and 23rd streets is a largely gay social strip with relatively new places featuring foods from many nations.

- In **Greenwich Village**, tiny Cornelia Street has been blessed with a string of above-average places, and West 4th Street between 7th and 8th avenues is a haven of quaint neighborhood spots. MacDougal and Bleecker streets are both strong on Italian coffee parlors.

- In the **East Village**, head to East 6th Street between 1st and 2nd avenues for cheap Indian food. St. Mark's Place has many casual, eclectic cafés, some open far into the night.

- **SoHo** has many exciting and expensive little spots.

- **Chinatown** and **Little Italy** have many less attractive but economical options.

## Less Expensive Options

If you want to check out a high-end restaurant but lack the budget, consider **lunch** instead of dinner; in many restaurants the lunch menu can often be 25 percent cheaper than dinner, and reservations may be more available. Certain high-caliber restaurants participate in a seasonal or year-round $20 **prix-fixe** lunch special and may have a corresponding dinner special. The list of participating restaurants can be obtained from NYC & Company (➤ 36 and 46). Relatively inexpensive lunches can also be had at the bars and cafés listed. Many places also have less expensive **pre**- or **post-theater** menus.

## Reserving a Table

The most popular places can be booked before you arrive in New York.

■ Some upscale spots will accept reservations **30 days ahead**. Be aware that, even if you have reservations, some places require you to call the day of arrival to reconfirm.

■ If you don't like planning ahead, there are other tactics. You can call the night before you'd like to go or on the same day to find a last-minute **canceled table**. Be nice to the reservationist and mention that this is your one chance to come, etcetera, and you may get lucky.

■ It is also possible to have a pleasant, unreserved dinner at the **bar** in some restaurants.

■ A few places do not take reservations, so you will have to be prepared to **wait in line** or at the bar, which can be an enjoyable part of the scene, and at least you'll have a fighting chance for a table.

## Recommended Places to Eat and Drink

Each of the four zones in the book has a listing of recommended places to eat and drink. These have been listed alphabetically and price guidelines are displayed. The sales tax in New York is 8.25 percent, so most New Yorkers figure the tip by doubling the sales tax.

**Prices** The $ amounts indicate what you can expect to pay for an average, complete dinner for one person, including drinks, tax, and a 15–20 percent tip.

| $ under $30 | $$ $30–60 | $$$ over $60 |
|---|---|---|

### Diamond Ratings

AAA field inspectors evaluate each restaurant on the overall quality of food, service, decor and ambience – with extra emphasis given to food and service. Ratings range from **one diamond** (♦) indicating a simple, family-oriented establishment to **five diamonds** (♦♦♦♦♦) indicating an establishment offering superb culinary skills and an ultimate adult dining experience.

---

### Best...
...**breakfast:** Barney Greengrass
...**Chinese:** NY Noodle Town
...**coffee atmosphere:** Caffe Reggio
...**croissants (almond):** Ceci-Cela
...**fish:** Le Bernadin
...**Italian:** I Trulli
...**Japanese:** Nobu
...**NYC experience:** Sammy's Roumanian
...**pizza:** Lombardi's
...**scene:** Balthazar
...**steak:** Sparks
...**vegetarian:** Mavalli Palace
...**wine and food experience:** Montrachet

### Late-Night Dining

New York has quite a few options for eating and drinking after hours. Bars and cafés often serve food late, and these are a good bet:
Balthazar (➤ 157)
Carnegie Deli (➤ 70)
Corner Bistro (➤ 128)
First (➤ 128–129)
Florent (➤ 129)
John's Pizzeria (➤ 130)
Katz's Deli (➤ 158)
Lombardi's (weekends) (➤ 158)
N.Y. Noodle Town (➤ 159)
Second Avenue Deli (weekends) (➤ 130)

# Shopping

There is nothing you can't buy in New York City. There are entire blocks devoted to single items, such as jewelry on 47th Street between 5th and 6th avenues, flowers on 26th Street between 6th and 7th avenues, and fabrics on 38th Street between 6th and 7th avenues.

## Clothing

For chic but conservative **designer wear** and shops, choose 5th and Madison avenues, beginning at around 60th Street and heading Uptown. For **department-store shopping**, Midtown is the place. Probably the most famous stores are Macy's (Broadway and 34th Street) and Bloomingdale's (Lexington Avenue and 59th Street). Also head to SoHo for younger as well as **top trendy wear** and entertaining, **high-end boutique** browsing. For **discount clothing**, there's Loehmann's in Chelsea, Daffy's on 34th Street, and the Lower East Side. For unusual and **unique wear** and shops, head for the East Village and to "Nolita" (the newest shopping neighborhood east of SoHo) or the newer shops on the Lower East Side.

## Art

Uptown Madison Avenue, 57th Street and SoHo have the most galleries.

## Further Information

In New York everything can be bought at both the highest *and* the lowest prices. Many natives spend a good portion of their lives trying to stay on the right end of that dilemma by doing their homework and shopping around. There are entire **books** devoted to shopping in Manhattan, mostly organized according to the objects sought. One such book is Gerry Frank's *Where to Find It, Buy It, Eat It in New York*.

The Manhattan *Yellow Pages* is also a good source if you're searching for one quirky item. If you are looking for fashion bargains, designer sample sales have become the craze. They're not widely advertised, so check for **listings** in *New York* magazine and in *Time Out New York*. Sales of goods at these outlets are final and often cash-only. *New York* also has weekly listings of "Best Bets" and "Sales and Bargains."

## Prices

Prices are usually **nonnegotiable**, unless you are shopping in certain Midtown electronics stores, the older Lower East Side stores where the prices are not on the goods, or at a flea market. Avoid shopping for anything of value on the street (with the possible exception of flea markets). If you've found a deal that seems too good to be true, it probably is. Furthermore, do not take seriously "going out of business, everything must go" signs: They are often a scam. If you feel that a store has misrepresented a product and you wish to take action, call the Better Business Bureau (tel: 212/533-7500, extension 124).

## Opening Times

Hours change seasonally (some places are open later in the summertime), so call ahead. Department stores are best visited midmorning or after lunch on weekdays. Some are open well into the evening. Many Downtown stores (below 14th Street) are notorious for waiting till nearly lunchtime to open. Sunday is a big shopping day in many areas of the city, though you may find that parts of Midtown are closed up.

**Best...**
...**antiques center:** Chelsea Art & Antiques Building (➤ 133)
...**art supplies:** Pearl Paint (➤ 162)
...**bookstore:** Strand Bookstore (➤ 133)
...**bread:** Sullivan Street Bakery (➤ 161)
...**Chinese products:** Pearl River Mart (➤ 162)
...**cooking supplies:** Bridge Kitchenware (➤ 75)
...**cosmetics:** Kiehls (➤ 132)
...**curiosity shop:** E. Buk (➤ 161)
...**department store to browse:** Takashimaya (➤ 74)
...**electronics:** B&H Photo-Video (➤ 133)
...**flea market:** Chelsea Flea Market, weekends (➤ 133)
...**foodie haven:** Zabar's (➤ 104)
...**furniture shop for browsing:** Art & Industrial Design Shop (➤ 132)
...**housewares:** ABC Carpet & Home (➤ 132)
...**museum store:** Museum of Modern Art Design Store (➤ 75)
...**new designer for women:** Mark Montano (➤ 132)
...**old neighborhood to explore:** Lower East Side, Sundays (➤ 156)
...**print shop:** Pageant Book & Print Shop (➤ 161)
...**sporting goods:** Paragon (➤ 133)
...**teenage girl accessories:** Infinity (➤ 104)
...**toy store:** Enchanted Forest (➤ 161)

# Entertainment

New York City's reputation for nurturing creativity in the performing arts is well documented. The options in every medium range from mainstream presentations to the decidedly avant-garde. Likewise, when it comes to venues, the possibilities include gilded theatrical palaces, homey performance spaces and, in summer, the great outdoors.

## Theater, Dance and Music
The Broadway Theater district is technically on or just off **Broadway** between about 40th and 53rd streets, plus the Vivian Beaumont Theater at Lincoln Center. Musicals and classic revivals are the Broadway norm these days. **Off-Broadway** productions can be more artistically adventurous, and include more dramas. Even smaller and more low-profile – but often no less engaging – are the **Off-Off Broadway** productions, where your theater might be a formal space or a few folding chairs around a stage.

Among New York's prominent **dance** companies are the New York City Ballet and American Ballet Theater, both of which perform in Lincoln Center. In Chelsea is the Joyce Theater, which hosts local and visiting troupes of renown. The prime **classical music** venue is Lincoln Center, but performances take place all over the city, in small halls, museums, churches and parks.

For **opera**, head to Lincoln Center, where the New York City Opera and Metropolitan Opera perform. You can hear **jazz** throughout Manhattan, though two centers of activity are the Village and SoHo. For **offbeat music** of many genres, head to the Knitting Factory in SoHo.

## Information and Reservations
If you've got your heart set on attending a "hot" Broadway play or other production, do reserve ahead – with so many potential customers in the area, sellouts are common. If you're not the type to plan far ahead, have

no fear: There's so much happening that you're bound to find something to entertain you.

■ **Box offices**. Even with the most popular shows, it's worth a try to phone or drop by a particular theater's box office – you might score same-day tickets for a hit show: house seats, cancellations or single unsold seats. On show days, box offices are generally open from 10 am until just after showtime.

■ **Broadway Line** (212) 302-4111. Recorded information on this line includes story lines, themes and lead cast members of current shows. You can also purchase tickets.

■ **MovieFone** (212) 777-3456. Call this line for movie showtimes, theaters and offerings. For a nominal charge, you can reserve tickets; on weekends, when screenings often sell out, this can be a godsend (www.moviefone.com).

■ **NYC & Company** (212) 484-1222. Counselors at this New York Convention and Visitors Bureau number can advise you about current cultural activities. Phone (800) 692-8474 within the U.S. for literature (www.nycvisit.com).

■ **NYC/On Stage** (212) 768-1818. This service provides information about theater, performance art, dance, music and family entertainment, and you can order tickets (www.tdf.org).

■ **Prestige Entertainment** (212) 697-7788. This is one of many independent ticket agencies that just might help you secure tickets to that "sold-out" show.

■ **Tele-charge** (212) 239-6200 or (800) 432-7250. This charge-by-phone ticketing agency handles big and small productions and events. There's a small handling fee (www.telecharge.com).

■ **TKTS** (212) 221-0013. The TKTS booth sells discounted (from 25 to 50 percent off) day-of-performance tickets, depending on availability, to Broadway, Off-Broadway, dance, opera and occasionally symphony performances. There's a small service charge, and only cash and traveler's checks are accepted. Times Square booth, 47th Street and Broadway: Mon–Sat, 3–8 for evening shows; Wed and Sat, 10–2 for matinees; and 11–closing (usually by 7 pm) for Sunday matinees or evening performances (www.tdf.org).

### Further Information

Several publications carry comprehensive arts-and-entertainment listings. Check out *The New York Times* Friday Weekend sections (one for the performing arts, the other for the visual and fine arts) and the Sunday Arts and Leisure section. Other good sources are these weekly publications: *The New Yorker, New York* magazine, *The Village Voice* and *Time Out New York*. *Paper*, a slick monthly, also publishes full listings. For gay and lesbian events, look into *The New York Blade, HX* or *Next*.

Or check out these useful websites:

www.nytimes.com: *The New York Times*
www.newyorkmag.com: *New York* magazine
www.timeout.com/newyork: *Time Out New York* listings and city guide
www.villagevoice.com: *The Village Voice*
www.papermag.com: *Paper*
www.newyorker.com: *The New Yorker*

# Midtown
# Manhattan

# Getting Your Bearings

From glossy Times Square to glamorous 5th Avenue, Midtown Manhattan is New York at its showy best. You may have to brave crowds at times, but you'll find some of the city's most beloved attractions.

Midtown stretches from 42nd Street to 59th Street, where Central Park begins. Most of the sights to see lie between 8th Avenue to the west and Lexington Avenue to the east. Fifth Avenue splits the West Side from the East.

With some of Manhattan's highest rents, nearly every square inch of Midtown has been put to commercial use. Except on broad

COLUMBUS CIRCLE — CENTRAL

WEST 57TH S

NINTH AVENUE
EIGHTH AVENUE
BROADWAY

0 — 500 yards
0 — 500 metres

WEST 49TH STREET
CLINTON

THEATER

SC

DISTRICT

ELEVENTH AVENUE
TENTH AVENUE

**15** *Intrepid* **Sea-Air-Space Museum**

42nd Street-Port Authority Bus Terminal
Times Square

WEST 42ND STREET
AVENUE
Port Authority Bus Terminal
Times Squa
42nd Stre

Park Avenue, you may find the concentration of buildings and humanity a bit much, but it's hard not to get caught up in the district's delirious pace. New Yorkers were notorious multi-taskers before the high-tech world even coined the phrase. It's not uncommon to see someone marching briskly down the street, barking into a cell phone while munching on a hot dog bought from a street vendor. You needn't submit to this rat race – you're on vacation, after all – but it can be amusing to witness.

**Right: Disney's flagship store is on 5th Avenue**

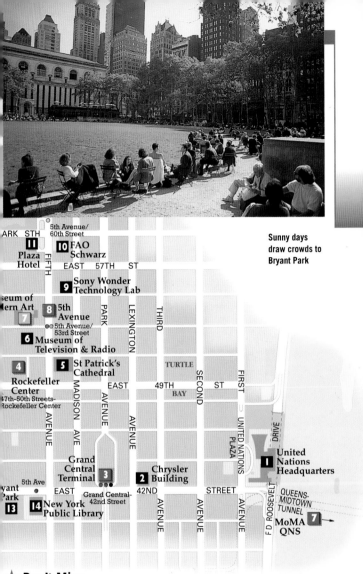

Sunny days draw crowds to Bryant Park

**11** Plaza Hotel
**10** FAO Schwarz
5th Avenue/60th Street
PARK STH
FIFTH
EAST 57TH ST
**9** Sony Wonder Technology Lab
eum of ern Art
**7**
**8** 5th Avenue
5th Avenue/53rd Street
PARK
LEXINGTON
THIRD
**6** Museum of Television & Radio
**5** St Patrick's Cathedral
TURTLE
**4** Rockefeller Center
47th-50th Streets-Rockefeller Center
MADISON AVE
AVENUE
EAST 49TH
SECOND
BAY
ST
FIRST
UNITED NATIONS PLAZA
AVENUE
F D ROOSEVELT DRIVE
Grand Central Terminal
**3**
**2** Chrysler Building
**I** United Nations Headquarters
5th Ave
yant Park
**13**
**14** New York Public Library
EAST Grand Central-42nd Street
42ND
AVENUE
STREET
AVENUE
AVENUE
QUEENS-MIDTOWN TUNNEL
MoMA QNS **7** →

## ★ Don't Miss

## At Your Leisure

Icons of culture and commerce beckon on this tour
of the heart of Manhattan.

# Midtown Manhattan in a Day

## 9:00 am

Catch rush hour's end at **3 Grand Central
Terminal** (right, ➤ 52–55). As stressed
commuters streak madly by, you'll feel
doubly glad you're on vacation. Explore the
terminal and then head across Lexington
Avenue to the **2 Chrysler Building** (➤ 65).
Walk up Lexington to 46th Street,
make a left, and continue west
to 5th Avenue.

## 10 am

Check out
the art-
deco **8 Fred
H. French
Building**
(➤ 62) at 45th Street and 5th Avenue (to
get the full-length view of the exterior,
cross to the west side of 5th Avenue).
Then walk north on 5th Avenue to 50th
Street. Atlas, or to be more precise a
sculpture of him, bears the weight of the
world on his shoulders at **4 Rockefeller
Center** (➤ 56–59). Across the street is
**5 St. Patrick's Cathedral** (left, ➤ 66).

## 11:30 am

Stroll along **8 5th Avenue** (➤ 61–62)
between 50th and 59th streets, resting
your feet in the lobby of the **11 Plaza
Hotel** (➤ 67) before exiting on
Central Park South (59th Street,
along the north side of the hotel)
and heading west (left). At 7th
Avenue make a left.

# 12:30 pm

For a pricey lunch in elegant surroundings, make a reservation at the
French restaurant Petrossian (182 West 58th Street at 7th Avenue,
tel: 212/245-2214) in the Alwyn Court apartment building, a cornucopia of
terra-cotta detailing. Caviar is among the house specialties. For a more down-
scale but no less atmospheric repast, continue south on 7th Avenue past
Carnegie Hall (at 57th Street) to the raucous Carnegie Deli (➤ 70).

# 2:00 pm

From either restaurant, head south to 53rd Street and make a right. At
Broadway make a left.

That brash,
noisy district
to the south
is **12** **Times
Square** (left,
➤ 63–64).

# 4:30 pm

Head east on 42nd Street to **13** **Bryant Park** (➤ 67–68) to relax, then continue
east on 42nd Street to the **14** **New York Public Library** (➤ 68–69).

# 5:30 pm

Walk east one block to Madison Avenue, turn left, walk up to 52nd Street and
turn right. Inside the **Seagram Building** (➤ 66) have a restful cocktail prior to
your prix-fixe, pre-theater dinner at the haute-modernist Four Seasons Grill and
Pool Room. Consider stopping for a drink even if you don't stay for dinner.

# 8:00 pm

It's show time.

# 3 Grand Central Terminal

You needn't be a student of architecture to recognize the design achievements of Grand Central Terminal. Natural light streams through high arched windows, artificial lights twinkle amid an overhead mural of major constellations, and crowds whisk by on polished marble floors. The terminal exudes class and prosperity, both in great supply in early 20th-century New York when the structure was built.

The movies have chronicled Grand Central's ups and downs. Fred Astaire glides through a gleaming Main Concourse in the 1953 musical "The Band Wagon," but by 1973's "The Seven-Ups" the exterior looks gray and dowdy, and fluorescent ads mar the concourse view in "Koyaanisqatsi" (1982). When commuters stop bustling and begin waltzing in "The Fisher King" (1991), joy momentarily pierces the disorder.

The city's economic recovery of the 1990s coincided with an upswing in Grand Central's fortunes. Much credit for the terminal's restoration went to Jacqueline Kennedy Onassis, who for two decades threw the weight of her celebrity behind the battle to stave off one of two outcomes: demolition or a scheme to plop a glass and steel skyscraper atop the historic site.

The main entrance faces south because, when construction began, the neighborhood between 23rd and 42nd streets was the city's most fashionable. The terminal's completion accelerated Manhattan's expansion northward. Crowning the building is Jules-Félix Coutan's 1,500-ton sculptural group – Mercury, the god of commerce (and speed, most appropriate for a train station), flanked by Minerva (goddess of wisdom) and Hercules (god of strength). A bronze statue of 19th-century railroad baron Cornelius Vanderbilt (1794–1877), who started the company that built the terminal, stands underneath the middle arch. Oak leaf and acorn patterns predominate outside and inside the building: "Mighty oaks from little acorns grow" was the Vanderbilt motto. Just inside the main entrance, you can see these patterns close up on the door frames and chandeliers in Vanderbilt Hall, the former waiting room. Because long-distance travelers no longer use the

**Above: The Main Concourse**

**Cornelius Vanderbilt, left, started the railroad company that constructed Grand Central**

terminal, the hall now hosts temporary events and exhibits.

As you glide north into the Main Concourse – go ahead, give 'em the old Astaire soft shoe – you may find your eyes darting from one architectural element to another. One of the terminal's designers believed that a train station should possess the vitality of a marketplace or an ancient bazaar, and the concourse does have an impact similar to that of a Greek or Roman public space. The floor marble, arranged in slightly varying shades according to Cartesian principles, subliminally assists commuters in judging their distance from each other. Stand on the east or west balcony and you'll see how, even when rushing, people rarely bump into each other.

If you know your astronomy, you'll notice that the constellations in the overhead mural are composed in reverse, and that Orion holds a club in his right hand instead of his left.

## VITAL STATISTICS

*CONSTRUCTION STARTED:* 1902
*COMPLETION DATE:* 1913
*RESTORATION COMPLETED:* 1998
*MAIN CONCOURSE CEILING HEIGHT:* 125 feet
*MAIN CONCOURSE SIZE:* 40,000 square feet

❑ Reed & Stem (Minneapolis), Warren & Wetmore (New York) were the original architects
❑ Beyer Blinder Belle (New York) handled the restoration
❑ More than 400,000 people pass through each day

➕ 197 D3 ✉ 42nd Street between Vanderbilt and Lexington avenues ☎ (212) 532-4900 🕐 Daily 5:30 am–1:30 am 🍴 Dining Concourse ($); Michael Jordan's The Steakhouse N.Y.C. ($$); Métrazur ($$–$$$) 🚇 Grand Central (4, 5, 6, 7, S) 🚌 M42, M98, M101, M102, M104 🚆 Metro North

Classy Grand Central serves thousands of passengers every day

Whether the reversal was intentional or not is a matter of minor debate: Some historians suspect that the artist, Paul Helleu, goofed, as he most certainly did with Orion's hand. There is a tale (probably apocryphal) that when one of the Vanderbilts questioned Helleu about his layout, he responded that he'd assumed they'd wanted the stars depicted from God's point of view.

The east staircase, a late-1990s addition, matches the original one on the west. Tenements existed east of the terminal in the early 1900s, so the original design gave that side short shrift. The restoration architects arranged to reopen the quarry that supplied the original marble for the station so that the new stone on the staircase and elsewhere would match the old.

Grand Central serves thousands of passengers daily, but it's also a modest-sized shopping center, part of a plan by the Metropolitan Transportation Authority to generate income to maintain the space. Cafés and restaurants line the lower-level Dining Concourse.

Two high-profile restaurants – a steakhouse bearing the name of the basketball player Michael Jordan, and Métrazur, a stylish brasserie overseen by celebrated chef Charlie Palmer – do business, respectively, on the west and east balconies of the Main Concourse.

*Above: Huge chandeliers light Vanderbilt Hall*

*Opposite: A 1,500-ton sculptural group tops the terminal*

## TAKING A BREAK

For a mid-20th century New York experience, sidle up to the lunch counter (for a more sedate meal, head to the more expensive sit-down restaurant) at the lower-level **Oyster Bar & Restaurant**, order some oyster stew, and listen to the chatter of the cooks, waiters and regulars.

*Sit-down dining at The Oyster Bar & Restaurant*

GRAND CENTRAL
TERMINAL

## GRAND CENTRAL: INSIDE INFO

**Top tip** On Wednesdays there's a **free tour** of the terminal at 12:30 pm. Join the group at the information kiosk (under the clock) in the center of the Main Concourse. For a perspective on the mural that isolates a few of its features, head up the escalator toward the north entrance, and then immediately board the down escalator. On the ride down, you'll see the central portion of the mural framed by two columns. In this section Orion holds his club over Taurus, with Capricorn nearby. The isolated portion looks very much smaller in scale as you reenter the Main Concourse.

**Hidden gem** Off the west balcony opposite Jordan's restaurant is a small staircase leading to the intimate **Campbell Apartment bar**. John Campbell, a friend of the Vanderbilts, furnished his office/pied à terre in the 1920s like a room in a 13th-century Florentine palazzo. The bar's designers reprised the motif and retained the stained-glass windows by Louis Comfort Tiffany.

# ❹ Rockefeller Center

People the world over recognize Rockefeller Center mostly by its parts: the art-deco towers, the sunken ice-skating rink, the statue of Prometheus and, of course, the annual Christmas tree. With 6.5 million square feet of office space, this 19-building "city within a city" is first and foremost a bastion of corporate commerce. Wander through the outdoor esplanades, and retail, dining and entertainment spaces, though, and you'll sense their appealing combination of grandeur and accessibility.

When the Great Depression made impossible the construction of a new Metropolitan Opera House centered on the blocks between 48th and 51st streets and 5th and 6th avenues, John D. Rockefeller Jr. (1874–1960) reconceived the project to house radio and television broadcasters and other tenants. Architects headed by Raymond Hood created a cohesive group of skyscrapers clad in Indiana limestone and ornamented in a subtle art-deco style.

The main build-ings went up between 1931 and 1939. One design element attests to Rockefeller's prescience about how important television would become: Some studio floors of the RCA (now the General Electric, or GE) Building, occupied by the National

**Prometheus prompted chuckles the day of his dedication**

**Below: Flags flap in the breeze above the Outdoor Plaza**

Broadcasting Company (NBC), have no windows.

A committee developed a grandiose theme for choosing Rockefeller Center's artworks: "Man at the Crossroads Looking With Hope and Vision to the Choosing of a New and Better Future." Art by committee doesn't always succeed, but by and large the group selected artists of merit.

Begin at Lee Lawrie's statue of Atlas, across 5th Avenue from St. Patrick's Cathedral at 51st Street in front of the International Building. Poke your head into the building's green-marble lobby. Here you'll find one of the earliest examples of an escalator incorporated as a major design component.

**Above: Atlas stands tall**

Head south to the Channel Gardens, so named because they separate the British Empire and French buildings. Follow the sloping walkway west and peer into the Outdoor Plaza. Paul Manship's gilded statue, *Prometheus* – body in midair, arms outstretched – presides over the plaza.

It's a tad ironic that Prometheus, the Titan known for stealing fire from the Greek gods and giving it to man, stands watch over wintertime ice-skating. That wasn't the original plan for the Outdoor Plaza, which was supposed to draw people into subterranean shops and restaurants but didn't. New refrigeration techniques saved the day, however. When New York City's first artificial outdoor skating rink opened on Christmas Day in 1936, the plaza began attracting more attention.

On the day of the golden boy's dedication in the early 1930s, one spectator mumbled something about Prometheus looking

### Lenin Pic Gets Rivera Mural Nixed

Jose Maria Sert's *American Progress*, an unabashed tribute to capitalism, replaced the original mural by Mexican painter Diego Rivera, who incited a furor by including a portrait of Lenin. The Rockefellers insisted the communist had to go, the artist refused, and the painting was destroyed.

➕ 196 C4 ✉ Between 48th and 51st streets and 5th and 6th avenues 🍴 Underground concourse restaurants ($–$$$) 🚇 47th–50th Streets/Rockefeller Center (B, D, F) 🚌 M4, M5, M27, M50

like he'd just leaped off the roof and was about to crash land. The story circulated, and before long the whole crowd was chuckling. The press picked up the story about "Leapin' Louie," and thereafter few people would take him seriously.

These days, though, playful Prommy perfectly suits his surroundings. Flags and banners wave above the upper promenade, skaters zip below (in summer the plaza is open for dining), and during the Christmas holidays he seems to bear with grace the weight of the center's large tree.

A painting by William Blake inspired *Wisdom*, the central panel of Lee Lawrie's limestone-and-glass frieze over the east entrance to the GE Building. The panel to

the left represents sound and the one to the right represents light, most appropriate for a building that still houses NBC. Jose Maria Sert's mural *American Progress* adorns the GE's east lobby, and two other Sert murals can be seen on the north and south walls.

South across 49th Street from the GE Building are the street-level studios for the "Today" morning news and interview show. Arrive between 7 and 10 on a weekday and you can compete with the masses for a moment on the TV. Walk north up Rockefeller Plaza. Just before you reach 51st Street you'll pass, on the left, Isamu Noguchi's *News* frieze. One of the abstract sculptor's rarer figurative works, it hangs over the entry to the Associated Press Building at 50 Rockefeller Plaza.

Turn left on 50th Street to reach Radio City Music Hall. Three rondels by Hildreth Meiere along the 50th Street side of Radio City Music Hall depict dance, drama and song. The hall's flashy original impresario, Samuel "Roxy" Rothafel, made the precision dancers the Rockettes (called the Roxyettes in the 1920s and 1930s) synonymous with Radio City.

Walk south on the east side of the Avenue of the Americas. Barry Faulkner used more than 1 million pieces of glass to create the frieze over the western entrance to the GE

**John D. Rockefeller's art budget was very generous**

**Opposite, above: Eye-catching art deco detail**

**Right: The neon-lit exterior of the Radio City Music Hall**

Building (under the awning at 1250 Avenue of the Americas). *Intelligence Awakening Mankind* honors human endeavor, from sports to the study of philosophy.

Cross the avenue and stand midblock between 50th and 49th streets for a good angle on Radio City Music Hall's neon-lit exterior. Directly across the street you'll notice that the architecture of the two buildings that flank the GE Building doesn't mirror the center's art-deco look. Their owners refused to sell out to Rockefeller.

### TAKING A BREAK

In good weather when the skating rink's not up, you can dine on the Outdoor Plaza level. The underground concourse contains takeout places and restaurants.

## VITAL STATISTICS

*ORIGINAL SIZE:* 12 acres
*CURRENT SIZE:* 22 acres
(now includes four buildings on the west side of Avenue of the Americas, plus a fifth on 7th Avenue)
*RINK DIMENSIONS:* 59 ft. by 122 ft.
*RINK SEASON:* mid-October to mid-April

❏ Radio City Music Hall Seating Capacity: 5,910

❏ Major architects: Hood & Fouilhoux; Corbett, Harrison and MacMurray; Reinhard & Hoffmeister

## ROCKEFELLER CENTER: INSIDE INFO

**Top tip** You can usually find the center's **walking-tour** pamphlet in the GE Building's east entrance lobby.

**One to miss** Forget the **expensive** Radio City Music Hall tour unless you really dig theaters or have located discount coupons in the lobbies of larger hotels.

# 7 Museum of Modern Art

"Had she been a man she could have commanded an army," said the architect Philip Johnson about Abby Aldrich Rockefeller, perhaps the most important person behind the creation of the Museum of Modern Art. Writer and art collector Gertrude Stein, an authority on modern art, had declared the notion of a museum of modern art an "impossibility," museums to her mind being by their very nature celebrants of the well established. MoMA, arguably the foremost repository of 20th-century art in the world, proved her wrong, not only introducing new artists and movements, but also redefining what constituted art itself.

The early 21st century finds MoMA reinventing itself. A major expansion and the complete remodeling of existing galleries (overseen by architect Yoshio Taniguchi) will close the museum's Midtown galleries from summer 2002 until late 2004 or early 2005. During this period, exhibitions will be held in Queens in a newly designed space, dubbed MoMA QNS, inside the former Swingline staple factory. Many, but not all, of the famous works by the MoMA all-stars – these include Constantin Brancusi, Jasper Johns, Frida Kahlo, Roy Lichtenstein, Henri Matisse, Joan Miró and Pablo Picasso – will be on display at MoMA QNS.

It's an easy subway ride to MoMA QNS. From Grand Central Terminal or Times Square, take the 7 train heading toward Queens/Flushing to 33rd Street station (five stops from Grand Central). Follow the signs in the subway station to MoMA QNS.

✚ 197, off F3 (Midtown galleries: 196 C5)  ✉ 45–20 33rd Street, Long Island City, Queens  ☎ (212) 708-9400  ◷ Sat–Mon, Thu 10–5, Fri 10–7:45; closed Tue, Wed, Thanksgiving, Dec 25  🍴 Café ($)  🚇 33rd Street (7)  🚌 Q32  💲 Moderate

# ⑧ 5th Avenue

Once famous for its grand mansions, 5th Avenue in Midtown evolved into an exclusive shopping district (▶ 74–75) in the early 20th century, as wealthy homeowners cashed in their fancy digs and moved farther uptown.

**Opposite: World-renowned MoMA helped redefine art**

**St. Patrick's Cathedral, squeezed between 5th Avenue skyscrapers**

As the new millennium unfolds, longtime retailers such as Tiffany & Co. (at 57th Street) and department stores Bergdorf Goodman (at 57th) and Saks Fifth Avenue (at 50th) do business alongside relative newcomers like the Niketown (at 57th) shrine to sportswear and the splashy Disney Store (at 55th).

Although 5th Avenue has become more blatantly commercial in recent years, an undeniable gentility endures. The stretch of 5th between 50th and 59th is the most chic. And the most crowded: At times it seems as though half of New York's tourists are out window-shopping. For a glimpse of Japanese style, step into the sleek Takishimaya (at 54th) department store. If it's

open, enter St. Thomas' Church (at 53rd) and note its main altar screen. Designed by Lee Lawrie, it's a complete contrast to his art-deco-style *Atlas* (► 57), which adorns Rockefeller Center (► 56–59). The avenue's architectural dazzlers (► box below) are worth a stroll in themselves.

### TAKING A BREAK

Take refuge from the crowds over a late-afternoon libation at the rooftop bar of the **Peninsula Hotel** (at 55th); the bar opens at 5 pm daily except Sunday. You can have a reasonably priced snack at the brassy (literally and figuratively) **Trump Tower** (at 56th), on the atrium's lower level.

Famed department store's flagship location from the 1920s

➕ 196 C3 🚇 5th Avenue/53rd Street (E); 5th Avenue/60th Street (N, R, W); 42nd Street/6th Avenue (B, D, F, Q, 7) 🚌 M1–5, M42, M50, M57

### A Dozen Dazzlers

New York's finest architects have contributed to the evolution of 5th Avenue, from the Gothic Revival and Beaux Arts buildings of the late 19th century to the art-deco stylings of the early 20th century to modernist and other creations after World War II. From south to north, below are a dozen dazzlers, with their current name and address, cross street, predominant style and year of completion:

* HSBC (452 5th at 40th; Beaux Arts, 1902)
* Fred H. French Building (551 5th at 45th; art deco, 1927)
* Benetton (597 5th near 48th; Beaux Arts, 1913)
* Versace (647 5th near 52nd; Italian Renaissance, 1905)
* Cartier (651 5th at 52nd; Italian Renaissance, 1905)
* 666 5th Avenue (at 52nd; International, 1957)
* St. Thomas' Church (1 West 53rd at 5th; Gothic Revival, 1914)
* University Club (1 West 54th at 5th; Florentine palazzo, 1899)
* St. Regis Hotel (2 East 55th at 5th; Beaux Arts/art nouveau, 1904 with major addition 1925)
* Peninsula Hotel (2 West 55th at 5th; Beaux Arts, 1905)
* Crown Building (730 5th at 57th; eclectic, 1921)
* 745 5th Avenue (at 57th; art deco, 1931)

See also: New York Public Library (► 68–69); Plaza Hotel (► 67); Rockefeller Center (► 56–59); St. Patrick's Cathedral (► 66).

# ⓲ Times Square

Splashy, flashy and no longer trashy, 21st-century Times Square is New York's way of telling the world the city is back and loving life again. Few places tweak one's consciousness so thoroughly. You can spin through the area in less than an hour and still get a strong sense of what makes this place tick.

Times Square bills itself as "The Crossroads of the World," and there's no denying its brilliance: Zoning laws require multiple illuminated signs on new buildings, which include several high-rise office towers and hotels.

Two structures of note, the art-deco Paramount Building and the gleaming 4 Times Square tower, sit across Broadway from each other at 43rd Street. "A Century in Times Square" (➤ 20–22) provides an overview of the area's history.

## Times Square Highlights

Times Square itself is the triangle formed by 42nd Street, Broadway and 7th Avenue. The Times Square business district lies roughly between 40th and 53rd streets from just west of 6th Avenue to 8th Avenue.

✚ 196 B3
🚇 Times Square/42nd Street (1, 2, 3, 7, N, Q, R, W, S); 42nd Street/8th Avenue (A, C, E)
🚌 M6, M7, M10, M42, M104

**Times Tower** (1 Times Square at 42nd Street): The place to be for the annual New Year's Eve celebration contains mostly vacant floors, but its owners collect millions in advertising fees for the building's signs.

**MTV studios** (Broadway between 44th and 45th streets): Music fans hang out on the street below the channel's second-floor studios. You can tell the hot bands by the T-shirts the kids wear.

It's the law: Developers *must* put lighted signs on Times Square buildings

**42nd Street** The E-Walk entertainment complex, 25-screen AMC multiplex, Madame Tussaud's wax museum, and the restored New Amsterdam Theatre are among the draws west of 7th Avenue.

**Paramount Building** (1501 Broadway at 43rd Street): A 1926 landmark that once housed the Paramount Theater, this globe-topped art-deco structure's several setbacks create a vaguely mountainous look.

*Modern office buildings tower over the Times Square area these days*

**TKTS booth** (47th Street between Broadway and 7th Avenue): Half-price day-of-performance tickets are sold (cash only) to some Broadway shows here.

**Palace Theatre** (1564 Broadway at 47th Street): During the vaudeville era, to have "played the Palace" represented the pinnacle of success.

**Times Square Visitor Center** (1560 Broadway at 47th Street): The restored former Embassy Theatre, an exclusive 1920s screening room, contains toilets, a currency exchange machine, Internet access and tourist services.

### TAKING A BREAK

The pretheater crowd turns **Café Un Deux Trois** (123 West 44th Street, tel: 212/354-4148) into a madhouse until show time, but the rest of the day the place is relatively serene.

### VITAL STATISTICS

*NUMBER OF BUSINESSES:* 5,000
*OFFICE SPACE:* 23.4 million square feet
*ANNUAL TOURIST VISITATIONS:* 26 million
*NEW YEAR'S EVE VISITATIONS:* 500,000
*THEATERS:* 39
*ANNUAL TICKETS SOLD:* 11.5 million
*SUPERSIGNS:* 50
*HOTELS:* 28, accounting for 20 percent of all rooms in NYC

### TIMES SQUARE: INSIDE INFO

**Top tip** To check out the facades of a few older theaters, walk west from Broadway on 44th, 45th or 47th Street. The revolving View bar atop the Marriott is tacky, but **the vistas are splendid.**

**One to miss** The souvenir shops in Times Square have some of **New York's highest prices**; you'll see that T-shirt or Statue of Liberty snow cone cheaper elsewhere.

# At Your Leisure

## ❶ United Nations Headquarters

Slaughterhouses once prospered in the area of Manhattan that now holds the complex of the United Nations, a bit of a paradox considering the organization's goal to promote world peace. Though the U.N.'s modernist exterior lacks vigor, the Bauhaus-inspired lines of some interior spaces do please the eye. Most of the U.N., including the General Assembly and Security Council chambers, can be seen only on tours. True to the institution's diplomatic mandate, the articulate guides adroitly sidestep visitors' questions concerning the transgressions of member nations.

➕ 197 F4 ✉ 1st Avenue between 42nd and 48th streets ☎ (212) 963-8687 🕐 Tours daily 9:30–4:45, Mar–Dec; Mon–Fri 9:30–4:45, Jan–Feb (no children under age 5). Closed Jan 1, Presidents' Day, Eid al-Adha, Good Friday, Memorial Day, Jul 4, Labor Day, Eid al-Fitr, Thanksgiving, Dec 25 🚇 Grand Central (4, 5, 6, 7, S) 🚌 M15, M27, M42, M50, M104 💲 Moderate

## ❷ Chrysler Building

American automaker Walter P. Chrysler was riding high, so to speak, in the late 1920s, so he splurged on what briefly reigned as the world's tallest building (► 6). His architect, William Van Alen, decorated the Chrysler Building's upper exterior with larger-than-life re-creations of auto parts – hood ornaments, hubcaps, radiator grills and the like – from 1929 Chrysler models. No expense was spared on one of New York's most

The Chrysler's magical peak

distinguished art-deco lobbies, whose noteworthy elements include "rouge flame" Moroccan marble walls, inset panels of Mexican white onyx, and muralist Edward Trumbull's exuberant ceiling, a homage to the building and to transportation old and new. The doors to the Egyptian King Tutankhamun's tomb inspired the multihued wood inlays of the elevator doors, and the motif continues in the elevators' pyramidal lamps.

➕ 197 E3 ✉ East 42nd Street and Lexington Avenue 🕐 Lobby: Mon–Fri 8–6, Sat–Sun limited viewing access 🚇 Grand Central (4, 5, 6, 7, S) 🚌 M1–4, M42, M101–104

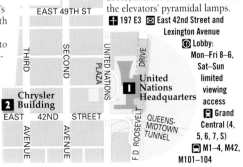

EAST 49TH ST

THIRD AVENUE

SECOND AVENUE

UNITED NATIONS PLAZA

F D ROOSEVELT DRIVE

Chrysler Building ❷

United Nations Headquarters ❶

EAST 42ND STREET

QUEENS-MIDTOWN TUNNEL

## Midtown Moderns

Midtown's skyline incorporates the best and worst of modern architecture. Because there's more that's bland than grand, it's easy to miss the extraordinary specimens. Below, from east to west, are a few highlights.

### Seagram Building

Mies van der Rohe's 38-story modernist milestone is notable for its outdoor plaza (a novel notion in 1958) and its use of vertical, instead of the usual horizontal, I-beams. Philip Johnson fashioned the interior spaces, including the spare yet classy Four Seasons restaurant and bar.

➕ 197 D5  ✉ 375 Park Avenue at 52nd Street

### Lever House

Buildings with glass-curtain walls had been erected as early as the 1910s, but Gordon Bunshaft's 1952 design for the blue-green 24-story Lever House was one of the first large-scale triumphs of the form.

➕ 197 D5  ✉ 390 Park Avenue at 53rd Street

### Sony Building

Postmodernism got a high-profile boost when Philip Johnson and John Burgee designed this structure as the headquarters for American Telephone & Telegraph. Noteworthy elements include the pinkish-gray granite facade, the vaulted minimalist central lobby with gold-leaf ceiling, and the Chippendale-like roof ornamentation.

➕ 197 D5  ✉ 550 Madison Avenue at 56th Street

### CBS Building

Finnish-born architect Eero Saarinen's only skyscraper, also known as "Black Rock," contains austere and majestic charcoal-gray, three-sided granite columns that shoot upward in a clean line from the ground to the roof.

➕ 196 C5  ✉ 51 West 52nd Street at Avenue of the Americas

## 5 St. Patrick's Cathedral

New York's cathedrals generally lack the sweep and solemnity of their European counterparts, but the Gothic Revival-style St. Patrick's has both to spare. James Renwick Jr., who designed Manhattan's other stylish house of worship, Grace Church, modeled the interior and exterior of St. Patrick's after several European cathedrals, most notably the ones at Reims, Cologne and Amiens. Construction began in 1858. The church opened in 1879, but the 330-foot spires weren't completed until 1888.

Midtown skyscrapers dwarf St. Patrick's, and Lee Lawrie's huge statue of the pagan archetype *Atlas* stands across 5th Avenue at Rockefeller Center, but the church more than holds its own, visually and spiritually. Its time-tested stone appears almost

to mock the slick pre-fab surfaces of its neighbors, and its elegant symmetry only accentuates *Atlas*' cartoonish features. Charles Connick, one of the premier stained-glass artists of the 20th century, designed the rose window. Tiffany & Co. created the St. Michael and St. Louis altar.

➕ 197 D4  ✉ 5th Avenue and 50th Street  ☎ (212) 753-2261  🚇 5th Avenue/53rd Street (E)  🚌 M1–5, M50  ♿ Free

## 6 Museum of Television and Radio

Cackles and occasionally sobbing break the usual hush at this museum, whose most popular section consists of consoles where patrons can view television comedies, dramas, talk shows, documentaries, commercials, news and sports broadcasts. Temporary exhibits and screenings within the pale limestone structure, designed by Philip Johnson and John Burgee, honor radio and television personalities and examine mass-media history.

🔲 196 C5 ✉ 25 West 52nd Street west of 5th Avenue ☎ (212) 621-6600 or (212) 621-6800 ⓘ Tue–Sun, noon–6 (also Thu 6–8 pm; Fri 6–9 pm, theaters only). Closed Jan 1, Jul 4, Thanksgiving, Dec 25 🚇 5th Avenue/53rd Street (E) 🚌 M1–5, M50 🎟 Inexpensive

## 🟑 Sony Wonder Technology Lab

You need to have your wits about you at this four-floor playground of high-tech interactive exhibits that entertain and engage the brain. Kids and adults can take part in a simulated recording session, learn about medical imaging or computer chips, or work on a graphic-arts project.

🔲 197 D5 ✉ 550 Madison Avenue at 56th Street ☎ (212) 833-8100 ⓘ Tue–Wed and Fri–Sat 10–6; Thu 10–8; Sun noon–6. Closed Jan 1, Easter, Jul 4, Thanksgiving, Dec 25 🚇 5th Avenue/53rd Street (E) 🚌 M1–4, M31, M57 🎟 Free

## 🔟 F.A.O. Schwarz

It's been said that retail stores are society's true museums. If so, this repository of stuffed animals, high-tech and low-tech toys, Barbie dolls, Hello Kitty merchandise, and model cars, planes and railroads is the Louvre of toy stores. The array

staggers the mind, and so too does the high cost of some people's diversion (a few Christmases back, actor Eddie Murphy and some pals purchased three pint-size, motorized Mercedes runabouts for $2,200 each). The annual appearance of Santa Claus is a well-attended event.

🔲 199 E1 ✉ 767 5th Avenue at 58th Street ☎ (212) 644-9400 🚇 5th Avenue/60th Street (N, R, W) 🚌 M1–5, M31, M57

## 🔟 Plaza Hotel

Henry J. Hardenbergh designed two memorable Manhattan structures, the Dakota Apartments (► 98) and the 19-story Plaza Hotel, which opened in 1907, replacing an eight-story structure of the same name that also was popular with New York society. Hardenbergh's sprightly Plaza has a cheery white-brick exterior topped by weathered green dome turrets. Twinkling lights and horse-drawn carriages outside and the plush, marble-bedecked lobby within complete a picture of old-style grandeur of the type novelist F. Scott Fitzgerald immortalized in his novels (he and his wife Zelda partied famously here).

Dress up a little and you'll blend with the smart set for high tea in the Palm Court or a manhattan in the Oak Bar. It was at the Plaza's ballroom that writer Truman Capote tossed the Black and White Ball, *the* society soirée of the mid-20th century.

🔲 199 E1 ✉ 5th Avenue and Central Park South ☎ (212) 759-3000 🚇 5th Avenue/60th Street (N, R, W) 🚌 M1–5

## 🔟 Bryant Park

It's fitting that, love of nature being a primary theme of his poetry, William Cullen Bryant (1794–1878) should have this patch of greenery behind the New York Public Library named in his honor. A statue of the author of *Thanatopsis* and a longtime editor of *The New York Evening Post* stands midway between an indoor restaurant

and an outdoor café (in nice weather a great stop for a drink or a meal). From the café west to 6th Avenue spreads a large lawn flanked on both sides by tree-lined paths. The fashion industry occasionally takes over the park for promotional events, and movie classics screen on summer Monday evenings.

🚇 196 C3 ✉ 6th Avenue and West 42nd Street 🚇 42nd Street/6th Avenue (B, D, F, 7) 🚌 M1–4, M42, M104 👋 Free

### 🔢 New York Public Library

Two marble lions flank the exterior staircase of the Beaux Arts-style main library, the crowning achievement of the architectural firm of Carrère and Hastings. Arches abound in the all-marble main rotunda, Astor Hall. The

**Tea or a meal at the Palm Court is always a swank affair**

staircase to the left leads to the third floor, where large murals by Edward Lansing depict the history of the printed word. The nearly two-block-long Rose Reading Room to the west looks like a ballroom. Venetian paintings were the inspiration for

CLIN'

🔢 Intrepid Sea-Air-Space Museum

ELEVENTH AVENUE

W

**Fighter plane at *Intrepid* museum**

## Speciality Museums and Centers (phone for opening times)

### American Craft Museum
The line between crafts and "art" blurs at this handsome facility (40 West 53rd Street at 5th Avenue, tel: 212/956-3535), which exhibits works in metal, wood, clay, fiber and other media.

### International Center of Photography
Exhibits at this well-respected center (1133 Avenue of the Americas [6th Avenue] at 43rd Street, tel: 212/860-1777) examine photography's role in contemporary life.

### American Folk Art Museum
In a spiffy new building, this museum (45 West 53rd Street at Sixth Avenue, tel: 212/595-9533) exhibits grassroots American art in traditional and unconventional media.

the salmony clouds that feature in the room's ceiling murals. The library's generally well-conceived exhibits explore the many and varied facets of New York life and culture.

🚻 196 C3 ✉ 5th Avenue and 42nd Street ☎ (212) 930-0830; (212) 869-8089 for exhibition information 🕐 Mon and Thu–Sat 10–6; Tue–Wed 11–7:30 (exhibitions until 6). Closed Jan 1, Martin

attacked it) and later took part in space-capsule recovery missions, has been transformed into a well-organized, comprehensive three-part museum. In addition to the namesake attraction, whose flight deck holds historic aircraft, you can tour a submarine, a destroyer and several other vessels, and view exhibits about the U.S. Navy and air, sea and space technology. Interactive high-tech exhibits – not to mention

Luther King Day, Presidents' Day, Memorial Day, Jul 4, Labor Day, Columbus Day, Veterans' Day, Thanksgiving, Dec 25 🚇 42nd Street/6th Avenue (B, D, F) 🚌 M1–4, M42, M104 🎟 Free

### 🔢 *Intrepid* Sea-Air-Space Museum
The aircraft carrier USS *Intrepid*, which saw duty in World War II (when Japanese kamikaze planes

Hudson River breezes – make this anything but a stuffy museum experience.

🚻 196, off A4 ✉ 12th Avenue and West 46th Street ☎ (212) 245-0072 🕐 Mon–Fri 10–5, Sun 10–6, Apr–Sep; Tue–Sun 10–5, Oct–Mar. Last tickets sold 1 hour prior to closing. Closed Thanksgiving, Dec 25 🚇 42nd Street/8th Avenue (A, C, E); 42nd Street/Times Square (1, 2, 3, 7, N, Q, R, W, S) 🚌 M42, M50 🎟 Moderate

# Where to...
# Eat and Drink

**Prices** The $ amounts indicate what you can expect to pay for an average, complete dinner for one person, including drinks, tax and tip.
$ = under $30          $$ = $30–60          $$$ = over $60

## RESTAURANTS

### Beacon $$$

This dynamic place is the baby of Waldy Malouf, well-respected N.Y.C. chef formerly of The Rainbow Room. The focus is on straightforward, earthy food, much of which is prepared in wood-fired ovens. Specialties include roast suckling pig, wood-roasted trout and lobster. For dessert, soufflés such as chocolate chip need to be ordered ahead, or else there's the lush caramelized apple pancake or some wood-roasted fruit. There is an extensive wine list.

➕ 196 C5 ☒ 25 West 56th Street between 5th and 6th avenues ☎ (212) 332-0500 ⓖ Lunch Mon–Fri noon–2 pm; dinner Mon–Thu 5.30 pm–10:30 pm, Fri, Sat 5:30–11 pm. Closed Sun, national holidays

### Le Bernardin $$$

Possibly the finest of the French restaurants, Le Bernardin is run by the formidable Maguy Le Coze. Legions of waiters swoop about, serving some of the most elegant seafood dishes available anywhere in New York. There is a prix-fixe, three-course menu, as well as two tasting menus. The fricassee of

shellfish is divine, as are the hearty fish dishes, with such adornments as squab jus and foie gras. The desserts feature exotic ingredients and compelling combinations. Jackets are required for men.

➕ 196 B5 ☒ 155 West 51st Street between 6th and 7th avenues ☎ (212) 489-1515 ⓖ Lunch Mon–Fri noon–2:30; dinner Mon–Thu 5.30–11, Fri–Sat 5.30–11.30. Closed Sun, national holidays

### Broadway Diner $

Though no longer associated with one another, these once-sister diners (one also on Lexington Avenue; cash only) excel at standard versions of all-American classics – think burgers, salads, milk shakes and the like. But avoid the Americanized versions of ethnic dishes, both because they fall short and because you can get the real thing in New York if you want it. Service is quick and prices are low.

➕ 196 B5 ☒ 1726 Broadway at 55th Street ☎ (212) 765-0909 ⓖ Lunch Mon–Fri 11:30–4; dinner daily 4–10:30

### Carnegie Deli $

You'll get an authentic New York eating experience here, with gargantuan sandwiches, idiosyncratic service and close quarters. Don't miss it. It's a good opportunity to try the tongue, or settle for magnificent corned-beef sandwiches served with pickles, coleslaw and Russian-dressing dip. The desserts are divine.

➕ 197 D5 ☒ 590 Lexington Avenue at 52nd Street ☎ (212) 486-8838 ⓖ Lunch 11–4; dinner 3–10. Closed Thanksgiving, Easter, Dec 25, Sun

### Churrascaria Plataforma $$

Experience a popular Brazilian import: the all-you-can-eat barbecue. It's quite lively and best for a meat-craving, hungry group. You pay the prix fixe and eat for as long as you like, simply signaling the meat bearers with a red light/green light paddle system. *Caipirinhas* are the

➕ 196 B5 ☒ 854 7th Avenue at 55th Street ☎ (212) 757-2245 ⓖ Daily 6:30 am–4 am 🗐 Cash only

excellent national cocktail, and there are incredible amounts of beef, chicken, sausages and innards, as well as an impressive array of dishes available at a vast self-service buffet.

✚ 196 A4 ⬛ Belvedere Hotel, 316 West 49th Street between 8th and 9th avenues ☎ (212) 245-0505 Ⓒ Lunch daily noon–5; dinner daily 5–midnight

### ▼▼▼ Dawat $$

This is the place for top-quality Indian cuisine, where food expert Madhur Jaffrey has helped conceive the menu, and where you can suffuse your life with spices in an elegant setting. The breads are fantastic.

✚ 199, off F1 ⬛ 210 East 58th Street between 2nd and 3rd avenues ☎ (212) 355-7555 Ⓒ Lunch Mon–Sat 11:30–2:45; dinner Mon–Sat 5:30–11, Sun 5:30–10

### East $

This popular minichain of Japanese restaurants fills a void in Midtown – high-quality, reasonably priced food

of any kind. The draw here is sushi – fresh, quick and well prepared – especially during happy hour, where most pieces are two-for-one. There are vegetarian and traditional Japanese dishes too, and service is attentive and friendly. A Lower East Side location draws a more exotic, local clientele.

✚ 196 B5 ⬛ 253 West 55th Street ☎ (212) 581-2240
✚ 197 E4 ⬛ 210 East 44th Street ☎ (212) 687-5075

### ▼▼▼ Felidia $$$

Here is a rare opportunity to experience authentic Northern Italian cuisine, in particular the little-known specialties from Trieste, the birthplace of owner/chef Lidia Bastianich. Pastas are homemade, the risottos are superb, and so are the hearty braised meat dishes. If you go in the fall, you might, at some expense, have the fresh pasta with shaved white truffles along with a Barbera or Barbaresco. It doesn't get much better than this.

✚ 199, off F1 ⬛ 243 East 58th Street between 2nd and 3rd avenues ☎ (212) 758-1479 Ⓒ Lunch Mon–Fri noon–2:30; dinner Mon–Thu 5–10.45, Fri–Sat 5–11:15. Closed Sun, national holidays

### ▼▼▼ La Grenouille $$$

This New York top-of-the-line French restaurant is the place to come if you want to experience grand contemporary French cuisine in a romantic setting. Dishes such as seafood quenelles and frogs' legs are masterfully executed by chef Richard Pommeis, and his creations are complemented by impeccable formal service amid the lovely floral decorations. The menu at both lunch and dinner is prix fixe, with lunch significantly less expensive.

✚ 197 D5 ⬛ 3 East 52nd Street between 5th and Madison avenues ☎ (212) 752-1495 Ⓒ Lunch Tue–Sat noon–2:30; dinner Tue–Sat 5:30–11.30. Closed Sun, Mon, national holidays, Aug

### Keens Chophouse $$

A classic New York steak joint, atmospherically decorated in a 19th-century spirit. The service is alert and the food straight steakhouse. The best menu selection is the "Legendary Mutton Chop," a formidable beast with a distinct flavor, perfectly cooked to your liking. The mashed potatoes and creamed spinach should be ordered and shared; skip the appetizers.

✚ 196 C2 ⬛ 72 West 36th Street between 5th and 6th avenues ☎ (212) 947-3636 Ⓒ Lunch Mon–Fri 11:45–3; dinner Mon–Sat 3–10. Closed Sun

### Kum Gang San $

One of the finest selections in "Korea Town," this may be a once-in-a-lifetime opportunity to sit in a grotto by a waterfall under a white baby grand piano. The food here is fresh and features some of the best classic Korean dishes. There is a sushi bar, but you're better off with the Korean selections, such as the barbecue, where you grill your own marinated beef at the table, or the delicate but comforting beef and dumpling soup. In Korean tradition, you automatically receive a barrage of small condiment and vegetable dishes and sometimes a little soup, such as sweet potato.

➕ 196 C2 ⊠ 49 West 32nd Street at Broadway ☎ (212) 967-0909
🕒 24 hours

### ▼▼▼ Lespinasse $$$

In addition to AAA's highest diamond rating, chef Christian Delouvrier has been awarded four stars by *The New York Times* for his splendid execution of contemporary French cuisine with an emphasis on classic flavors. There's nothing brash about the setting, with well-spaced tables, big chairs and hushed tones. The wine service is as impressive as the food. Jackets required for men.

➕ 197 D5 ⊠ St. Regis Hotel, 2 East 55th Street between 5th and Madison avenues ☎ (212) 339-6719
🕒 Dinner Tue–Fri 6–10, Sat 5:30–10; closed Sun, Mon

include the rabbit stew with allspice and cloves, and lamb shank braised in a clay pot with orzo.

➕ 196 B5 ⊠ 871 7th Avenue between 55th and 56th streets ☎ (212) 582-7500 🕒 Lunch daily 12:30–3; dinner Mon–Fri 5:30–11:30, Sat 5–midnight, Sun 5–11. Closed Dec 25

### Oyster Bar at Grand Central $–$$

Where else but in New York could you eat oysters in the bowels of the most beautiful and gloriously renovated train station? There is a briny scent in the air, and the atmosphere is casual, with several dining options, including tables with red-checked tablecloths in the bright and cavernous main room or in the dim and clubby bar, as well as horseshoe-shaped lunch counters. From the seats at the counter you can watch the oysters being shucked and cooks executing the highly recommended pan roasts, made from any of about 25 varieties of oysters. If you're in the

### ▼▼▼ March $$$

True food-lovers will enjoy savoring chef Wayne Nish's radical menu of dishes, superbly created and served strictly in tasting portions. The setting is quite romantic, intimate and small, with a garden for the occasional cool summer evening. Co-owner Joseph Scalice should be solicited for his extensive knowledge of wines to pair with the extraordinary foods.

➕ 199, off F1 ⊠ 405 East 58th Street between 1st Avenue and Sutton Place ☎ (212) 754-6272 🕒 Dinner Mon–Sat 6–11, Sun 6–10:30; closed Thanksgiving, Dec 25, Jan 1

### Molyvos $$

Around the corner from Carnegie Hall lurks a cavernous restaurant evoking a small Greek fishing village. The food is full of flavor, the ouzos fragrant and the service professional. An excellent opener is the mezes, small and fabulous bites of Greek cheese fritters and taramosalata. Main-course dishes

market for a cheaper meal at the counters, make sure to ask for the sandwich menu.

➕ 197 D3 ⊠ Grand Central, lower level at 42nd Street and Vanderbilt Avenue ☎ (212) 490-6650 🕒 Mon–Fri 11:30–9:30 (also Sat noon–9:30 pm)

### Rosa Mexicano $$

The chance to sample top-class Mexican cooking is rare this far north of the border. Chef/owner Josefina Howard creates fabulous dishes like lamb shanks with *guajillo* peppers steamed in beer, pork *posole* and great guacamole (prepared tableside) to enjoy with the pomegranate margaritas.

➕ 199, off F1 ⊠ 1063 1st Avenue at 58th Street ☎ (212) 753-7407 🕒 Dinner daily 5–midnight; closed Thanksgiving

### Sparks Steakhouse $$$

The steaks are the draw here, as is the old-fashioned, masculine atmosphere. The place is famous as the location of a murder. Mob man

Paul Castellano was shot out front one night after dinner. You're safe, especially if you keep to the basic New York strip, dry-aged in-house and absolutely an exquisite piece of meat, served unadorned. The lamb chops are also notable. Have a tomato and blue cheese salad to start, and ask for asparagus (not on the menu). The wine list is the best, famous for offering good buys on fantastic selections. Retire to the bar for the cigar menu and a big single-malt Scotch selection.

🗺 197 E4 ⊠ 210 East 46th Street between 2nd and 3rd avenues ☎ (212) 687-4855 Ⓓ Lunch Mon–Fri noon–3; dinner Mon–Sat 5–11. Closed Sun, national holidays

## BARS

### FireBird (and FireBird Cafe, next door)

It's as if you had walked into a St. Petersburg mansion, and it puts you in the mood for any of the many vodkas available. A light,

pretheater menu can be made of *zakvska*, Russian hors d'oeuvres.

🗺 196 A4 ⊠ 365 West 46th Street between 8th and 9th avenues ☎ (212) 586-0244 Ⓓ Mon–Sat 11:30–10, Sun 5–9:30

### King Cole Bar

Here you can sit before Maxfield Parrish's giant mural, *Old King Cole*, and delight in his delights as you indulge in a classic cocktail or two in this elegant bar. You can select from a range of reasonable light meals.

🗺 197 E4 ⊠ St. Regis Hotel, 2 East 55th Street between 5th and Madison avenues ☎ (212) 339-6721 Ⓓ Mon–Thu 11:30 am–1 am, Fri and Sat "later," Sun noon–midnight

### Oak Bar

See where Cary Grant began his suspense-filled escapade in "North by Northwest." Have a martini here. The bar isn't fancy or precious, but it is masculine and smoky and formidable in scale and

ambience. Bar and lunch menus are available.

🗺 199 E1 ⊠ Plaza Hotel, 768 5th Avenue at Central Park South ☎ (212) 546-5330 Ⓓ Daily noon–1 am

### P. J. Clarke's

Surrounded by a sea of skyscrapers, housed in a renegade tiny building, lies a classic New York saloon – lively, inexpensive and publike. Burgers are on the small menu.

🗺 197 E5 ⊠ 915 3rd Avenue at 55th Street ☎ (212) 355-8857 Ⓓ Daily 11:30 am–4 am

### Rainbow Grill Bar

Formerly the stylish Rainbow Promenade Bar, this toned-down version (note: no jacket required) atop Rockefeller Center lets piano music and the Midtown skyline create the perfect Manhattan backdrop for the perfect manhattan. The building's lobby warrants a quick tour too – the intricate ceiling murals can play even more tricks on your eyes after a drink or

two. No reservations are necessary for drinks only.

🗺 196 C4 ⊠ 49 West 49th Street, 65th floor, inside Rockefeller Center ☎ (212) 632-5000 Ⓓ Sun–Thu 5–midnight, Fri–Sat 5–1 am

### Solera

This is a perfect place for a drink and a light meal. You sit at the low-key, long and curving bar and select from an array of flavorful tapas, sherries, wines by the glass and wonderful Spanish cheeses. The staff is knowledgeable and courteous, and you can certainly indulge in a pleasant meal here.

🗺 197 E5 ⊠ 216 East 53rd Street between 2nd and 3rd avenues ☎ (212) 644-1166 Ⓓ Mon–Fri noon–10, Sat 5 pm–1 am

### Whiskey Bar

Come here for a glimpse of "cool" New York – but not so cool the "regular" people can't get in. Actually, this is more like "cooled-off" New York, a once white-hot A-list nightspot that nowadays draws more of an out-of-town, hotel crowd (it's in the lobby of Ian Schrager's chic Paramount Hotel). But an occasional celebrity sighting is not unheard of, and the crowd does have its share of beautiful people. Dress like you mean it – black on black – and you'll be taken seriously.

➕ 196 B4 ✉ 235 West 46th Street 🕿 (212) 819-0404 🕘 Mon–Sat 4–4, Sun 4–3 am

## CAFÉS

Despite its central position, Midtown does not have any cafés worthy of note, though many of the better hotels serve a delicious afternoon tea. The St. Regis, the Plaza's Court and the Waldorf are all good destinations catering for this. There is one tiny, off-the-beaten-track spot for good coffee and a range of mouth-watering cakes:

### Cupcake Café

This low-key spot amid the multi-ethnic food purveyors on 9th Avenue has about three tables and little or no atmosphere and there's often a crowd, *but* they make such lovely-looking cakes and cupcakes with the most beautiful flowers on them that you might consider a stop here.

➕ 196 A3 ✉ 522 9th Avenue at 39th Street 🕿 (212) 465-1530 🕘 Mon–Fri 7–7, Sat 8:30–6:30, Sun 9–5

### easyInternetCafe

"Café" doesn't quite do justice to this mammoth Times Square operation with 800 PCs – it's more like a hyperactive college library. But it's open 24/7, the phone and computer rates are inexpensive, and the coffee's not bad either.

➕ 196 B3 ✉ 234 West 42nd Street (between 7th and 8th avenues) 🕿 (212) 398-0775 or (212) 398-0724 🚇 42nd Street/Times Square (1, 2, 3, 7, N, Q, R, W, S); 42nd Street/8th Avenue (A, C, E)

# Where to... Shop

Midtown is the home of shopping and shoppers, with major department stores, jewelry and the flagship headquarters of many international businesses. Some of 5th Avenue has been usurped by corporate stores, but there are still classy shops between 47th and 60th streets.

**Takashimaya** (693 5th Avenue) is an interesting department store, offering a beautiful array of Japanese goods, old and new, displayed impeccably. **Henri Bendel** (712 5th Avenue) is a boutique department store with one-of-a-kind designs in clothing and housewares. **Bergdorf Goodman** (5th Avenue and 59th Street) is another New York classic, with a men's outpost across the

street. As for other department stores, **Macy's** (34th Street and Herald Square) is the biggest, so big you could get lost there. **Bloomingdale's** (59th Street and Lexington Avenue) is the quintessential New York department store, better than any branch elsewhere.

**Tiffany & Co.** (5th Avenue and 57th Street) is always a good place to browse for jewels, and the windows at **Harry Winston** (718 5th Avenue) may give you an idea of what the most fabulous people wear for decoration. For diamonds and gold, 47th Street between 5th and 6th avenues is the district, and includes the **Jewelry Exchange** (15 West 47th Street), where small dealers occupy booths in huge marketplaces. Some other notables on the block are **Roberta Antiques Jewelry** (73 West 47th Street) and **Mark Jewelry** (32 West 47th Street) for silver. At **Jean's Silversmiths** (16 West 45th Street) you'll find odd silver pieces and sets at a discount.

Take a look at the former Vanderbilt mansion and some over-the-top designs when you visit **Gianni Versace** (647 5th Avenue). If you can handle the commotion, you could check in at famous toy store **F.A.O. Schwarz** (767 5th Avenue; ▶ 67). Save some money for the huge **Toys 'R' Us** store in Times Square. Other interesting stops include the **Museum of Modern Art Design Store** (44 West 53rd Street), with goods based on MoMA's design collection, and **Felissimo** (10 West 56th Street), with multicultural housewares, clothes and accessories.

There are several noteworthy bookstores. Wood-paneled **Rizzoli** (31 West 57th Street) specializes in the arts and architecture, **Urban Center Books** (457 Madison Avenue) in urban planning and conservation, and **Argosy** (116 East 59th Street) in rare books.

Madison Avenue harbors shops for men, such as **Brooks Brothers** (346 Madison Avenue) for classic clothes, and **Crouch & Fitzgerald** (400 Madison Avenue) for fancy leather bags and briefcases.

For antique dealers, try the **Manhattan Art & Antiques Center** (1050 2nd Avenue at 56th Street). For upscale art galleries, go to 57th Street between Madison and 6th avenues, and consult *New York* magazine or *The New Yorker* for listings.

The Garment district (West 38th Street between 6th and 7th avenues) is fun to prowl around if you're into fabrics, notions and samples. Consult *Time Out New York* or *New York* magazine about sample sales. **Hersh 6th Avenue Buttons** (1000 6th Avenue) has a dizzying array of fabrics, buttons, ribbons and other trimmings.

If you still smoke, **Nat Sherman** (500 5th Avenue) has its own brand of cigarettes in wild colors. **Bridge Kitchenware** (214 East 52nd Street) has all manner of professional cooking and baking equipment and fun gadgets. For a good New York City souvenir selection, there's **NYC 57** (24 West 57th Street).

# Where to...
## Be Entertained

### THEATER

See Entertainment (▶ 45–46) in Finding Your Feet for information about Broadway theaters, ticket availability and reservations.

**Roundabout Theater**

Serious dramas are the specialty of this acclaimed theater company, though it also presents musicals and comedies. Its main stage is the American Airlines Theatre, a restored classic.

🚹 196 B3 ⌂ 227 West 42nd Street
☎ (212) 719-1300

**Manhattan Theatre Club**

This is a showcase for contemporary plays, but it also presents readings and workshops.

🚹 196 B5 ⌂ 131 West 55th Street
☎ (212) 581-1212

### DANCE

**City Center**

Top modern-dance and ballet companies perform here.

🚹 196 C5 ⌂ 131 West 55th Street
☎ (212) 212/581-1212

### MUSIC

*Classical/Jazz*

**Birdland**

Cool and classy (candles and linens), this jazz supper club has superb acoustics.

🚹 196 A4 ⌂ 315 West 44th Street
☎ (212) 581-3080

## Carnegie Hall

The world's finest classical and jazz musicians perform at the renowned hall.

✚ 196 A5 ⊠ 311 West 57th Street ☎ (212) 247-7800

## Iridium Jazz Club

Musical greats like Ahmad Jamal and Abbey Lincoln play in a swank new setting near what was the hot spot for jazz during the mid-20th century.

✚ 196 B5 ⊠ 1650 Broadway ☎ (212) 582-2121

## Contemporary

## B.B. King's Blues Club & Grill

The blues singer's Manhattan outpost has a snappy décor, and prices to match. Expect great music.

✚ 196 B3 ⊠ 243 West 42nd Street at 8th Avenue ☎ (212) 997-4144

## Le Bar Bat

The funky space presents R&B, soul, occasionally jazz and also has a disco.

✚ 196 A5 ⊠ 311 West 57th Street ☎ (212) 307-7228

## Radio City Music Hall

Pop, rock, country and other stars appear at the famed art-deco hall.

✚ 196 C4 ⊠ 1260 6th Avenue at 50th Street ☎ (212) 247-4777

## Roseland

Contemporary rockers perform at this retro yet modern-looking venue.

✚ 196 B5 ⊠ 239 West 52nd Street ☎ (212) 777-6800

## Town Hall

The historic venue books world, jazz, rock and other performers.

✚ 196 C3 ⊠ 123 West 43rd Street ☎ (212) 840-2824

## Caroline's on Broadway

New and emerging comics strut their funny stuff near Times Square.

✚ 196 B4 ⊠ 1626 Broadway near 49th Street ☎ (212) 757-4100

## Don't Tell Mama

A piano bar and two small cabarets keep things lively at this convivial club.

✚ 196 A4 ⊠ 343 West 46th Street ☎ (212) 757-0788

## FireBird Café

This upscale jazz cafe (there's also a separate restaurant) books established acts. You'll appreciate the great acoustics.

✚ 196 A4 ⊠ 363 West 46th Street ☎ (212) 586-0244

## Oak Room

Sophisticated jazz singers are the staple of this intimate, atmospheric space.

✚ 196 C4 ⊠ Algonquin Hotel, 59 West 44th Street ☎ (212) 840-6800

## Stardust Theatre

The Stardust plays hilarious "Forbidden Broadway" and "Forbidden Hollywood" spoofs.

✚ 196 B5 ⊠ Broadway at 51st Street ☎ (212) 239-6200

The state-of-the art **Loews** and **AMC** cineplexes on 42nd Street near 8th Avenue have 38 screens between them.

## Museum of Television and Radio

Screenings of old TV shows take place daily at the museum (▶ 66–67).

✚ 196 C5 ⊠ 25 West 52nd Street ☎ (212) 621-6600

## Paris

Art and independent movies screen at this handsome theater near the Plaza Hotel.

✚ 199 E1 ⊠ 4 West 58th Street ☎ (212) 688-3800

## Ziegfeld

With 1,400 velvet seats, this place is well worth a visit whatever's playing.

✚ 196 C5 ⊠ 141 West 54th Street at 6th Avenue ☎ (212) 765-7600

# Uptown and Central Park

# Getting Your Bearings

The 19th-century northward advance of New York's wealthy culminated with the creation of Central Park, which cuts a wide green swath through the two neighborhoods they settled: The Upper East Side and the Upper West Side.

Uptown begins at 59th Street. Museums and chichi shops are the main attractions on the Upper East Side; performing-arts venues and more shops are the lures of the Upper West Side. As Central Park West's name suggests, this extension of 8th Avenue straddles the park's western edge; 5th Avenue borders the park on its eastern side.

The upper-upper crust of New York society – the heirs of Astors, Vanderbilts and their ilk – preferred the East Side, which partly accounts for its stuffy reputation among locals. Egalitarian types rarely set foot here except to attend a museum show. Though the Upper East Side is hardly inert, the Upper West Side is livelier, its shops a little hipper, its clubs a bit more happening. Fine architecture lines Central Park on either side, but the greenery in between is just as apt to seduce you.

## ★ Don't Miss

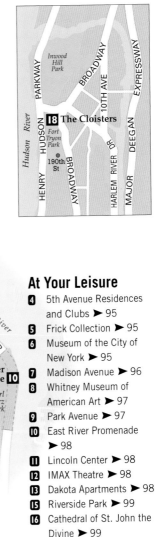

125th St
EAST 125TH ST

Marcus Garvey Park

PARK
FIFTH AVENUE
AVENUE

EAST 116TH ST

AVENUE

em
er

EAST 106TH ST

**6** 103rd St
**Museum of the City of New York**

THIRD
SECOND
FIRST

EAST 96TH STREET

F D ROOSEVELT DR

East River

**Solomon R Guggenheim Museum**
**3**

EAST 86TH STREET
86th St
AVE
AVE
AVE

**East River Promenade** **10**

Carl Schurz Park

**Metropolitan Museum of Art** **2**

**UPPER**

**9 Park Avenue**

EAST 79TH STREET

**EAST SIDE**

77th St

**5th Avenue Residences and Clubs** **4**

FIFTH

**Whitney Museum of American Art** **8**

EAST 72ND STREET

**Frick Collection** **5**

68th St–Hunter College

**Madison Avenue**
**7**

AVENUE
PARK

Lexington Ave

**5th Avenue Residences and Clubs** **4**

5th Ave/
60th St
AVE
Lexington Ave
59th St

EAST 57TH ST

Inwood Hill Park

PARKWAY
BROADWAY
10TH AVE
EXPRESSWAY

Hudson River
HUDSON
DEEGAN

**18 The Cloisters**

Fort Tryon Park

HENRY
190th St
BROADWAY
HARLEM RIVER DR
MAJOR

## At Your Leisure

# Uptown and Central Park in a Day

## 8:30 am

Begin your day by taking in a bit of ❶ **Central Park** (▶ 82–86). Enter at 5th Avenue and 66 Street and stroll north along the path closest to 5th Avenue. At 79th Street return to 5th Avenue and head north for three blocks.

## 9:30 am

Beat the crowds and be in front of the ❷ **Metropolitan Museum of Art** (▶ 87–91) when the doors open at 9:30, having already chosen a few must-see exhibits.

## 11:30 am

Have an early lunch a few blocks south and one block east of the Met at casually hip Serafina Fabulous Pizza (1022 Madison Avenue at 79th Street), which also serves salads and Italian entrées.

## 12:45 pm

If you're up for viewing more art, head north on 5th Avenue past the Met to the ❸ **Guggenheim Museum** (▶ 92–93); after touring the Guggenheim, follow 5th Avenue back to the Met, behind which you'll see Cleopatra's Needle poking into the sky. Otherwise, backtrack west from Serafina on 79th Street to Central Park (left) to Cleopatra's Needle, veering left at the Shakespeare Garden. Due east a few steps, Belvedere Castle looms merrily over the garden. Ascend the tower stairs for sweeping park views.

## 1:30 pm

Looking west from the castle's tower you can see your next stop, the ❿ **American Museum of Natural History** (▶ 94). The museum – don't miss those dinosaurs – is just south of the park's West 81st Street exit.

## 3:30 pm

The Beatle John Lennon lived at the tan-brick **13 Dakota** (► 98) at Central Park West and 72nd Street. Reenter Central Park at 72nd Street and you'll run right into serene Strawberry Fields (left), dedicated to Lennon's memory. A bit east of Strawberry Fields is Bethesda Fountain.

## 4:15 pm

With all this strolling you've earned a rest. Grab a snack or a drink north of the fountain at the Loeb Boathouse (right), which overlooks the Lake. Exit the park at West 67th Street.

## 4:45 pm

Along West 67th Street are tall red-brick buildings, among them Nos. 17 and 27, whose "studios" – actually large, window-filled apartments – attracted well-to-do painters and other artistic types during the early 20th century. At Columbus Avenue make a left; you'll soon arrive at **11 Lincoln Center** (► 98).

## 5:15 pm

Backtrack up Columbus to 71st Street, turn right, and stop in at humble Café de la Fortuna (69 West 71st Street), where the decor, tunes, and Italian ices and pastries will prepare you for a night at the opera.

## 8:30 pm

If you're not heading to Lincoln Center for a performance, you certainly have made reservations at Café des Artistes (► 104), on the ground floor of one of the abovementioned studios, where you're in for an ultraromantic night.

# ❶ Central Park

At certain times – watching a play under the stars at the Delacorte Theater, taking in the stark beauty of a snowstorm's aftermath, or joining what seems like half of New York for a stroll on a warm spring weekend – Central Park becomes one of the most magical places on earth. The rest of the time this lush pocket of nature is merely splendid.

With their Greensward Plan, landscape architects Frederick Law Olmsted and Calvert Vaux set out not so much to tame the terrain between 59th and 110th streets (though they did accomplish that) as to create a space so unequivocally rustic that city residents would feel transported from their urban setting.

The concept, greatly influenced by London's public parks and private gardens, was as revolutionary sociologically as it was artistically. *The New York Herald* newspaper fretted in 1858 that the park might become "nothing but a great beer-garden for the lowest denizens of the city," but from its inception it has worked nobly as public space for the amusement of rich and poor alike.

Of course, things move a bit faster these days. At the Bandshell, the site of decorous Sunday concerts during the 19th

**The park has attracted ice skaters since its inception**

🕂 199 D3 ✉ Bordered by 59th Street (Central Park South), Central Park West, 110th Street (Central Park North) and 5th Avenue ☎ (212) 360-3444 🕐 6 am–1 am 🍴 Leaping Frog Café ($); Boathouse Express ($); Boathouse Café ($$–$$$); Tavern on the Green ($$–$$$) 🚇 West Side (various stops along Central Park West; A, B, C, D); 1, 2 (to Columbus Circle); East Side (5th Avenue/60th Street; N, R, W) 🚌 M1–4 (East Side); M66, M72, M79, M86, M96, M106 (crosstown buses through park); M10 (West Side) 🎫 Free

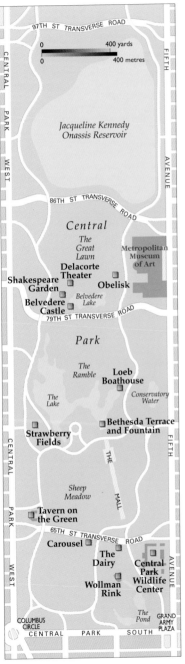

Jacqueline Kennedy
Onassis Reservoir

**Central**

The
Great
Lawn

**Delacorte
Theater**

**Shakespeare
Garden**

**Obelisk**

*Belvedere
Lake*

**Belvedere
Castle**

79TH ST TRANSVERSE ROAD

97TH ST TRANSVERSE ROAD

0        400 yards
0        400 metres

86TH ST TRANSVERSE ROAD

CENTRAL PARK WEST

FIFTH AVENUE

Metropolitan
Museum
of Art

*Park*

The
Ramble

**Loeb
Boathouse**

*The
Lake*

*Conservatory
Water*

**Bethesda Terrace
and Fountain**

**Strawberry
Fields**

THE MALL

*Sheep
Meadow*

**Tavern on
the Green**

65TH ST TRANSVERSE ROAD

**Carousel**

**The
Dairy**

**Central
Park
Wildlife
Center**

**Wollman
Rink**

*The
Pond*

COLUMBUS
CIRCLE

GRAND
ARMY
PLAZA

CENTRAL     PARK     SOUTH

and early 20th centuries, boom boxes blare on weekend afternoons, when rollerbladers and skateboarders rule. But if the scene's more raucous these days, it's no less entertaining, and just steps away you can find the peace of Sheep Meadow.

**Ready to roll in Central Park**

You haven't "done" New York until you've explored Central Park, so venture in. One good route is northwest from the entrance at Grand Army Plaza, at 59th Street and 5th Avenue, past the Mall, Bethesda Fountain, the Lake, the Ramble and Belvedere Castle; you can exit the park at this point or continue on to the Great Lawn, the reservoir and beyond.

Another route is the mid-park loop. Begin from the B or C subway train exit at 72nd Street. Just inside the park is Strawberry Fields. Follow the path east to Bethesda Fountain. Pass south under the arches for a look at the Bandshell and Mall, then walk back to the fountain and continue east to the Boathouse.

From the Boathouse, walk east to the Conservatory Water and *Alice in Wonderland* statue, then backtrack to the Boathouse. Wander north along the eastern edge of the Ramble to Belvedere Castle. From the third floor you can view Turtle Pond and the Great Lawn. Head west from the castle, dropping by the Shakespeare Garden before you exit the park at West 81st Street.

## The Best of Central Park

**Belvedere Castle.** The fanciful castle (left), atop Vista Rock, houses the Henry Luce Nature Observatory, where you can pick up information about the park's animal and plant life. Head to the tower for a 360-degree view.
✉ Midpark at 79th Street

**Bethesda Terrace and Fountain.** Carvings of flora and fauna decorate the grand staircase that leads from the upper terrace at the north end of the Mall under the 72nd Street Transverse to the landing and fountain below. Emma Stebbins carved the fountain's bronze sculpture, *Angel of the Waters*, whose four cherubs represent Purity, Health, Peace and Temperance.
✉ Midpark at 72nd Street

**Carousel.** Wooden horses bob and twirl around this circus-theme merry-go-round inside an octagonal brick structure.
✉ Midpark at 64th Street

**Central Park Wildlife Center.** Modern habitats and its manageable size make the Central Park Zoo's current incarnation a pleasant stop. From 5th Avenue you can peer into the sheep, goat and cow corrals; the polar bears can sometimes be seen from the promenade near the Leaping Frog Café.
✉ South of East 65th Street   🎫 Inexpensive

**Conservatory Garden.** Away from the hubbub elsewhere in Central Park, this 6-acre plot (► 174) contains formal English, French and Italian gardens. Docents give Saturday tours at 11 am from mid-April to mid-October.
✉ 5th Avenue and East 105th Street

**Conservatory Water.** Model-boating enthusiasts steer their vessels along this pond's surface. To the north, the title character of *Alice's Adventures in Wonderland* perches on a toadstool, flanked by the Mad Hatter and the White Rabbit. To the west are Hans Christian Andersen and his allegorical Ugly Duckling.
✉ East Side at 74th Street

**Dairy.** Children visiting in the 19th century sipped milk and munched on snacks here, but these days the Victorian building houses a visitor center.
✉ Midpark at 65th Street

**Delacorte Theater.** Each summer at this outdoor facility the very fine Public Theater mounts two productions, at least one of them Shakespearean. Tickets

### Carriage Trade
Tour the park as the 19th-century gentry did, in a horse-drawn carriage (left). A quick spin of 20 to 30 minutes costs about $35.

are available after 1 pm on the day of the show. The line forms as early as 9 am for well-reviewed plays.

✉ Midpark at 81st Street (closer to West Side)

**Great Lawn.** This is the site of summer concerts and other large events.

✉ Midpark between 80th and 84th streets

**Jacqueline Kennedy Onassis Reservoir.** After her death, the reservoir was named for Onassis in appreciation of her efforts to promote the park's rehabilitation.

✉ East Side between 87th and 96th streets

**The Lake.** The focal point of the midpark area attracts attention whether packed with boaters or serenely quiet on an icy winter's day. Bow Bridge arches over the Lake, separating the more manicured areas to the south and the wilder Ramble to the north.

✉ Midpark between 72nd and 77th streets

**Loeb Boathouse.** You can rent boats or stop by for a snack and a lake view. In cool weather, a fire keeps things cozy.

✉ Midpark at 74th Street

**The Mall.** Rows of American elms arch over the bench-lined walkway between the Dairy and Bethesda Terrace. In the 19th century, this was the only acceptable place for young men and women to promenade unchaperoned, which accounted in part for the area's immense popularity.

✉ Midpark between 66th and 72nd streets

**Obelisk.** Hieroglyphics on this 71-foot granite column, a gift from Egypt, recount the accomplishments of the Egyptian pharaoh Thothmes II. Though it's popularly known as Cleopatra's Needle, the Egyptian queen probably never saw the Obelisk.

✉ Behind Metropolitan Museum of Art at 81st Street

**The Ramble.** A patch of green amid a largely metropolitan stretch beneath the Atlantic flyway (an avian route between the Arctic and the tropics), Central Park attracts about a third of the major bird species in North America. Watch them in this 37-acre maze of paths and foliage.

✉ Midpark between 74th and 79th streets

**Sheep Meadow** (above). Sheep really did graze here until the early 1930s. Nowadays lazing is the chief activity in this quiet zone, where sports are prohibited.

✉ West Side at 67th Street

## VITAL STATISTICS

*ACRES:* 843
*ANNUAL VISITATIONS:*
20 million people
*COST FOR LAND AND BUILDINGS:*
$7.4 million (1858 dollars)
*TREES, SHRUBS, VINES PLANTED:*
500,000 (1858–73)

❑ Years/number of workers to
landscape: 15 years/20,000
workers

**Shakespeare Garden.** The plantings are strictly by the Bard at this restful spot west of Belvedere Castle.
✉ West Side at 79th Street

**Strawberry Fields.** John Lennon's widow, Yoko Ono, provided seed money and an endowment for this international peace garden a few hundred yards east of their home, the Dakota (➤ 98). Embedded in the sidewalk is a mosaic in black and white of the word "imagine," the title of one of Lennon's post-Beatles signature songs.
✉ West Side at 72nd Street

**Tavern on the Green.** Deliriously overdone, with chandeliers, mirrored hallways and dizzying floral rugs, this restaurant in the park's former sheepfold (Sheep Meadow is nearby) draws folks more for its ritzy ambience than for its unchallenging American cuisine. If the bar's open, pop in for a drink.
✉ West Side at 66th Street

**Wollman Rink.** The skating's on ice in winter and on a smooth surface in summer at this concession, where equipment is available for rent.
✉ East Side near 63rd Street   💲 Moderate; does not include skate rental

### TAKING A BREAK

You can pick up a snack at the **Leaping Frog Café** (near the wildlife center at about 64th Street) and the **Boathouse Express** (midpark near 74th Street),

both of which have indoor and outdoor seating. The **Boathouse Café** is an upscale restaurant (no lunch in winter). For a splurge, head to **Tavern on the Green** at West 66th Street.

The atmosphere's festive
year-round at Tavern on
the Green

### CENTRAL PARK: INSIDE INFO

**Top tips** Vendors charge top dollar for refreshments, so bring your own if you're on a budget. The park is **extremely safe on weekend days**, but be more alert on weekdays. Except for a cultural event **it's best not to come after dark**.

**One to miss** The western section of the park south of 66th Street hasn't much of interest, though **the Carousel is a must** if you're traveling with children.

**Hidden gems** The **Conservatory Garden** and **Belvedere Castle** are two of the park's most delightful spots.

# 2 Metropolitan Museum of Art

With more than 3 million artworks and objects, the Metropolitan Museum of Art, also known as the Met, is so big it's impossible to see everything in a day or even two. So the pressure's off. Have a leisurely go at it: Check out the holdings in your favorite periods, sip some coffee at the café, swing by the Egyptian Temple of Dendur (to the right of the front desk), have a rest in one of the sculpture courts, and perhaps explore a particular artist or era on a docent-led tour.

The Met's collections span the past 5,000 years, but the stars are the European paintings (particularly the works by Rembrandt, Vermeer, and the Impressionists and Post-impressionists); European sculpture and the decorative arts; the paintings, sculpture and decorative arts in the American Wing; and the Egyptian holdings.

Consider yourself a genius if you tour the Met (a notoriously confusing place) without getting completely disoriented a couple of times. But there is help. Though they may not be able to identify precise artworks, most of the guards can direct you to particular galleries.

➕ 199 E4  ✉ 1000 5th Avenue at East 82nd Street  ☎ (212) 535-7710 (recorded information) or (212) 879-5500  🕐 Tue–Sun 9:30–5:30 (also Fri–Sat 5:30–9); closed Jan 1, Thanksgiving, Dec 25  🍴 Cafeteria ($); café and bar ($); restaurant ($$)  🚇 86th Street (4, 5, 6)  🚌 M1–4, M79  🎟 Moderate; admission fee includes same-day visit to Cloisters (➤ 100)

## The Best of the Met

**American Wing.** Paintings by Winslow Homer, John Singer Sargent, Thomas Cole, Mary Cassatt and Thomas Eakins are among the highlights here, but don't miss the Living Room From the Little House, on the first floor. Architect Frank Lloyd Wright designed this coolly beautiful space that's heavy on the oak but very modern in form for 1912–14. Several works by Louis Comfort Tiffany, among them the iridescent-tile *Garden Landscape and Fountain* and stained-glass *Autumn Landscape*, line the walls of the adjacent Charles Engelhard Court.

**Arts of Africa, Oceania and the Americas.** Masks, sculptures, utensils, weapons, reliquaries and other objects render a fascinating portrait of the lives and spirits of the peoples of these regions. Along the far south wall – the one with the windows looking out on Central Park – *mbis* poles (used for funeral rituals)

A bit of Egypt in Central Park: The Temple of Dendur

Opposite: The arch-resplendent Great Hall provides a suitably grand entrance

stand tall. Other large ceremonial and functional artifacts from Oceania are also displayed here.

**Egyptian Art.** The Met constructed an entire wing to shelter the Temple of Dendur, built in 15 BC by the Roman emperor Augustus. The carvings in the sandstone walls honor Egyptian and Nubian gods and goddesses. (You can also see the scratched-in names of European tourists from the early 1800s.) In the Egyptian galleries, the well-preserved 4,000-year-old wooden figures in Gallery 4, which were unearthed in the tomb of a high-ranking official, yield many clues about daily life in Egypt.

**European Sculpture and Decorative Arts.** Gian Lorenzo Bernini's *A Faun Teased by Children* and the Flemish tapestries *The 12 Ages of Man* are among the many noteworthy pieces in this wing. The Grand Salon from the Hôtel de Tessé, an exquisite example of Louis XVI style, glitters with gold in the Wrightsman galleries, which contain other period rooms from France, Great Britain and elsewhere.

Above: Napoleon swiped *Perseus With the Head of Medusa* from Italy

**Greek and Roman Art.** The intricate decorations on the functional objects in these galleries will give you a feel for how the Greeks and Romans incorporated aesthetics into everyday life. The *Statue of a Kouros* (Youth) is one of the most understatedly beautiful sculptures in the Met's entire collection. Off the Great Hall, near the south coat check, seven rare Roman frescoes line the Cubiculum from Boscoreale, a room from a villa near Pompeii.

**Medieval Art.** Some of the Met's finest medieval works are at the Cloisters, which makes the richness of the collection here in the main building all the more astonishing. Look for the painted limestone *Virgin and Child* attributed to Claux de Werve in the Medieval Sculpture Hall. The adjacent Medieval Treasury holds secular and religious works.

**20th-Century Art.** Picasso always said Gertrude Stein would come to look more and more like his portrait of her that hangs in the modern-art galleries, and she did. Nearby are Henri Matisse's masterly *Nasturtiums With Dance I* and Wassily Kandinsky's *The Garden of Love (Improvisation Number 27)*.

**Asian Art.** Buddhas of all media and incarnations populate the Asian galleries. Among the stunners is the *Avalokiteshvara, the Bodhisattva of Infinite Compassion, Seated With Royal Ease* (Cambodia or Thailand), in the South and Southeast Asian Art section. Tucked away in a third-floor annex that holds Tibetan and Nepalese art is the marvelously sensuous *Standing Maitreya*.

**Chinese Art.** At well more than a story high, the *Standing Bodhisattva* stands tall indeed in the Arthur M. Sackler Gallery, also the home of a 49-foot-wide 15th-century wall painting, *The Assembly of the Buddha Shakyamuni*, which outlines Buddhist principles. The rare *Seated Buddha* and *Standing Buddha* reside in the adjacent Charlotte C. Weber Galleries. The serene Astor Court is modeled on a scholar's court.

**Renaissance Paintings.** The paintings of Giotto, Fra Filippo Lippi, Raphael and others hang in galleries 3 to 7 of the Italian galleries. Jan van Eyck's *The Crucifixion, The Last Judgment* (Dutch) is usually on display in Gallery 23. Pieter Bruegel the Elder's *The Harvesters* (Dutch) hangs in Gallery 25.

Edouard Manet was summering with Renoir and Monet when he painted *Boating*

**17th- and 18th-Century European Paintings.** Rembrandt's works, including a famous self-portrait, grace Room 14 of the European galleries. *Young Woman With a Water Jug*, by Johannes Vermeer (Room 12), and Nicholas Poussin's *The Rape of the Sabine Women* (Room 10) are two must-sees in the R. H. Macy Gallery.

**19th-Century European Paintings and Sculpture.** Paintings by Claude Monet, Jean Renoir, Paul Cézanne and Vincent van Gogh hang in the Annenberg Galleries. The Havemeyer Galleries contain many works by Edgar Degas.

**Robert Lehman Collection.** The European works Robert Lehman collected were donated to the museum. His prize selections include *The Annunciation* by Botticelli and *Figure in Front of a Mantel* by the French painter Balthus.

**Islamic Art.** Mihrabs (niches that point toward Mecca) and Turkish prayer rugs are exhibited in the Islamic galleries, along with impressive scrolls and paintings.

**Japanese Art.** The galleries here display costumes, period rooms, scrolls and shoji screens from several centuries. The 12th-century wooden sculpture *Fudo Myo-o* depicts one of Buddha's guards.

## VITAL STATISTICS

*ESTABLISHED:* 1870
*OPENED IN CENTRAL PARK:* 1880
*EXHIBITION SPACE:* 2 million square feet
*ANNUAL VISITATION:* 5.2 million
*STAFF:* 1,800 full-time; 900 volunteers

The architectural firm Kevin Roche John Dinkeloo and Associates has designed all the Met's additions since the 1970s.
The Proconneian Garland Sarcophagus, a Roman coffin, was the Met's first acquisition.

## TAKING A BREAK

The museum's cafeteria and café serve sandwiches and American entrées; pastas and contemporary cuisine are served at the restaurant. For a view of Central Park, head to the European sculpture court, where a beverage stand is set up.

A former exterior wall is now part of the enclosed Petrie Sculpture Court

## METROPOLITAN MUSEUM OF ART: INSIDE INFO

**Top tips** Avoid weekend days, which are crowded. Weekday mornings are less so, and Friday and Saturday evenings, when a classical-music ensemble plays in the Great Hall Balcony, aren't usually congested. If you're traveling in a group, **pick a meeting place and time**; especially on a busy day it's easy to get separated. The museum's director, Philippe de Montebello, narrates a tour of the museum's highlights that's available on audio in the Great Hall.

**One to miss** Although the Met has some choice 20th-century holdings, that era is not the museum's strong suit.

**Hidden gem** Sculptures and a gorgeous view of Central Park and the Manhattan skyline make the roof garden, where beverages and sandwiches are served, **a most romantic spot**. It's open from May to mid-November.

# ❸ Guggenheim Museum

Architect Frank Lloyd Wright capped his illustrious career with the spiral-shaped Guggenheim Museum. Many visitors come solely to view his highly sculptural 1959 building, but the permanent collection and engrossing temporary exhibitions make this one of New York's premier showcases for modern and contemporary art.

In the action movie "Men in Black," actor Will Smith loops up the Guggenheim's circular exhibition ramp chasing a bad guy. Smith's stunt lacks the solemnity Frank Lloyd Wright intended for this "temple of the spirit," but it does illustrate the fluidity of his design.

Unlike standard museums of boxlike, connecting rooms, the Guggenheim's main space is continuous, with, as Wright put it, "no meeting of the eye with angular or abrupt changes of form." The walls slope slightly backward because Wright believed this provided the best viewing perspective and would reduce

✚ 199 E5  ✉ 1071 5th Avenue at East 89th Street  ☎ (212) 423-3500  🕐 Sun–Wed 9–6, Fri–Sat 9–8 pm; closed Jan 1, Martin Luther King Day, Presidents' Day, Memorial Day, Jul 4, Labor Day, Columbus Day, the 4th Fri in Nov, Dec 25  🍴 Museum Café ($)
🚇 86th Street (4, 5, 6)  🚌 M1–4  💲 Moderate

the glare on paintings. Famously imperious, the architect responded to criticism of the low ceilings in the main space: "If the paintings are too large, cut them in half!"

Wright intended for patrons to take the elevator to the top floor and view an exhibition as they descended the ramp, but shows here generally begin at the base and wind up to the seventh level. The Guggenheim isn't ideal for all exhibitions, but when viewing a chronological survey, you can experience the progression of an era's style or an artist's output much more easily than in a conventional space.

The circular ramp contains the main temporary exhibit. The tower section, completed in 1992 and based on Wright's original design, holds the permanent collection and larger artworks. The Guggenheim's strengths include its paintings by Wassily Kandinsky, Paul Klee, Pablo Picasso, Robert Delaunay and Joan Miró. Supplementing Solomon R. Guggenheim's original holdings are works by Paul Cézanne, Edouard Manet, Vincent van Gogh and other artists acquired in the 1970s.

Look up for a view of Wright's striking skylight

Opposite: The Guggenheim itself is a work of art

## TAKING A BREAK

The museum's café, which serves espresso drinks, coffee and tea, and light snacks, is directly across from the entrance.

---

### GUGGENHEIM MUSEUM: INSIDE INFO

**Top tips** During popular shows, the wait to get inside can be a half-hour or more. Try to **arrive early and avoid weekends and holidays** if possible. On Friday from 5 to 8 a jazz band plays in the rotunda. You can sip wine or soda while you listen. From 6 to 8 on Friday, "pay what you wish" to enter. You can easily tour the Guggenheim in two hours.

**Hidden gem** Look straight up as you enter. Wright based the museum's dome on Mesopotamian ziggurat designs. From the fourth floor of the tower you can get a good perspective of both the small and large rotundas as well as the circular supporting columns. **Gaze straight down from the seventh level** (hold the rail if you're prone to vertigo) for an angle on the ground-floor layout. Notice how the circular pattern of the floor complements the curves of the fountain, ramp, main desk and tower entrances.

# 14 American Museum of Natural History

Soaring ceilings, neoclassical columns and mid 20th-century dioramas of animal habitats lend this illustrious museum the splendor of an old-time science hall, though with modernized dinosaur displays and the 21st-century Rose Center for Earth and Space this facility has more than kept up with the times.

The museum's star exhibits examine the lives and history of dinosaurs in grand and minute detail. Gigantic skeletons immediately catch your eye, but you can also look through a magnifying glass at a fossilized embryo still in its egg. The squealing of awestruck children generally adds to the enjoyment. The museum's other strengths include its gem and mineral collections, halls of mammals, world culture exhibits and the high-tech museum and planterium show at the Rose Center's Hayden Planetarium (constructed as a solid sphere inside a transparent cube).

A barosaurus poised to attack greets visitors inside the main entrance

Head to the fourth-floor dinosaur exhibits, and then to the first floor to the halls of meteorites, gems and minerals. If you have more time, see the halls of mammals and the Northwest Coast exhibit.

## TAKING A BREAK

**Café 4**, the nicest of the museum's eateries, serves soups, sandwiches, salads, desserts and espresso.

➕ 198 C4 ✉ Central Park West at West 79th Street ☎ (212) 769-5100 🕐 Daily 10–5:45 (also Fri–Sat 5:45–8:45); closed Thanksgiving, Dec 25 🍴 Museum Food Court ($); Café 77 ($); Café 4 ($) 🚇 81st Street (B, C) 🚌 M10, M79 💷 Moderate

# At Your Leisure

## EAST SIDE

### 4 5th Avenue Residences and Clubs

Apartment buildings, a few of them quite handsome, have replaced most of the early mansions and town houses north of the Plaza Hotel on what was known as Millionaires Mile. The few remaining single-family dwellings now serve as schools, consulates or foundation headquarters. Buildings of note include the Italianate-style Metropolitan Club (1 East 60th Street); the Federal Revival-style Knickerbocker Club (2 East 62nd Street); the Italian Renaissance-style apartment house at 817 5th Avenue near 63rd Street; the Louis XVI-style Frick Mansion (1 East 70th Street); the neoclassical Commonwealth Fund (1 East 75th Street); the twin French-style town houses at 972 and 973 5th Avenue at 79th Street; the Beaux Arts town house of the American Irish Historical Society (991 5th Avenue); and the French-style mansion occupied by the Neue Galerie (1048 5th Avenue).

🚇 199 E2  ✉ Between East 59th and East 110th streets  Ⓜ Various stations (4, 5, 6, N, R, W)  🚌 M1–4, M66, M72, M79, M86, M96

### 5 Frick Collection

If you find the hordes and the surfeit of artworks at the Metropolitan Museum of Art too daunting, consider this gem of a museum inside the stately home architect Thomas Hastings designed for Henry Clay Frick (▶ 28). The steel baron proved as shrewd in collecting art as he was in business: His small but staggering collection includes pivotal works by Titian, El Greco, Fragonard, Fra Filippo Lippi, Turner, Corot, Vermeer, Rembrandt and Gainsborough, and you get a glimpse of how New York's wealthy lived. In the restful interior courtyard you can reflect on the exhibits and Frick's luxurious life. Children under age 10 are not admitted.

🚇 199 E3  ✉ 1 East 70th Street  ☎ (212) 288-0700  🕐 Tue–Sat 10–6, Sun 1–6, Election Day, Nov 11 1–6; closed Jan 1–2, Jul 4, Thanksgiving, Dec 24–25  Ⓜ 68th Street (6)  🚌 M1–4; M72  💲 Moderate

### 6 Museum of the City of New York

Way uptown, but worth the trip if you're a history buff, is this repository of city artifacts, from historical memorabilia and games (New York has long been a center for toy manufacturing) to theatrical and other costumes. Check out two exquisitely crafted period rooms, on the fifth floor, from John D. Rockefeller's 5th Avenue mansion. Past temporary exhibitions include cartoons from *The New Yorker* magazine, 200 years of Broadway history, and architectural drawings of 20th-century skyscrapers.

**Millionaires Mile mansions were often heavy on ornamentation**

## Specialty Museums and Centers (phone for opening times)

### Asia Society
This organization mounts sterling exhibits to achieve its goal of helping Americans better understand Asia's history and cultures.
✚ 199 F3  ✉ 725 Park Avenue at East 70th Street  ☎ (212) 288-6400

### Cooper-Hewitt National Design Museum
Past, present and future uses of design – from the mundane to high art – are the focus of this fascinating museum in the former mansion of the steel magnate and philanthropist Andrew Carnegie.
✚ 200 C1  ✉ 2 East 91st Street at 5th Avenue  ☎ (212) 849-8400

### El Museo del Barrio
Rare pre-Columbian works and several hundred *santos* (carved wooden saints) from Puerto Rico and elsewhere are among the many works of interest at this museum devoted to Latin American arts and culture.
✚ 200 C3  ✉ 1230 5th Avenue at East 104th Street  ☎ (212) 831-7272

### National Academy of Design
The mansion (don't miss the Stone Room) of philanthropist Archer M. Huntington and his wife Anna, a sculptor and academy member, contains a superb collection of mostly American art.
✚ 199 F5  ✉ 1083 5th Avenue at 89th Street  ☎ (212) 369-4880

### Jewish Museum
The largest Jewish museum in the Western hemisphere surveys 4,000 years of Jewish arts, culture and history.
✚ 200 C1  ✉ 1109 5th Avenue at East 92nd Street  ☎ (212) 423-3200

If you're taking public transportation, it's better to ride the bus, because a housing project and a park block the obvious route from the subway station. The museum has announced plans to move to the Tweed Courthouse in Lower Manhattan, though for political and other reasons this may not happen. If the move does occur, it probably won't be before 2003. Call the museum for details.
✚ 200 C3  ✉ 1220 5th Avenue at East 103rd Street  ☎ (212) 534-1672
🕓 Wed–Sat 10–5, Sun noon–5; closed Jan 1, Jul 4, Election Day, Nov 11, Thanksgiving, Dec 25  🚇 103 Street (6)
🚌 M1–4  💲 Moderate

### 7 Madison Avenue
Couturiers, antiques dealers and other purveyors of upscale merchandise pay among the highest rents per square foot in the world for retail space on Madison Avenue between 59th and 72nd streets. On a window-shopping excursion you might spot your favorite international celebrity slipping into Gianfranco Ferre, Moschino or some other salon. Much of the exterior commercial design is mundane, though one of the exceptions – the Giorgio Armani Boutique (760 Madison Avenue at East 65th Street), a chic, sleek 1990s take on 1960s minimalism – is a knockout. Don't forget to look up when you get to the next corner north. It probably won't surprise you that one of the architects of the delirious neo-Gothic apartment building (45 East 66th Street) also designed theaters. Many exclusive antiques shops and art galleries do business alongside clothing designers in the blocks north of 70th Street.
✚ 199 F2  ✉ Between East 59th and East 72nd streets  🚇 Lexington Avenue/59th Street (4, 5, 6, N, R, W); 68th Street (6)  🚌 M1–4, M66, M72

American masters receive due respect at the Whitney, now enjoying a renaissance

## 8 Whitney Museum of American Art

Local artsy types love to dish the Whitney, which appeared to have lost its aesthetic footing in the 1990s. Purists lambasted the curators for valuing politics over technique, especially in the selections for the Whitney Biennial Exhibition, which takes place during even-numbered years. Defenders asserted that the works selected by the museum merely reflected the preoccupations of contemporary American artists. Maybe so, but for many patrons and a segment of the press, the institution founded by Gertrude Vanderbilt Whitney, a sculptor and collector, became less essential. Things are looking up these days, though. Several career retrospectives of major artists have gained high praise, and the curators seem more discerning about the adventurous new art they exhibit. The permanent collection contains stellar works by Edward Hopper, Georgia O'Keeffe, Alexander Calder and other American masters.

🞣 199 F3  ✉ 945 Madison Avenue at East 75th Street  ☎ (212) 570-3676
🕓 Tue–Thu and Sat–Sun 11–6, Fri 1–9; closed Jan 1, Thanksgiving, Dec 25
🚇 77th Street (6)  🚌 M1–4, M72, M79
🎫 Moderate

## 9 Park Avenue

A broad median often brightened by flowers separates the east and west sides of one of New York's most glamorous thoroughfares. Now dotted with sturdy redbrick apartments built in the 1910s and 1920s, the former 4th Avenue was, in the 19th century, a soot-filled corridor for trains heading in and out of the old Grand Central Depot.

The opening of Grand Central Terminal in 1913 spurred development north of 42nd Street. As real-estate prices rose, the wealthy began giving up their town houses and mansions and embraced apartment living. One appeal was convenience: The previous dwellings generally had several levels, requiring lots of stair climbing, whereas even the grandest apartments generally spread out over a single floor. A recent *Vanity Fair* article proclaimed the choicest Park Avenue addresses to be between 85th and 95th streets, but don't thumb your nose at folks in the 60s or 70s – their digs are among New York's most expensive, too.

🞣 199 F2  ✉ Between 59th and 96th streets  🚇 Various stations (6 local; 4, 5 at 59th and 86th streets; N, R, W at 5th Avenue/60th Street only)  🚌 M1–4, M66, M72, M79, M86, M96

### Map labels

EAST 106TH ST
103rd St
**6 Museum of the City of New York**
THIRD
SECOND
EAST 96TH STREET
FIFTH AVENUE
PARK AVE
FIRST
F D ROOSEVELT DR
**UPPER**
**3 Solomon R Guggenheim Museum**
**East River Promenade 10**
EAST 86TH STREET
86th St
AVE
AVE
AVE
Carl Schurz Park
**2 Metropolitan Museum of Art**
**EAST SIDE**
**9 Park Avenue**
EAST 79TH STREET
**4 77th St 5th Avenue Residences and Clubs**
**8 Whitney Museum of American Art**
FIFTH
EAST 72ND ST
**5 Frick Collection**
68th St-Hunter College
**Madison Avenue 7**
AVENUE
Lexington Ave
**4 5th Avenue Residences and Clubs**

## 🔟 East River Promenade

On a muggy summer afternoon when even Central Park is stifling, river breezes usually make this bench-lined walkway above FDR Drive pleasant for a stroll. The views include the borough of Queens and several bridges and islands. Wealthy New Yorkers live in the apartment buildings overlooking the promenade, and trees shade the uncrowded Carl Schulz Park, which abuts the walkway and often hosts weekend crafts or other fairs. Gracie Mansion, the official residence of the city's mayor since 1942, stands at the park's northern end.

➕ 199, off F5 ✉ From 81st to 90th streets east of East End Avenue 🚇 86th Street (4, 5, 6) 🚌 M15, M31, M79, M86

## WEST SIDE

## 1️⃣1️⃣ Lincoln Center

After serving as the set for the 1961 movie "West Side Story," more than 500 buildings in the San Juan Hill neighborhood were razed to make way for the Lincoln Center, an austere modernist cultural complex that opened in phases during the 1960s. It has provided homes for the New York Philharmonic, the New York State Theater and the celebrated Juilliard School for the Performing Arts among others.

The best time to visit the white travertine center is at night, when you can view the Marc Chagall murals behind the glass-walled front of the Metropolitan Opera House. Curtains cover them during daylight hours. Evening is also when New York's culture vultures head to ballet, opera, dance, music, theater and film events at several theaters. A daytime must for opera buffs is a backstage tour (tel: 212/769-7020) of the Metropolitan Opera House; less compelling, but still informative, are the tours of the entire complex (tel: 212/875-5350). Damrosch Park, south of the opera house, and the main plaza often host festivals and concerts.

➕ 198 C2 ✉ Broadway between West 62nd and West 66th streets ☎ (212) 546-2656 🚇 66th Street/Lincoln Center (1, 2) 🚌 M5, M7, M11, M104

## 1️⃣2️⃣ IMAX Theatre, Sony Lincoln Square

Large-format movies on sports, nature and other themes play in 2-D and 3-D at the Sony multiplex's IMAX facility. The story line of "Across the Sea of Time: New York 3-D," which screens on most days, veers toward the sappy but combines authentic stereoptic photographs (a precursor to 3-D) from the early 20th century with contemporary three-dimensional cinema. The juxtaposition of past and present is often quite stunning.

➕ 198 C2 ✉ 1998 Broadway at West 68th Street ☎ (212) 336-5000 🚇 66th Street/Lincoln Center (1, 2) 🚌 M5, M7, M104 ✋ Moderate

## 1️⃣3️⃣ Dakota Apartments

Singer sewing machine president Edward S. Clark became the butt of jokes when he financed an apartment building in the then sparsely populated area west of Central Park. A friend joked that the turreted tan-brick structure, which was completed in 1884, was so far from civilization it might as well be in the Midwestern territory of Dakota. Clark went with the gag, named his gamble the Dakota, and got the last laugh: Its 85 apartments quickly filled up with rich New Yorkers. Henry J. Hardenbergh, who also designed the Plaza Hotel, gave the building its fanciful yet slightly brooding look. Arts and entertainment types from Boris Karloff to Lauren Bacall have lived here, so it's perhaps fitting that the Dakota's fame derives in part from its appearance in movies, most notably Roman Polanski's "Rosemary's Baby." (Mia Farrow, who played the mother of the satanic baby, lives next door at the Langham.) Musician John Lennon was murdered at the entrance in 1980; his widow, Yoko Ono, still maintains their seventh-floor apartment, under the flag-pole, facing Central Park West.

➕ 198 C3 ✉ 1 West 72nd Street 🚇 72nd Street (B, C) 🚌 M10

## 15 Riverside Park

West Siders flock to this lengthy sliver of green to avail themselves of its playgrounds, dog runs, recreational facilities and Hudson River views. Despite all the traffic whizzing by on Henry Hudson Parkway, the feel in this designated scenic landmark is almost bucolic. Edgar Allan Poe gave Mount Tom, the rocky knob at 83rd Street, its name; he used to sit atop the hill and stare at the Hudson. Riverside Drive (another designated scenic landmark) straddles the eastern edge of the park. At Riverside and 122nd Street are the Gothic-style Riverside Church (if it's open, ascend the 22-story-high tower for great water views) and Ulysses S. Grant's Tomb, the

resting place of the U.S. president and victorious leader of the Northern troops during the Civil War. Follow the directions at the end of the Uptown Stroll (▶ 174) to return to Downtown by bus; the area above 122nd Street contains less of interest than the parts below.

➕ 198 A4 ✉ Between West 72nd and West 125th streets and West 135th and 155th streets ⓢ Various stations (1, 2, 3) 🚍 M5

## 16 Cathedral of St. John the Divine

Greeters at the Episcopalian St. John's unfailingly remind visitors that it's "the largest Gothic cathedral in the world." Though the boast is made humbly and to encourage donations to fund the completion of the structure, on which construction began in 1892, the declaration nevertheless strikes a coarse note. This isn't a good thing, because unlike Westminster Abbey in London or the Cathedral of Notre Dame in Paris, St. John's isn't a place one warms to immediately, unless perhaps the choir's in session – sopranos sound crisp and saintly here. The congregation's ecumenical spirit will likely grow on you, however, as you walk past altars honoring New York's fire department and commemorating victims of genocide and AIDS, or notice the wall sculpture paying homage to the musician John Coltrane and the fanciful altar triptych by Keith Haring, the last work he created.

➕ 198, off B5 ✉ Amsterdam Avenue and West 112th Street ☎ (212) 316-7540 ⓣ Mon–Sat 7–6 (plus Sun 6–7 pm) ⓢ 110th Street/Cathedral Parkway (B, C, 1) 🚍 M4, M11, M104 💲 Inexpensive

## 17 Harlem

The name Harlem usually inspires two images, the whirlwind Harlem Renaissance of the 1920s and the neighborhood's decades-long battle against poverty and crime. Neither truly represents the district. The

**Rose window at the Cathedral of St. John**

**Cotton Club** evokes the Renaissance, but African-Americans could only enter it to serve white patrons or entertain them. Clubs frequented by African-Americans received less national publicity than whites-only ones. As for poverty, sections of Harlem are solidly middle class. And crime is less of a problem these days. During daylight hours the main drags – among them boisterous Martin Luther King Jr. Boulevard (125th Street) and Malcolm X Boulevard (Lenox Avenue) – are generally safe.

Entertainers from Ella Fitzgerald to James Brown have performed at the **Apollo Theater** (253 West 125th Street, tel: 212/531-5300; tours by appointment only). The **Studio Museum** in Harlem (144 West 125th Street, tel: 212/864-4500) exhibits the works of artists of African descent. Both facilities are east of the 125th Street subway station (A–D lines). The office of former U.S. president Bill Clinton is at 55 West 125th Street, though he doesn't receive drop-in guests. A half block east of the museum you can hop on the 2 or 3 subway train or walk the ten blocks to 135th Street. Near the 135th Street subway station is the **Schomburg Center for Research in Black Culture** (515 Malcolm X Boulevard, tel: 212/491-2200), which mounts superb exhibits.

If you get up this far, continue north and west to the architecturally significant homes and apartments known as **Striver's Row** (202–250 and 203–271 West 138th Street and 202–252 and 203–269 West 139th Street). Stanford White (▶ 24)

designed the snazzy Italian Renaissance-influenced row between 203 and 269 West 139th. Two musical talents were neighbors on 139th Street: Fletcher Henderson (No. 228) and W.C. Handy (No. 232). The pianist-songwriter Eubie Blake lived at 236 West 138th Street. Harlem Spirituals Gospel & Jazz Tours (tel: 212/391-0900) conducts guided trips through Harlem.

🚉 200 B5 ✉ From 110th Street (125th Street on western portion) to 151st Street 🚇 125th Street (at Broadway: 1; at Frederick Douglass Boulevard: A, B, C, D; at Lenox Avenue/Malcolm X Boulevard: 2, 3) 🚌 M1–4; M18, M100, M101, M104

### 🔢 The Cloisters

The Metropolitan Museum's northern Manhattan outpost, high on a hill overlooking the Hudson River, houses medieval artifacts. Among the major draws are the intricate Unicorn Tapestries (Brussels, about 1500), whose layered symbolism illustrates their era's dominant religious, cultural and social attitudes.

Other highlights include the various chapels and the Treasury, which holds liturgical and secular objects made of gold and other precious metals and stones. Although in Europe you can see such chapels in situ, the museum's more or less chronological arrangement of whole interiors and fragments yields strong impressions of the evolution of European spirituality and architecture. Try to come on a sunny day, to enjoy the three outdoor gardens. You can take a bus that loops from the subway station to the museum's front door, or walk north through Fort Tryon Park.

🚉 198, off B5 ✉ Fort Tryon Park north of West 190th Street ☎ (212) 923-3700 🕐 Tue–Sun 9:30–5:15, Mar–Oct; Tue–Sun 9:30–4:45, Nov–Feb. Closed Jan 1, Thanksgiving, Dec 25 🚇 190th Street (A) 🚌 M4 💲 Moderate; fee includes same-day admission to Metropolitan Museum of Art

**The Cloisters holds medieval treasures**

# Where to...
## Eat and Drink

**Prices** The $ amounts indicate what you can expect to pay for an average, complete dinner for one person, including drinks, tax and tip.
$ = under $30    $$ = $30–60    $$$ = over $60

## RESTAURANTS

### ⇝ Aureole $$$

An elegant town house, with a peaceful back courtyard open in good weather, provides the setting. The style of food is contemporary American and Charles Palmer's version of it is bold, the presentations artful and impressive – particularly the desserts, which often tower so high it's difficult to know how to approach them. The wine list is extensive, with a large American list. Prix-fixe menus are available at both lunch and dinner, and there is a six-course tasting menu at night.

✚ 199 F1 ☒ 34 East 61st Street between Madison and Park avenues ☎ (212) 319-1660 ⏰ Lunch Mon–Fri noon–2:30; dinner Mon–Sat 5:30–11. Closed Sun, Dec 25

### Avenue $$

This all-purpose venue is several notches above the others. Chef Scott Campbell creates a menu that changes seasonally. Dishes come in various sizes so that you can design your meal portions: three small, two medium or one large plate. The cuisine is contemporary French-American with strong references to tradition. The decor is fairly casual,

brasserielike, with exposed brick walls and modern fixtures. The breakfast here is self-service.

✚ 198 C5 ☒ 520 Columbus Avenue at 85th Street ☎ (212) 579-3194 ⏰ Daily 8 am–11:30 pm

### Barney Greengrass $

Smoked fish is the specialty of the "Sturgeon King," and very popular it is. The frenzy is significant on weekends, but things are more relaxed during the week, when seating is in the very casual dining room next to the store. Obviously, smoked fish is the thing, and you'd better have bialys with the scallion cream cheese to go with it.

✚ 198 B5 ☒ 541 Amsterdam Avenue between 86th and 87th streets ☎ (212) 724-4707 ⏰ Tue–Fri 8:30–4, Sat–Sun 8:30–5

### Carmine's $$

Come here for a throwback to those black-and-white-tiled Italian restaurants of yesteryear where large, boisterous groups came, sat, and the

food didn't stop until someone died. Though nothing as extreme, this place cranks out family-style dishes that could easily feed a family of four. All the classic pasta, veal, chicken and seafood entrees are here, so you'd better arrive hungry and in the mood for food. Famished hordes line up along Broadway hopping for a table (weekends can be impossible), so call ahead for a reservation. Pronto.

✚ 198 B5 ☒ 2450 Broadway (between 90th and 91st streets) ☎ (212) 362-2200 ⏰ Lunch daily 11:30 am–3 pm; dinner daily 3 pm–midnight

### ⇝ Daniel $$$

One of New York City's renowned chefs, Daniel Boulud, has relocated his flagship restaurant to this stately space and restored it to its 1920s Renaissance-inspired splendor, complete with pilasters, balustrades and an 18th-floor coffered and stenciled ceiling. The atmosphere is rich and the cuisine contemporary French, with the menus changing seasonally. Boulud can be trusted to expertly apply classic French technique, yet surprise his diners with new combinations. The wine list is impressive, with a unique vertical selection of Château-Latour dating from 1945 to 1990.

➕ 199 F2 ☒ 60 East 65th Street between Madison and Park avenues ☎ (212) 288-0033 ⓒ Lunch Tue–Sat noon–2:15 pm; dinner Mon–Sat 5 pm–1 am. Closed Sun, national holidays

### Gabriela's $

This is a popular spot for casual but tasty Mexican food. It is bustling, particularly in the evening, so you may have to wait outside or send an envoy ahead. The guacamole is good, as are the fresh chips. A favorite main course is the rotisserie chicken seasoned with "Yucatan spices" and served with several side dishes.

➕ 198, off B5 ☒ 685 Amsterdam Avenue at 93rd Street ☎ (212) 961-0574 ⓒ Lunch and dinner daily 11:30 am–midnight

### ⬳ Jean Georges $$$

Jean Georges Vongrichten has given his name to this home of five-diamond dining. The restaurant, overlooking Central Park, sports subtly dramatic decor and is eternally chic, modern and minimalist. The menu, based on French-American cuisine, follows the seasons, with the chef producing unusual yet harmonious combinations such as sea scallops with a raisin-caper emulsion and cauliflower, or loin of lamb with black truffle mushrooms and leek purée. See Nougatine, below, for Vongrichten's lower-priced enterprise.

➕ 198 C1 ☒ Trump International Hotel, 1 Central Park West between 60th and 61st streets ☎ (212) 299-3900 ⓒ Lunch Mon–Fri noon–2:30; dinner Mon–Sat 5:30–11. Closed Sun

### Nougatine $$

The front bar area of Jean Georges contains this less formal restaurant with its own a la carte menu. The food emanates from the same

kitchen, providing a viable and perhaps more accessible alternative. Jackets are required in the evening.

➕ 198 C1 ☒ Trump International Hotel, 1 Central Park West between 60th and 61st streets ☎ (212) 299-3900 ⓒ Breakfast Mon–Fri 7–11, Sat 8–11; brunch Sun 11–3; lunch daily noon–3; dinner daily 5:30–11

### Ollie's Broadway $

This Chinese mini-chain was popular on its own merits even before Upper West Sider Rosie O'Donnell, America's reigning Queen of Daytime Talk, started singing its praises on air. But Ollie's didn't let its newfound celebrity go to its head. The same litany of praise-worthy noodle soups, dumplings and standard Chinese dishes can be found at any of their locations (four at last count, and all on Broadway). The decor doesn't invite lingering, but both Upper West Side locations are directly across the street from multiplexes, so patrons in a rush to catch their movies hardly notice.

➕ 198 C2 ☒ 1991 Broadway at 67th Street (also at 84th and 116th streets) ☎ (212) 595-8181 ⓒ Lunch daily 11:30–3 pm; dinner daily 3 pm–midnight

### Pampa $

A very popular, no-reservation spot, with moderately priced grilled steaks and other Argentinian delights. Don't miss the fabulous morcilla sausage, the steak and the mixed grill.

➕ 198, off B5 ☒ 768 Amsterdam Avenue between 97th and 98th streets ☎ (212) 865-2929 ⓒ Dinner daily Mon 4–11, Tue–Fri 4–midnight, Sat–Sun noon–midnight; closed national holidays

### ⬳ Payard Patisserie and Bistro $$

This is a grand spot for classic bistro fare and brilliant pastries and chocolates by François Payard of Daniel restaurant fame (▶ 101).

➕ 199 F3 ☒ 1032 Lexington Avenue between 73rd and 74th streets ☎ (212) 717-5252 ⓒ Lunch Mon–Sat noon–3; dinner Mon–Thu 5:45–10:30, Fri–Sat 5:45–11. Closed Sun

## Picholine $$$

This has long been one of the best restaurants in the neighborhood. It serves Mediterranean-style food in a well-appointed room with a country feel. A specialty of the house is the superb salmon in a horseradish crust, and the daily specials are worth trying as well. The knowledgeable staff will guide your choice of wine and menu options, and throw light on the legendary cheese selection.

⊞ 198 C2 ⊠ 35 West 64th Street between Broadway and Central Park West ☎ (212) 724-8585 ⓖ Lunch Tue–Sat 11.45–2; dinner Mon–Thu 5.15–11, Sat 5.15–11.45, Sun 5–9. Closed national holidays

## Shun Lee $$

At this upscale Chinese restaurant you'll find finer cuts and more costly ingredients than in Chinatown, with elaborate dishes such as rack of lamb. A specialty is Beggar's Chicken, baked in clay, which needs to be ordered the day before. There's also a café next door:

## Shun Lee Café $

A more casual eating spot than the full-service restaurant, the café serves dim sum, good for a light supper or snack before a performance at Lincoln Center.

⊞ 198 C2 ⊠ 43 West 65th Street between Columbus Avenue and Central Park West ☎ (212) 595-8895 ⓖ Restaurant: lunch daily noon–4; dinner daily 4–midnight. Café: lunch Sat–Sun; dinner daily

## Spazzia $$

The emphasis here is on food from Liguria, the "Italian Riviera," with some French Provençale aspects. Chef Dave Hart is a known expert on the region's food and signature dishes include a rich Ligurian fish soup, grilled squid served on black rice and the hearty Veal Three Ways. The service is upbeat and enthusiastic.

⊞ 198 C4 ⊠ 366 Columbus Avenue at 77th Street ☎ (212) 799-0150 ⓖ Lunch Mon–Fri 11.30–3; dinner Mon–Fri 5.30–10, Sat–Sun 5–11.30

avenues ☎ (212) 873-7411 ⓖ Mon–Sat noon–midnight, Sun 11 am–midnight

## Elaine's

Owned by the notorious Elaine Kauffman, this is the hangout of literati and other notable New York personalities. The kitchen is open late for night owls.

⊞ 199, off F5 ⊠ 1703 2nd Avenue between 88th and 89th streets ☎ (212) 534-8103 ⓖ Daily 6 pm–2 am

## CAFÉS

## Café Guy Pascal

Now reopened, with French pastries by veteran New York pastry chef from the famous French restaurant La Cote Basque. Try Le Delice cake with chocolate mousse, coffee buttercream and toasted almonds.

⊞ 199 F5 ⊠ 1231 Madison Avenue at 89th Street ☎ (212) 831-2340 ⓖ Mon–Sat 7.30 am–10 pm, Sun 8 am–10 pm

## BARS

Many bars and restaurants line Columbus and Amsterdam avenues on the Upper West Side, and 2nd Avenue on the East Side. Plenty are acceptable, none spectacular. If you do find yourself Uptown and in the mood for a drink, there are a few enduring favorites among New Yorkers to try:

## Brandy's

A fun piano bar with a friendly straight and gay local crowd who know their show tunes.

⊞ 199, off F5 ⊠ 235 East 84th Street between 2nd and 3rd avenues ☎ (212) 650-1944 ⓖ Daily 4 pm–4 am

## Café Luxembourg

White-tile walls and art-deco touches make this longtime popular spot near Lincoln Center a pleasant place to have a drink or a snack.

⊞ 198 B2 ⊠ 200 West 70th Street between Amsterdam and West End

# Where to... Shop

Uptown provides some long avenues lined with many small shops interspersed among a multitude of neighborhood services for residents. On the West Side, Columbus Avenue and Broadway between 72nd and 86th streets are teeming with life, with interesting stores tucked in among many food shops, restaurants and more. The biggest local institution is **Zabar's** (2245 Broadway), where hungry shoppers choose from some of the best food in the city. Upstairs is a great kitchen store with quality items at good prices.

Other notable stops include **April Cornell** (487 Columbus Avenue), featuring lovely Indian fabrics in clothes and linens, and

## Le Pain Quotidien

This Belgian bakery has great bread and aromatic café au lait, as well as tasty and imaginative sandwiches.

✚ 199 F5 ⬚ 1131 Madison Avenue between 84th and 85th streets
☎ (212) 327-4900 ⓒ Mon–Fri 7:30–7, Sat–Sun 8–7

## Parlor at Café des Artistes

Located across from its mother restaurant, the Parlor is like a tiny version, with the same menu as in the restaurant, or just coffee and pastries.

✚ 198 C2 ⬚ 1 West 67th Street between Columbus Avenue and Central Park West ☎ (212) 877-3500
ⓒ Daily 5–midnight

## Payard Patisserie and Bistro

Take a detour here for the brilliant pastries by François Payard. Sweets are delicious, and include *canneles*, small glazed cinnamon cakes that are a Bordeaux specialty.

✚ 199 F3 ⬚ 1032 Lexington Avenue between 73rd and 74th streets ☎ (212) 717-5252 ⓒ Mon–Sat 7 am–11 pm

**Pickle-Licious Gourmet** (580 Amsterdam Avenue) with delicious housemade pickles and spreads. **Shoofly** (465 Amsterdam Avenue) has gorgeous children's shoes, and **Unique Science** (410 Columbus Avenue) has amusing magic tricks and models for all ages. The **Performing Arts Shop/ Metropolitan Opera Shop** (136 West 65th Street) specializes in products (books, CDs, gifts) relating to the arts performed at Lincoln Center.

## Upper East Side

On the East Side, Madison Avenue between 60th and 72nd streets is a strip of some of the city's ritziest designer clothing boutiques and art galleries. **Calvin Klein** (654 Madison Avenue) has a sleek new flagship store that's worth a visit just to look at the store itself.

**Barney's** department store (660 Madison Avenue) sells beautiful clothes and accessories; it caters mainly to men, though there are

some selections for women, too. **Shanghai Tang** (714 Madison Avenue), an upscale Chinese department store, sells a huge variety of imported merchandise.

Try **Moschino** (803 Madison Avenue) for surreal fashions, or **Mackenzie-Childs** (824 Madison Avenue) for whimsical housewares and a minimansion exhibit (admission charged). Get those cowboy boots of your dreams at **Billy Martin's** (220 East 60th Street).

**Fred Leighton** (773 Madison Avenue) has lovely antique jewelry. If there's an adolescent girl in your world, **Infinity** (1116 Madison Avenue at 83rd Street) is a must for clothing and accessories.

Some of the best closets in the world get cleaned out in this neighborhood, so the several upscale thrift stores in the East 80s provide good opportunities for smart shoppers and they benefit charities, too. For real bargains visit **Out of the Closet** (220 East 81st Street) or the **Irvington**

Institute Thrift Shop (1534 2nd Avenue at 82nd Street).

An amazing collection of buttons new and old lives at **Tender Buttons** (143 East 62nd Street). One of the world's best culinary book selections is at **Kitchen Arts & Letters** (1435 Lexington Avenue). All manner of games for children and adults can be purchased at **Game Show** (1240 Lexington Avenue), which has a sister branch in Greenwich Village. For a well-edited collection of Americana, investigate **Steve Miller American Folk Art** (17 East 96th Street, No. 11A, tel: 212/348-5219). Who knows, you just might find that perfectly patinated 19th-century weather vane or primitive painting you've been looking for.

For an only-in-New York experience, check out **Weitz & Coleman Rare Books and Bindings** (1377 Lexington Avenue, tel: 212/831-2213). Be prepared for a wonderful chat, and it's best to offer a subject of interest or two.

# Where to...
# Be Entertained

## THEATER

### Lincoln Center Theater
The Vivian Beaumont hosts Broadway shows, the Mitzi E. Newhouse presents smaller productions.

➕ 198 B2 ⊠ 150 West 65th Street ☎ (212) 362-7600

### New York Shakespeare Festival
Summer brings two outdoor productions, at least one by the Bard.

➕ 199 D4 ⊠ Central Park, Delacorte Theater ☎ (212) 539-8500

## DANCE

### American Ballet Theater
This top-flight company's season begins in May and lasts two months. City Center hosts the two-week fall series. The opera house also presents other dance ensembles.

➕ 198 C2 ⊠ Lincoln Center, Metropolitan Opera House, Broadway at 64th Street ☎ (212) 362-6000

### Dance Theater of Harlem
This troupe's concerts (in Harlem and elsewhere) are always a treat.

☎ (212) 690-2800

### Lincoln Center Out of Doors
Watch for free summer dance events.

➕ 198 C2 ⊠ Lincoln Center Plaza, Broadway at 64th Street ☎ (212) 875-5108

### New York City Ballet
This troupe upholds the tradition of past choreographers Jerome Robbins and George Balanchine. The main season, from mid-November to early March, includes a month of *The Nutcracker*. An eight-week season begins in late April or early May.

➕ 198 C1 ⊠ New York State Theater, Broadway at 63rd Street ☎ (212) 870-5570

## MUSIC

### Classical and Jazz

### Kaufmann Concert Hall at 92nd Street Y
Classical and some jazz artists perform at this acoustically superior hall.

➕ 200 C1 ⊠ 1395 Lexington Avenue ☎ (212) 996-1100

### Lincoln Center
New York Philharmonic plays Avery Fisher Hall from late September to early June. Chamber Music Society performs at smaller Alice Tully Hall. Other offerings at Lincoln Center include Mostly Mozart and Great Performers series and student concerts at The Juilliard School.

Wynton Marsalis, musical director of Jazz at Lincoln Center, emphasizes the classics.

➕ 198 C2 ⊠ Broadway and 64th Street 🕾 (212) 546-2656 (recorded info), (212) 721-6500 (tickets)

## Contemporary

### Apollo Theater
African-American musical acts play here; Wednesday is amateur night.

➕ 200, off A5 ⊠ 253 West 125th Street 🕾 (212) 749-5838

### Beacon Theater
Name pop, rock and other acts play the ornate, historic venue.

➕ 198 B3 ⊠ 2124 Broadway 🕾 (212) 496-7070

### Central Park Summer Stage
This outdoor summer showcase presents music, dance and other concerts.

➕ 199 E3 ⊠ Rumsey Playfield, midpark at 72nd Street 🕾 (212) 360-2777

## OPERA

### Metropolitan Opera
The season runs from October to mid-April, with free June performances in city parks.

➕ 198 C2 ⊠ Lincoln Center, Metropolitan Opera House, Broadway and 64th Street 🕾 (212) 362-6000

### New York City Opera
The splendid company performs from September to November and in March and April.

➕ 198 C1 ⊠ Lincoln Center, New York State Theater, Broadway and 63rd Street 🕾 (212) 870-5570

## COMEDY AND CABARET

### Café Carlyle/Bemelmans Bar
Regular performers include Eartha Kitt and, every Monday, Woody Allen and his Dixieland Band. A pianist, and sometimes singers, perform at Bemelmans Bar, whose walls were illustrated by Ludwig Bemelmans. Dress up.

➕ 199 F3 ⊠ 36 East 76th Street 🕾 (212) 570-7189

### Comic Strip
Head Uptown for some sharp and contemporary comedy.

➕ 199, off F4 ⊠ 1568 2nd Avenue 🕾 (212) 861-9386

### Stand-Up New York
Silly stuff happens here daily.

➕ 198 B4 ⊠ 236 West 78th Street 🕾 (212) 595-0850

## Other interesting venues for classical music

Cathedral of St John the Divine
⊠ 112th Street and Amsterdam Avenue 🕾 (212) 662-2133

Church of St Ignatius Loyola
⊠ 980 Park Avenue 🕾 (212) 288-2520

Metropolitan Museum of Art
⊠ 5th Avenue at 82nd Street 🕾 (212) 870-6700

## MOVIES

### IMAX Theatre/Sony Lincoln Square
This is the nicest of the Uptown multiplexes showing Hollywood movies.

➕ 198 C2 ⊠ Broadway and 68th Street 🕾 (212) 336-5000

### Lincoln Plaza Cinemas
Art and independent films screen at this small multiplex.

➕ 198 C2 ⊠ Broadway at 63rd Street 🕾 (212) 757-2280

### New York Film Festival
A range of American and foreign films play this two-week festival in September.

➕ 198 C2 ⊠ Lincoln Center (various theaters), Broadway and 65th Street 🕾 (212) 875-5610

### Walter Reade Theatre
Silent movies, art films and videos screen at this versatile facility.

➕ 198 C2 ⊠ 165 West 65th Street at Broadway 🕾 (212) 496-3809

# Empire State to Greenwich Village

# Getting Your Bearings

The Empire State Building and Greenwich Village represent two extremes of the Manhattan psyche. With nary a trace of sentiment, a businessman demolished the cherished original Waldorf-Astoria Hotel and replaced it with the Empire State Building. For two centuries, the general reflex of Greenwich Villagers, on the other hand, has been to question, if not impede, development.

Now itself a beloved symbol of the city, the Empire State Building stands at the western edge of the Murray Hill neighborhood. Below Murray Hill on the East Side are Gramercy Park, Union Square and the East Village. To the west of the Empire State is the Garment district, south of which are Chelsea and Greenwich Village.

"Greenwich Village" originally referred to the land bordered by the Hudson River, 14th and Houston streets, and 4th Avenue. Real-estate folk came up with the label East Village in the 1960s. These days a reference to the Village, the West Village or Greenwich Village probably means the same place – the streets west of 5th Avenue. East Village generally refers to points east of 4th Avenue to about Avenue C or D.

Both "villages" have had reputations for historic preservation and the acceptance of freethinkers. A favorable 19th-century real-estate covenant has preserved much of Chelsea's residential character as well.

GARMENT
DISTRICT

WEST 34TH ST

Madison
Square
Garden

NINTH

EIGHTH

TENTH

*Chelsea Park*

23rd St

WEST 23RD STRE

Chelsea

**10**

Hote
Chel

**11**

TWELFTH AVENUE

Chelsea
Piers **12**

AVENUE

AVENUE

AVENUE

14th St

WEST 14TH STRE

HUDSON

GREEN
AVE

Greenwic
Villag

CHRISTOPHER
STREET

Previous page:
In the old days
they called it
the Empty State
Building

You really can
see for miles
from the Empire
State Building

EAST 42ND ST

PARK

Morgan
Library

MURRAY

FIFTH

HILL

**1**

EAST 34TH ST

**2** Empire State
Building

AVENUE

33rd St

St-
ld Sq

Madison
Square Park

THIRD

PARK

AVE

**3**

23rd St

rd St

EAST 23RD STREET

**4**

SECOND

Flatiron
Building

AVE SOUTH

**5**

FIFTH

Gramercy
Park

FIRST

0                    ½ mile

0                    1 km

Union
Square **6**

St

14th St-
Union Square

Stuyvesant
Square

●●○ EAST          14TH          STREET

**7** Forbes
Magazine
Galleries

FOURTH AVE

AVENUE

AVENUE

Tompkins
Square
Park

AVE

4th St-
hington Sq

8th St-
NYU

Astor
Place

**8** East
Village

AVENUE

AVENUE

C

Washington
Square Park

NEW

COOPER
SQUARE

EAST    7TH    STREET

YORK

LA GUARDIA
PLACE

UNIVERSITY

NOHO

BROADWAY

BOWERY

2nd Ave

WEST HOUSTON ST

**Vendors sell food and
flowers at Union
Square's Greenmarket**

Follow a visit to New York's most celebrated landmark with forays into four distinctive neighborhoods.

# Empire State to Greenwich Village in a Day

## 9:00 am

Arrive early at the **2 Empire State Building** (➤ 112–115). The first elevator soars skyward at 9:30.

## 11:30 am

Around the corner at East 36th Street and Madison Avenue, the **1 Morgan Library's** courtyard is a splendid spot for lunch (➤ 124).

## 1:00 pm

South on Madison Avenue lies **3 Madison Square Park** (➤ 124). Though it's not the tallest building in the park area, that sleek sliver the **4 Flatiron Building** (left, ➤ 124–125) steals the show.

## 1:30 pm

Head south on Broadway to East 21st Street. Make a left and walk two blocks to always-pristine **5 Gramercy Park** (➤ 125). Head south on Irving Place to East 17th Street and make a right.

## 2:00 pm

Students, shoppers, vendors and traffic keep historic **6 Union Square** (➤ 125) forever bustling. From here walk west on 12th Street to catch the whimsical exhibits at the **7 Forbes Magazine Galleries** (➤ 126).

# 2:45 pm

Walk or catch a cab heading east on 10th Street into the raffish ⑧ **East Village**
(➤ 116–119) past St. Mark's-in-the-Bowery Church. Fortify yourself with a
cannoli at Veniero's (➤ 32) on East 11th Street, then browse the shops on and
off 1st Avenue and Avenue A between East 11th and East 6th streets.

# 4:15 pm

Exit the East Village heading west on St. Mark's
Place, which eventually
becomes 8th Street. Make
a left at University Place.
The stately houses lining
⑨ **Washington Square Park**
(➤ 121) provide a
delightfully incongruous
backdrop for the
skateboarders, rollerbladers
and street artists who keep
the park in a state of
constant commotion.

# 5:00 pm

To loop through ⑨ **Greenwich Village** (➤ 120–123), head south on MacDougal
Street, make a right at Minetta Lane, cross 6th Avenue, and make a left on
Carmine Street. But for the cars you'll swear you've time-traveled to the 19th
century as you walk along St. Luke's Place, just west of 7th Avenue South. A few
blocks north is Manhattan's narrowest residence, the quirky 75½ Bedford Street.

# 6:00 pm

You'll only have returned to the early
20th century by the time you get to the former
speakeasy Chumley's (➤ 131). The decor
has changed little since F. Scott Fitzgerald
and other literary lights chatted and tippled
here. Stop in for some cider or a beer – and
a gallon of atmosphere.

# 6:30 pm

From Chumley's continue
west on Bedford a few
steps to Grove Street and
make a right.
Make a left at Bleecker
Street and poke through
its shops.

# 8:00 pm

Join New York's well-heeled set for new American cuisine at the discreetly chic
Gramercy Tavern (➤ 129) or at the more mellow and less expensive (but no
less chic) Grange Hall (50 Commerce Street, tel: 212/924-5246). Reservations
are essential at both restaurants.

# 2 Empire State Building

For a building whose style architectural handbooks describe as "low-key" art deco, the Empire State Building certainly attracts a lot of attention. King Kong climbed it, a B-25 bomber collided with it, daredevils have parachuted off it, and

lightning strikes the building an average of 100 times annually. About 3.5 million people drop by for a visit each year; just under 100 million have done so to date. Even Fidel Castro put the building on his New York City itinerary. For pure romance – not to mention unbeatable views of the city and nearby New Jersey – no skyscraper can compete.

To make way for the Empire State, developer John Jacob Raskob tore down the original Waldorf-Astoria, one of New York's fanciest hotels. Raskob, an executive at General Motors, wanted his skyscraper to rise higher than the 77-story Chrysler Building, which was completed in 1930 by a rival automaker, Walter P. Chrysler. Though some say Chrysler's building won in the looks department, the Empire State, which opened on May 1, 1931, surpassed the Chrysler as the world's tallest structure and held the title for four decades.

Not content with 86 stories of useable office space, the Empire State is capped by a 16-story observation tower that's crowned by telecommunications antennas and a lightning rod. The top of the building was originally planned to be a mooring mast for dirigibles, but after several test-run fiascoes (it was too windy up that high) the plan was eventually abandoned.

Designed to look like a pencil, the Empire State has a deliberately functional exterior. Gone are the frills and frou-frou of the Beaux Arts and neoclassical periods and even early art deco. The exterior celebrates the role of mass production in the building's construction. The designs in both the limestone façade and the chromium-steel window ornamentation are machine-stamped. Even the red paint on the window frames, the color used for priming steel, accentuates the building's industrial components.

State-of-the-art methods and a round-the-clock schedule resulted in a construction time of a mere 14 months.

---

🏠 196 C2  ✉ 350 5th Avenue at East 34th Street  ☎ (212) 736-3100  🕐 Mon–Fri 10 am–midnight, Sat–Sun 9:30 am–midnight  🚇 34th Street/ Herald Square (B, D, F, N, Q, R, W)  🚌 M1–7, M16, M34  💰 Moderate

Unfortunately for Raskob – who had proclaimed in a 1929 article titled "Everybody Ought To Be Rich" that prosperity was an "endless chain" – the U.S. stock market crashed before the old Waldorf had even been completely demolished.

Tenants were so scarce during the 1930s and early 1940s that the skyscraper was dubbed the "Empty State Building." For several years it was the income from the observation-deck admissions, not office rentals, that covered the taxes.

From the beginning the building has been used as a prop in feature films (about 125 to date), documentaries and news-reels, though the most famous cinematic sequence involving the Empire State – King Kong, with actress Fay Wray in hand, scaling the building and swatting away planes before his eventual demise – was shot in Hollywood.

**The Empire State casts its shadow over the East Side**

## VITAL STATISTICS

*HEIGHT, INCLUDING ANTENNA:* 1,454 feet
*OBSERVATION DECK (102ND FLOOR):* 1,224 feet
*OBSERVATION DECK (86TH FLOOR):* 1,050 feet
*NUMBER OF STEPS TO 102ND FLOOR:* 1,860
*VIEW ON A CLEAR DAY:* 50+ miles
*CONSTRUCTION COSTS:* $25 million
*COST OF LAND:* $16 million
*WEIGHT:* 73,000,000 pounds, 36,500 tons

The Empire State never moves off center more than one-quarter inch even in the highest winds, but people in its early days questioned the building's structural stability. Any doubts about this were erased when in 1945 an Army Air Forces plane crashed between the 78th and 79th floors. An explosion and fire ensued and 14 people died, but damage was contained to nearby floors, and the structural integrity of the building was unharmed.

On two occasions, pairs of para-chutists have sailed off the building.

### Color Chart

The white lights that bathe the Empire State Building at night sometimes give way to colors that celebrate events, holidays and various causes. Below are a few of the annually scheduled color changes.

**Red, black, green** Martin Luther King Day (third Mon in Jan)
**Green** St. Patrick's Day (Mar 17), Rainforest Awareness (Apr)
**Red, white and blue** All legal holidays
**Red** Valentine's Day (Feb 14)
**Yellow, white** Easter Week
**Lavender, white** Gay Pride (last weekend of Jun)
**Pink, white** Race for the Cure (for breast cancer; Sep)
**No lights** Day Without Art (AIDS Awareness; Dec 1)

Police only caught up with one of the four, a British tourist who leaped in 1986.

### TAKING A BREAK

The coffee shops and other eateries in the Empire State are of average quality. Except on Monday you can get a fancy light lunch or take afternoon tea at the nearby **Morgan Court Café** (37th Street and Madison Avenue, tel: 212/689-9016) at the Morgan Library (▶ 124). You don't have to pay museum admission to dine at the café.

### Star Attraction

"King Kong" provided the Empire State Building with its first great role, but the hits have kept on coming, among them:
"An Affair To Remember"
"Annie Hall"
"Easter Parade"
"The French Connection"
"Independence Day"
"Manhattan"
"New York, New York"
"Sleepless in Seattle"
"Taxi Driver"
"When Harry Met Sally"

**Right:** King Kong on a rampage

**Left:** There's marble everywhere in the building's 5th Avenue lobby

## EMPIRE STATE BUILDING: INSIDE INFO

**Top tips** Waiting in line for a ticket and then for the elevator can take hours. You'll save time if you **buy your tickets in advance** at the electronic ticketing booth (credit cards only) at the NYC & Company visitor center (▶ 36). Another option is to buy a Citypass (▶ 190); you can go straight to the elevator line, which will save you as much as an hour on a busy summer day. You can also buy tickets in advance (additional service charge) at the building's website: www.esbnyc.com

A final option is to **buy a combination ticket** for the observation deck and the New York SkyRide. The good news is that you can buy it at the SkyRide's ticket booth (tel: 212/279-9777, 10–10), whose line is much shorter than the deck's. The bad news is that the seven-minute motion-simulator ride, which whips you past two-story-high television projections of top city attractions, is only mildly diverting. Hydraulically powered seats move 320 degrees per second to reinforce the visceral impact of the projected imagery. (If you're the type to get woozy, forgo the experience.)

**One to miss** There's no need to head up to the cramped 102nd-floor observation deck, which in any case isn't always open. The view's no better than the one from the **86th floor**.

**Hidden gem** Although the main action at the Empire State takes place high in the sky, **don't ignore the deco lobby**, clad in rich floor-to-ceiling marble from quarries in Belgium, France, Germany and Italy.

# 8 East Village

Past and present clash in curious ways in the East Village. For much of the 20th century the area east of 4th Avenue between Houston and 14th streets was a haven for European immigrants and a nexus of leftist political activism. These days, though, it's as likely to harbor refugees from Ohio as from outside the United States, and radical pique has for the most part given way to radical chic.

Colorful and scruffy, the East Village is a great place to shop, stroll and soak up the atmosphere. Boutiques sport Day-Glo colors, multihued tattoos adorn the people, and the action on and off the streets is nothing if not eccentric. The **Burp Castle Temple of Beer Worship** (41 East 7th Street at 2nd Avenue, tel: 212/982-4576), a dark-wood, ecclesiastical-motif bar operated by "Brewist monks" garbed in hooded brown robes, is but the tip of this quirky iceberg.

Accessorize your outfits or your body at East Village emporiums

The term East Village came into use in the 1960s; before then the neighborhood was part of Greenwich Village (and shared its radicalism), with demographic links to the Lower

Kitsch baubles and pop collectibles lure customers to "LSD"

East Side. The many Yiddish theaters along 2nd Avenue during the early 20th century earned the street the moniker Jewish Rialto, and Germans and Italians lived here in large numbers.

Sections of the East Village look the way they did 100 years ago. Fast-food chains and graceless recent construction mar the fantasy somewhat, but many tenement buildings and historical sites remain (the latter mostly unmarked). The neighborhood's multitude of diners and thrift and vintage-clothing stores celebrate a more recent past, the 1950s and 1960s.

## East Village Landmarks

If you like to shop for clothing, housewares, new and used records, or kitschy memorabilia, you could spend an enjoyable day in the East Village focused entirely on the present. The past does bleed through, though, and you may find yourself curious about what went on here. Below, from west to east, are a few places that made neighborhood history.

• **Grace Church**, 802 Broadway at East 10th Street. James Renwick Jr., the architect of St. Patrick's Cathedral (► 66), designed this Gothic Revival-style Episcopal church, whose stained-glass windows are among its noteworthy features. During the 19th century, this was the church of New York's high society. The marriage of Newland Archer and May Welland in Edith Wharton's novel *The Age of Innocence* takes place here.

• **Colonnade Row**, 428–434 Lafayette Street south of Astor Place. Believe it or not, this decrepit row of Greek Revival houses (there were nine originally) was the classiest address in 1830s New York when John Jacob Astor, who made millions trading furs and speculating in Manhattan real estate, moved in along with other wealthy folks. Their homes had Manhattan's first indoor plumbing.

• **Merchant's House Museum**, 29 East 4th Street east of Lafayette Street, tel: (212) 777-1089, open: Thu–Mon 1–5

---

195 F3　Astor Place (6); Lower East Side/2nd Avenue (F); 8th Street/NYU (N, R)　M1, M8, M9

(inexpensive). Gertrude Tredwell, who lived in this 1832 Federal and Greek Revival-style house (her father was the titular merchant), was reputedly the inspiration for the heiress in the Henry James novel *Washington Square*. Embittered by a failed romance, Tredwell became a recluse and died in 1933 at age 93. Because her house immediately became a museum, its furnishings are mostly original and the detailing remains largely intact.

• **Cooper Union Foundation Building**, 51 Astor Place at 3rd Avenue. Peter Cooper, an industrialist (he built one of the first locomotives) and philanthropist who was one of 19th-century America's great self-made men, started the college headquartered in the eight-story brownstone that looms over Astor Place. Abraham Lincoln gave a memorable speech in the building's Great Hall that bolstered his bid to become president of the United States.

• **The Bowery**. During the 19th century and much of the 20th, the Bowery – 3rd Avenue below Astor Place – was synonymous with crime, derelicts and flophouses. The tough neighborhood had its edges softened somewhat in the play and 1937 Humphrey Bogart movie "Dead End."

• **St. Mark's-in-the-Bowery**, 131 East 10th Street at 2nd Avenue. Ecumenical religious services and wild happenings – anything from poetry slams to performances of the works of the Marquis de Sade – take place at this fieldstone church erected in 1799. The stern 17th-century Dutch governor Peter Stuyvesant, who's buried outside (the church is on the site of his family's chapel), would doubtless not approve.

• **Second Avenue Deli**, 156 2nd Avenue at East 10th Street, tel: (212) 677-0606. Plaques embedded in the sidewalk in front of the deli honor the stars of the Yiddish theater. The Molly Picon Room inside the restaurant contains pictures and posters of one of the most famous of them all. The traditional

**Hang onto your kids**

deli food looks and tastes
quite fine.
• **Fillmore East**,
Emigrant Savings Bank,
105 2nd Avenue at East
6th Street. Big Brother and
the Holding Company,
fronted by Janis Joplin,
opened this short-lived
(1968–71) rock palace,
where the Allman
Brothers, Frank Zappa's
Mothers of Invention, and
other groups cut live
albums. Only the building's
upper facade remains.
• **Ottendorfer Library
and German Dispensary**,
135–137 2nd Avenue at
St. Mark's Place. These
two handsome buildings
of red-orange brick com-
bine Queen Anne and
Italian Renaissance style.
One was the first truly free
and public library in New
York, the other was a
clinic whose facade
includes busts of famous
men of medicine. A news-
paper publisher and his
wife donated the struc-
tures to New York's
German community.

The folks back
home will love
your new
jewelry!

## TAKING A BREAK

A cross-section of the Village drops by the 24-hour Ukrainian
restaurant **Veselka** (144 2nd Avenue at East 9th Street,
tel: 212/228-9682) for its hearty meals and exuberant ambience. For a trendier bite, stop in at the 1950s-style **Stingy
Lulu's Luncheonette** (129 St. Mark's Place at Avenue A,
tel: 212/674-3545) or one of the other cafés on its block.

### EAST VILLAGE: INSIDE INFO

**Top tips** The neighborhood's commercial heart is along 1st and 2nd avenues
and avenues A and B. With some exceptions the **most interesting shops are between
5th and 11th streets**. An often stoned crowd hangs out in Tompkins Square Park,
between avenues A and B and 7th and 10th streets; it's generally safe during the
day, but you may find the scene intimidating.

**One to miss** Don't stray east of **Avenue B**. Not much of interest goes on, and the
several housing projects farther east can be dangerous.

# 9 Greenwich Village

Successive generations of old timers have declared that Greenwich Village isn't what it used to be. Maybe so, but though this former bohemian enclave has largely been gentrified, with even modest houses selling for $1 million, it retains an anarchic vibe.

Henry James chronicled the Washington Square area's brief 19th-century reign as an enclave of high society, the Provincetown Players performed the early works of Eugene O'Neill here in the 1920s, Bob Dylan and Jimi Hendrix wowed the faithful in local bars and coffeehouses in the 1960s, and a 1969 riot at a Christopher Street bar (➤ 19) jump-started the gay-liberation movement. Even before its avant-garde days, though, residents expressed their individuality: When New York's grid plan was established in the early 1800s, vehement protests on the western side thwarted efforts to impose a more uniform layout south of 14th Street. (You'll be acknowledging their victory each time you're required to consult your map.)

**Opposite: Christopher Park sculpture commemorates gay lib.**

✚ 194 B3  🚇 West 4th Street/Washington Square (A, C, E, F)
🚌 M1, M5–8, M10–11

**Wrought iron and ivy along Grove Street**

## Greenwich Village Highlights

Below, from east to west, are a few neighborhood highlights. The West Village walking tour (➤ 177–179) passes by these sites and more.

- **Washington Square Park**, base of 5th Avenue. Rollerbladers, street entertainers and tart-tongued regulars keep things lively at this former potter's field and place of public executions (the large elm in the park's northwestern corner was reputedly used for hangings as late as the 1820s). Designed by Stanford White, Washington Arch is a marble reproduction of the wooden original, erected to celebrate the 100th anniversary of George Washington's inauguration as president of the United States.

- **The Row**, Washington Square Park North, east and west of 5th Avenue. The mostly Greek Revival town houses along Washington Square Park North were built in the early 1830s, just as the park neighborhood was coming into fashion. Later occupants of the Row included painter Edward Hopper, at No. 3.

- **Washington Mews**, off 5th Avenue north of Washington Square Park North. The impressive residences along this private alley were carriage houses or stables for the Row.

- **MacDougal Alley**, off MacDougal Street north of Washington Square Park North. Gertrude Vanderbilt Whitney, the artistic heiress, sculpted in one of the MacDougal Alley structures. The first incarnation of the Whitney Museum, which she founded, was around the corner at 8 West 8th Street.

- **Jefferson Market Library**, 425 6th Avenue at West 10th Street. A former courthouse, this public library branch and neighborhood icon is a happy mishmash of Victorian Gothic architecture. Across the street is private Patchin Place, where the poet e. e. cummings and other artists lived and worked.

- **Christopher Park**, bordered by 7th Avenue South, West 4th Street, Christopher Street and Grove Street. George Segal's lifesize *Gay Liberation* sculpture, a standing gay male couple and two lesbians on a bench, was installed in this sliver of a park across from the site of the Stonewall Rebellion (➤ 19).

- **Grove Court**, between 10 and 12 Grove Street. An oval bed of ivy amid a well-trod brick patio stands in front of the six redbrick houses of this romantic private courtyard.

- **75½ Bedford Street**. The poet Edna St. Vincent Millay lived briefly in New York City's narrowest house, only 9.5 feet wide.

- **Chumley's**, 86 Bedford Street near Grove Street. Doors hidden behind bookcases and the lack of a sign are two clues that this evocative joint was a speakeasy during Prohibition. Generations of famous writers, many of whose book jackets line the walls, have hung out here.

- **St. Luke's Place**. One of the Village's handsomest blocks, this street of Italianate homes looks pretty much the way it did when they were built in the 1850s. The street lamps in front of No. 6, home of the jovial if corrupt Prohibition-era mayor Jimmy Walker, follow the custom from Dutch rule of placing lights in front of city officials' houses.

The poet W.H. Auden helped save the Jefferson Market Courthouse from demolition

Bookcases hid escape routes at the former speakeasy Chumley's

More than two centuries ago, the area north of Houston Street and east of the Hudson River symbolized health and well-being: During yellow fever and other epidemics, wealthy families from lower Manhattan took refuge in what became Greenwich Village.

By the 1840s, as Manhattan's population spread north, the Washington Square district became fashionable. So many African-Americans lived south of the square near MacDougal and Bleecker streets during this time that the area became known as Little Africa. Artists and intellectuals gravitated to Greenwich Village a few years later, the lure perhaps being the intellectual stimulation provided by New York University, which opened on the square in the 1830s.

Walt Whitman quaffed beers and waxed eloquent at Pfaff's, a saloon on Broadway near Bleecker Street, as did Edgar Allan Poe. Continuing the Village's literary traditions in the 20th century were poets Edna St. Vincent Millay and e. e. cummings, and writers like Djuna Barnes, James Baldwin and Allen Ginsberg. Cecil Taylor, John Coltrane and other jazz greats played the Village Vanguard, and 1960s folk and rock genres developed at Café Wha?, the Bitter End and other clubs.

## GREENWICH VILLAGE: INSIDE INFO

**Top tips** If you only have time for a quick taste of the neighborhood, follow steps 1–9 of the **West Village walking tour** (▶ 177–179).
• **Quirky shops** line Bleecker Street west of 6th Avenue. Arthur's Tavern (57 Grove Street, tel: 212/675-6879) is a moldy but **atmospheric jazz dive** that'll transport you back in time.

**One to miss** The area west of Hudson Street contains less of interest than the sections to the east.

Despite the irrevocable changes wrought by gentrification and "progress," you can still detect a real neighborhood here. Shopkeepers josh their regulars, and homey cafés and stores are shoehorned into peculiarly shaped spaces that leave customers no choice but to interact. Bleecker Street and Christopher Street are the two main east–west (more or less) commercial drags, but take time to wander off them.

## TAKING A BREAK

For pancakes, a sandwich, a zesty bowl of soup, and a heapin' helpin' of Village eccentricity, drop into **Shopsin's** (63 Bedford Street at Morton Street, tel: 212/924-5160). Less quirky but still appealing is the **Cornelia St. Café** (29 Cornelia Street near Bleecker Street, tel: 212/989-9318), where poetry readings and other arts events take place.

# At Your Leisure

J. P. Morgan researched in style

## 1 Morgan Library

Financier J. Pierpont Morgan collected illuminated books and other rare manuscripts – so many he had architect Charles McKim whip up a Renaissance-style palazzo to house them. The library's elaborate murals and mosaics and exquisite three-tiered shelving system alone warrant a visit. The Morgan Court Café (museum admission not required) serves lunch and afternoon tea in an enclosed courtyard.

✚ 197 D2 ✉ 29 East 36th Street at Madison Avenue ☎ (212) 685-0610 🕐 Tue–Sat 10:30–5 (also Fri 5–8, Sat 5–6), Sun noon–6; closed Jan 1, Jul 4, Thanksgiving, Dec 25 🍴 Morgan Court Café ($) 🚇 33rd Street (6) 🚌 M2–4 💵 Moderate

## 3 Madison Square Park

New York's wealthiest mid-19th-century families lived near Madison Square Park, but their swath for promenading had become a seedy mess by the 1980s. The emergence of "Silicon Alley" software, design and

Internet businesses helped revive the neighborhood and park, which holds several important sculptures. Augustus Saint Gaudens sculpted the finest, the bronze of Admiral David Farragut, a hero of the Northern States in the Civil War. The figures *Courage* and *Loyalty* flank the admiral on the semicircular pedestal, designed by Stanford White to resemble a ship's bow.

East of the park is the Metropolitan Life Insurance Tower (► 7) – the one with the clocks – briefly the world's tallest building.

✚ 195 D5 ✉ Bordered by 23rd and 26th streets and Madison and 5th avenues 🚇 23rd Street (N, R) 🚌 M1–3, M5–7

## 4 Flatiron Building

Painter Childe Hassam and photographer Alfred Stieglitz are among the many artists who have immortalized the 22-story Italian Renaissance-style skyscraper that rises so gracefully from a triangle formed by the

intersection of three major streets. Architect Daniel Burnham and others remarked that his building resembled a flatiron, and the inelegant name stuck. Its patrician bearing and playful terra-cotta detailing are the Flatiron's hallmarks, but the skyscraper's completion in 1903 represented the demise of the neighborhood's genteel lifestyle, depicted in novels like Edith Wharton's *The Age of Innocence*. Contrary to local folklore, the Flatiron was never the world's tallest building, and police used – but didn't coin – the phrase "23 skidoo" to disperse men angling for a look at women's ankles, revealed when the severe downdraft created by the structure raised ladies' full-length skirts.

🔁 195 D5 ✉ 175 5th Avenue at Broadway and 23rd Street 🚇 23rd Street (N, R) 🚌 M1–3, M5–7

## 🖪 Gramercy Park

Few places evoke New York's mid- to late 19th-century Gaslight Era better than this exclusive neighborhood, modeled on the residential squares of London, which borders the city's only private park. Those living along the park received keys to it, a tradition that survives to this day. Plaques at the park's north and south gates describe the Greek Revival and Italianate town houses to the west and other nearby structures. On the south

Gas still powers some of the lamps along Gramercy Park

side, at 15 and 16 Gramercy Park South, are two famous and still active clubs, the National Arts Club and the Players Club. Artists started the first, actors the second.

🔁 195 D5 ✉ Lexington Avenue between East 21st and East 20th streets 🚇 23rd Street (6) 🚌 M1–3, M101–103

## 🖪 Union Square

The site of at least one demonstration supporting the Northern States during the Civil War, and of labor rallies in succeeding years, the square is a civilized spot to sip coffee and people-watch. Sculptor Anthony de Francisci's exceptionally well-rendered figures of pioneer families, African-Americans, laborers and Native Americans animate the bronze relief that circles the base of the Independence Flagstaff, in the square's center. You can sample home-baked breads and cookies at the Greenmarket held on Monday, Wednesday, Friday and Saturday. During the summer on the north side, the Union Square Café opens a concession for outdoor dining and snacking.

🔁 195 D4 ✉ Bordered by 14th and 17th streets and Union Square West and East 🚇 14th Street/Union Square (L, N, Q, R, W, 4, 5, 6) 🚌 M1, M2, M3, M9, M14

## 7 Forbes Magazine Galleries

The late jet-setting magazine magnate Malcolm Forbes collected art and cultural artifacts with the same zeal with which he chronicled the world of business. Toy boats, toy soldiers, vintage Monopoly games, artifacts by Peter Carl Fabergé, and the papers of U.S. presidents are assembled here with wit and whimsy, making the galleries an enjoyable half-hour stop.

➕ 194 C4 ✉ 62 5th Avenue at West 12th Street ☎ (212) 206-5549 🕐 Tue–Wed and Fri–Sat 10–4; closed Jan 1, Martin Luther King Day, Presidents' Day, Good Fri, Memorial Day, Jul 4, Labor Day, Thanksgiving, Fri after Thanksgiving, Dec 25 🚇 14th Street (F); 14th Street/Union Square (L, N, Q, R, W, 4, 5, 6) 🚌 M1–3, M5, M101–103 📱 Free

## 10 Chelsea

When Joni Mitchell woke up and "it was a Chelsea morning," she was singing about the West Side neighborhood north of Greenwich Village and south of the Garment district. Mitchell had a ground-floor apartment during the 1960s at 41 West 16th Street. Educator Clement Clark Moore, best known for the poem that begins "Twas the night before Christmas," owned much of this land in the 1800s. The covenants in Moore's will limited commercial uses of the area, which accounts for the preservation of many of its historic homes. East of his holdings, along 6th Avenue and Broadway, was Ladies Mile, a major 19th-century shopping district. The cast-iron former Hugh O'Neill Dry Goods Store (655–671 6th Avenue near 21st Street) is one of several commercial structures from this era still standing. As SoHo rents have soared, many galleries have relocated to Chelsea. Most are west of 10th Avenue between 22nd and 29th streets. Check out the Dia Center for the Arts (548 West 22nd Street, tel: 212/989-5566; open: Wed–Sun noon–6) for contemporary art.

➕ 194 B5 ✉ North of 14th Street, west of 6th Avenue, south of 23rd Street 🚇 14th Street (A, C, E, F, L, 1, 2, 3); 23rd Street (C, E, F, 1, 2, 3) 🚌 M10, M11, M14, M23

## 11 Hotel Chelsea

It may have been crumbling inside and out for decades, but that didn't stop the Hotel Chelsea from attracting a veritable A-list of high and low culture. Past residents included writer Thomas Wolfe, singer Janis Joplin, feminist Germaine Greer and the composer Virgil Thomson – quite an array for what was essentially a dump for most of the 20th century, although in recent years it has been tidied up a bit. Also on the short- or long-term guest list: poets Edgar Lee Masters, Dylan Thomas and Leonard Cohen; rock musicians Bob Dylan, Jimi Hendrix, Patti Smith and the guys of Pink Floyd; sci-fi writer Arthur C. Clarke; suspense writer Patricia Highsmith; "superstars" Edie Sedgwick and Viva (immortalized in Andy Warhol's film "Chelsea Girls"); punk rocker Sid Vicious; and the mad Wrapper Christo. Stand across 23rd Street from the redbrick Victorian Gothic structure to view the architectural detailing: Lacy black wrought-iron balconies done in sunflower motifs span the facade, and a bit of greenery

**Artistic types loved the Hotel Chelsea's ornate exterior**

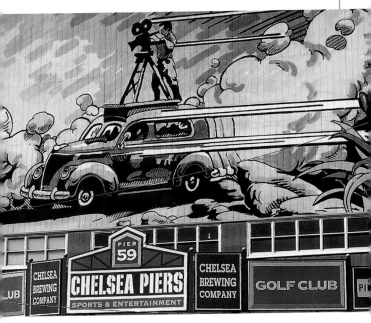

Movie and TV production takes place on piers, alongside multi-faceted diversions

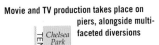

from the rooftop garden creeps into view over the angled dormers. At the time of its construction in 1884, the Chelsea was among the finest cooperative apartment buildings in the city and the first to have a penthouse. It became a hotel in 1905. Artists behind in their rent "donated" some of the artworks hanging on the lobby walls.

➕ 194 B5  ✉ 222 West 23rd Street
☎ (212) 243-3700  🚇 23rd Street (C, E, F, 1, 2)  🚌 M10, M23

## 🅸🅲 Chelsea Piers

Golfers drive balls into nets stretching over Pier 59, where the doomed luxury liner the RMS *Titanic* was to have ended its maiden voyage. The driving range is near the southern edge of the Chelsea Piers sports and entertainment complex, a raucous place to let off a little steam. You can test your skill in the baseball batting cage, rack up some strikes and spares during an Xtreme bowling session (pop music blaring, disco lights flashing), or zip around ice or roller rinks. The Chelsea Brewing Company serves good brews and decent food.

➕ 194, off A5
✉ Piers 59–62 between 16th and 23rd streets at West Side Highway
☎ (212) 336-6666  🚇 23rd Street (C, E; transfer to M23 bus heading west)  🚌 M14, M23

# Where to...
## Eat and Drink

**Prices** The $ amounts indicate what you can expect to pay for an average, complete dinner for one person, including drinks, tax and tip.

$ = under $30   $$ = $30–60   $$$ = over $60

## RESTAURANTS

### America $

Eat your way across the U.S.A. at this cavernous spot, where the menu is presented as a culinary road map to American regional cuisine. From complex New Orleans Cajun flavors, to spicy Southwestern dishes, to plain old peanut butter and jelly (PBJ) sandwiches, this menu can please any palate. It's the perfect spot for families and larger parties – it's big enough to keep waits to a minimum.

195 D4 9 East 18th Street
(212) 505-2110

### Babbo $$$

Celebrated Babbo touts chef Mario Batali in the kitchen. He and experienced restaurateur Joseph Bastianich have created a lovely setting. Wonderfully conceived and prepared dishes highlight Italian technique and seasonal ingredients. Specialties include homemade filled pastas and robust Italian meat dishes. The atmosphere is sophisticated, the wine list excellent, and the service professional.

194 C3 110 Waverly Place between 6th Avenue and MacDougal Street (212) 777-0303 Dinner
Mon–Sat 5:30–11:30, Sun 5:30–11

### Corner Bistro $

This is a simple, popular bar with a tiny dining room and with very low-priced, large and delicious burgers. The best seats are up front, and the best burger is the Bistro Burger, with cheese, bacon, lettuce and tomato. The BLTs are very good, too.

194 B3 331 West 4th Street at 12th Street (212) 242-9502
Daily 11:30 am–4 am

### Daily Chow $$

Owner Brad Kelley has taken to the latest trend in New York dining and transformed his Korean restaurant into a hip Pan-Asian destination, with a sleek bar upstairs and a handsome dining area on both levels. Be sure to have some Bibimbop, the house specialty, a delicious rice cooked in a special vessel to produce a crusty bottom layer blended with "wild mountain vegetables".

195 E2 325 Bowery at 2nd Street (212) 254-7887 Dinner
Mon–Thu 5:30–11, Fri–Sat 5:30–midnight

### Eisenberg's $

This is New York City lunch-counter dining at its best, with a well-reviewed tuna sandwich to boot. Try some Jewish specialties such as matzoh brei and other lunch-counter favorites. The place is very small and casual with lots of character, and it's bustling at lunchtime.

194 C5 174 5th Avenue between 22nd and 23rd streets
(212) 675-5096 Mon–Sat 7 am–5 pm. No dinner

### First $$

This spot is easily the best food destination in the East Village. The design is slick, with hammered tin and industrial fixtures, soft lighting and lively music. There are big, inviting booths for groups, and the bar has an eclectic menu of "nibbly bites." The wine list has good moderate selections, and they have 25 beers. For dessert you can make your own s'mores, an American delicacy of graham crackers, roasted marshmallows and melted chocolate.

## Holy Basil $–$$

A fresh sprig of basil accompanies most everything that comes out of the kitchen at this reasonably priced Thai favorite in the East Village. Spicy curry dishes are among the most popular, but the menu has satay and other Thai standbys, all prepared with the freshest ingredients. The main room looks like a cross between an elegant bordello and a set from "South Pacific". There's a tiny bar up front where you can compete for a Singh Ha while you wait for a table.

✚ 195 E3 ⊠ 149 2nd Avenue
(between 9th and 10th streets)
☎ (212) 460-5557 Ⓓ Dinner
Mon–Fri 5–11.30, Sat–Sun 5–midnight

## Il Bagato $

Don't let the Lower East Side location fool you – this cash-only place is not just cheap eats for starving neighborhood artists. The classic Italian dishes are almost as popular as the atmospheric downstairs bar, where a DJ holds court in the back

South
☎ (212) 477-0777 Ⓛ Lunch
Mon–Fri noon–2; dinner Sun–Thu
5.30–midnight, Fri–Sat 5.30–11.
Closed national holidays

## Grand Sichuan International $

You don't have to go to Chinatown for good Chinese food. The tea-smoked duck is sensational, the twice-cooked pork is rich and spicy. Ask if the delicious pea shoots are in season.

✚ 194 A5 ⊠ 229 9th Avenue at 24th
Street ☎ (212) 620-5200 Ⓛ Lunch
daily 11.30–5; dinner daily 5–11

## Hangawi $$

What you get here is Korean vegetarian food that will render you at once spellbound and virtuous-feeling. You sit on small cushions at low tables and eat mountain herbs, unfamiliar roots and interesting porridges.

✚ 197 D2 ⊠ 12 East 32nd Street
between 5th and Madison avenues
☎ (212) 213-0077 Ⓓ Lunch daily
noon–3; dinner daily 5–10

South American influences – duck quesadilla, molasses glazed tuna, pork with plantains – but you'll see the entire world parade by from this bright, airy spot on Greenwich Avenue

✚ 194 B3 ⊠ 89 Greenwich Avenue
between Bank and West 12th streets
☎ (212) 691-8080 Ⓛ Lunch Tue–Fri
11.30–3; dinner Tue–Thu 6–11, Fri–Sat
6–11.30, Sun 6–10

## ▼▼▼ Gramercy Tavern $$$

This popular restaurant can be visited either with a much sought-after reservation for the main dining room, or on a walk-in basis for the lower-priced Tavern Room (▲ 130). Chef Tom Colicchio is known for his excellent modern American fare, and pastry chef Claudia Fleming for her desserts. The vegetarian tasting menu, available in the main dining room, has a good range of vibrant dishes, and there is a fine cheese selection.

✚ 195 D5 ⊠ 42 East 20th Street
between Broadway and Park Avenue

✚ 195 F3 ⊠ 87 1st Avenue between
5th and 6th streets ☎ (212) 674-3823
Ⓓ Dinner Mon–Sat 6 pm–2 am, Sun
5 pm–1 am; brunch Sun 11–4

## Florent $

Long ago a luncheonette to the meat-market workers in the neighborhood, this has been a hip destination for some time, serving mostly French bistro fare such as steak *frites* and mussels, omelettes and *rillettes* (pork bread spread) to a colorful crowd. The scene here is during the wee hours, for the après-club crowd, and at brunch.

✚ 194 A3 ⊠ 69 Gansevoort Street
between Greenwich and Washington
streets ☎ (212) 989-5779
Ⓓ Sun–Thu 9 am–5 am, Fri–Sat
24 hours

## Good $$

The owners of Campo, the former Latin food restaurant, toned things down considerably when they re-opened. The fare now is more Americanized, with ambiguous

## Moustache $

This small and casual storefront restaurant has fabulous Middle Eastern food. The pita bread, made to order in a brick oven, goes well with the delicious salads and serves as a vehicle for the great merguez sandwich, satisfying and savory. The cheese-and-parsley pie is great, too.

➕ 194 B2 ⊠ 90 Bedford between Barrow and Grove streets ☎ (212) 229-2220 ⊚ Lunch and dinner daily noon–11

## I Trulli Enoteca $

This small wine bar charms with its many flights of interesting Italian wines. It is less expensive than the restaurant next door and has its own delicious menu (big portions) to enjoy. The informative staff make this a fun tasting experience.

➕ ⊠ (▶ above) ⊚ Mon–Fri noon–10 pm (also Fri 10–11 pm), Sat 5–11 pm

## John's Pizzeria $

John's is home to some of the best pizza pies in New York City, right from the brick oven, straightforward, delicious and satisfyingly crispy.

➕ 194 B2 ⊠ 278 Bleecker Street between 6th Avenue and 7th Avenue South ☎ (212) 243-1680 ⊚ Daily 11:30–11:30

## I Trulli $$$

As the name suggests, the food served in this lovely restaurant is based on dishes from Apulia in southern Italy (*trulli* are the strange, beehive-shaped dwellings characteristic of the region). Apulia is famous for its fish, which is often barbecued, and wood-roasted fish is on the menu here. Seasonal dining options include a table near the fire or one in the pleasant garden. The owners are friendly and knowledgeable about the wines of the region, and should be summoned for consultation.

➕ 197 D1 ⊠ 122 East 27th Street between Lexington Avenue and Park Avenue South ☎ (212) 481-7372 ⊚ Lunch Mon–Fri 12:30–3; dinner Mon–Thu 5:30–11, Fri, Sat 5:30–10:15. Closed national holidays

room. You're in for a wait if you have no reservations, so just grab a seat at the bar, have a drink, and people-watch the time away. Check out the wine bar, next door, for an after-dinner drink.

➕ 195 F2 ⊠ 192 East 2nd Street between avenues A and B ☎ (212) 228-0977 ⊚ Lunch Tue–Fri noon–5; dinner Tue–Thu 6:30–11:30, Fri–Sat 6:30–12:30, Sun 6–10.30. Closed Dec 25, Jan 1

## Second Avenue Deli $

Sample such delicacies as wonderful chopped liver and matzoh ball soup or *cholent* ("Jewish cassoulet") in this epitome of a New York deli. The simpler fare such as pastrami, corned beef and excellent smoked salmon is just as good.

➕ 195 E3 ⊠ 156 2nd Avenue at 10th Street ☎ (212) 677-0606 ⊚ Daily 7 am–midnight (also Fri–Sat midnight–3 am). Closed some Jewish holidays

## Tavern Room at Gramercy Tavern $$

The Tavern Room offers smaller, less expensive food than the sought-after Gramercy Tavern. "Tavern Tastes" are offered on a walk-in basis continuously throughout the afternoon and evening. This is a good way to experience the restaurant at a lower price, though the wait can be long.

➕ ⊠ (▶ 129) ⊚ Daily noon–11 pm (also Fri–Sat 11 pm–midnight)

## Patria $$$

Enter the colorful world of Latin America. Chef Andrew DiCataldo's creations are served in a spacious, multitiered room with a vibrant atmosphere. The wine list favors Spanish and Argentinian selections. It's one of the few upscale completely nonsmoking restaurants in town.

➕ 195 D5 ⊠ 250 Park Avenue South at 20th Street ☎ (212) 777-6211 ⊚ Lunch Mon–Fri noon–3; dinner Mon–Thu 5:30–11, Fri, Sat 5–midnight, Sun 5–11

## Tea & Sympathy $

This tiny storefront attracts a multitude of fans of the heartwarming foods of Great Britain, with delicious renditions of bangers and mash, Welsh rarebit, treacle pudding. They do a lovely full tea, served all day, with plenty of sweets and savories and featuring the best Devon clotted cream. The place has some of the best food and certainly the coziest atmosphere of any Village spot.

**✚ 194 B4 ⊠ 108 Greenwich Avenue between 12th and 13th streets ☎ (212) 807-8329 ⓦ Mon–Fri 11:30–10:30, Sat–Sun 10 am–10:30 pm**

## CAFÉS

## Anglers & Writers

Rustic and inviting, this quiet spot serves a good afternoon tea or coffee and baked goods, as well as heartier fare.

**✚ 194 B2 ⊠ 420 Hudson Street at Leroy Street ☎ (212) 675-0810 ⓦ Mon–Sat 9 am–11 pm (also Fri–Sat 11 pm–midnight), Sun 10–10**

## Café Pick-Me-Up

Great casual atmosphere for lounging and East Village people-watching.

**✚ 195 F3 ⊠ 145 Avenue A at 9th Street ☎ (212) 673-7231 ⓦ Mon–Sat 6:30 am–1:30 pm (also Fri–Sat 1:30 pm–2:30 am)**

## Caffe Reggio

Great atmosphere for lingering, good snacking and Italian cookies.

**✚ 194 C2 ⊠ 119 MacDougal Street between Bleecker and 3rd streets ☎ (212) 475-9557 ⓦ Sun–Thu 9 am–2 am, Fri–Sat 10 am–3 am**

## Danal

Delightful afternoon teas in a charming storefront restaurant.

**✚ 195 E3 ⊠ 90 East 10th between 3rd and 4th avenues ☎ (212) 982-6930 ⓦ Lunch and dinner daily; afternoon tea Fri–Sat from 4 pm; brunch Sat 10–3, Sun 10–3:30**

## Magnolia Bakery

Here's a real old-fashioned American bakery that specializes in awesome layer cakes, cupcakes, muffins and rare classic delights such as refrigerator cake and banana pudding made with Nilla wafers.

**✚ 194 B3 ⊠ 401 Bleecker Street at West 11th Street ☎ (212) 462-2572 ⓦ Mon–Fri 8–11:30 am, Sat–Sun 10 am–midnight**

## Tea & Sympathy

**✚ ⊠ (► left)**

## BARS

## Chumley's

This New York City classic lurks behind an unmarked door that's not easy to spot – a reminder of its speakeasy past. It is pleasantly old and dark, with fine ales on tap and a cozy feel in the winter with its working fireplace.

**✚ 194 B2 ⊠ 86 Bedford Street between Grove and Barrow streets ☎ (212) 675-4449 ⓦ Mon–Sat 6 pm–1 am (also Fri–Sat 1–2 am), Sun 4 pm–midnight**

## Corner Bistro

**✚ ⊠ (► 128)**

## I Trulli Enoteca

**✚ ⊠ (► 130)**

## McSorley's Old Ale House

Read Joseph Mitchell's description of this 19th-century pub before ordering your ale. They have their own brand, both light and dark, serving snacks of cheese, onions and crackers. Risk of lines on a Friday or Saturday.

**✚ 195 E3 ⊠ 15 East 7th Street between 2nd and 3rd avenues ☎ (212) 473-9148 ⓦ Daily noon–midnight**

## Temple Bar

Find the mysterious, barely marked entrance indicated by a dragon, then enter a sophisticated, upscale bar with sleek design and great drinks and snacks.

**✚ 195 D2 ⊠ 332 Lafayette Street between Bleecker and Houston streets ☎ (212) 925-4242 ⓦ Mon–Thu 5 pm–1 am, Fri, Sat 5 pm–2 am, Sun 7 pm–midnight**

# Where to... Shop

## West Village

The West Village is a charming area to wander about. Dip into the little places tucked away here and there. Many parts are more residential than commercial, though Bleecker Street and Christopher Street are good shopping strips.

Many shops have unusual specialties, such as **Chess Forum** (219 Thompson Street), where you can buy one of many chess sets or get up a game with locals, and **Peanut Butter & Jane** (617 Hudson Street), a cramped and vibrant toy store with some interesting new and vintage children's clothes. For altogether different pursuits, **Pink Pussycat** (167 West 4th Street) specializes in adult novelties and lingerie.

For the home there's **Kitschen** (380 Bleecker Street), which has a great selection of vintage kitchenware. **Susan Parrish Antiques** (390 Bleecker Street) has a fine collection of American folk art. The three **Amalgamated Homes** (9, 13 and 19 Christopher Street) have modern and tasteful household furnishings and hardware. **Mxyplzyk** (125 Greenwich Avenue and a neighboring annex) also has great home accessories to suit every taste. **Le Fanion** (299 West 4th Street) has beautifully made French ceramics. There is also great food. **Balducci's** (424 6th Avenue) where you can buy one of many chess sets or get up a game with locals, and **Murray's Cheese** (257 Bleecker Street) has one of the best selections anywhere. Bleecker Street is home to many an Italian pastry shop. **Li-Lac Chocolates** (120 Christopher Street) is a longtime destination for handmade chocolates.

## East Village to Union Square

The East Village has a fabulous array of one-of-a-kind small designer shops lurking on nearly every block, some consisting simply of people with sewing machines displaying what they have produced recently. East 9th Street between Avenue A and 2nd Avenue is particularly rich with such shops, some with vintage items as well as new, though East 5th, 6th and 7th streets should be explored thoroughly as well.

For good vintage, try **Atomic Passion** (430 East 9th Street). For glamorous and new, try **Mark Montano** (434 East 9th Street). **Patricia Field** (10 East 8th Street) is a classic stop for wild clothes and accessories.

For music, **Footlight Records** (113 East 12th Street) has an impressive classic vinyl collection, particularly by women vocalists. For all-natural cosmetics, follow the crowd to **Kiehls** (109 3rd Avenue). **Forbidden Planet** (840 Broadway) appeals to the collector with its huge selection of old and new comics, plus sci-fi paraphernalia of all kinds.

There is a lot of furniture to be had in this area and farther up, particularly on Bond Street between Lafayette Street and Bowery, and on Lafayette Street between Prince and Houston streets. The **Art & Industrial Design Shop** (399 Lafayette Street) has an entertaining display of older 20th-century furniture.

The zone for more formal antiques is 10th and 11th streets, University Place to Broadway. The huge home emporium **ABC Carpet & Home** (Broadway and 19th Street) carries an astounding array of old and new furniture and innumerable objets d'art. **Fishs Eddy** (889 Broadway) sells nifty old dinnerware from defunct restaurants and hotels.

Book lovers after cut-price new and secondhand books should not miss the "miles of aisles" at the **Strand Bookstore** (828 Broadway). **Paragon**, at Broadway and 18th Street, offers top sporting goods from all the major manufacturers, while the **Union Square Greenmarket** (open Mon, Wed, Fri and Sat) provides a gorgeous food and flower display, with an amazing selection during the peak growing season.

## Chelsea

Chelsea has several important centers of interest. A number of shops on 18th Street, between 5th and 6th avenues, specialize in used books and records, especially **Academy Records & CDs** (12 West 18th Street) for classical and jazz CDs, and **Books of Wonder** next door (16 West 18th Street) for vintage and new children's books.

You'll find some blocks with good, quirky shops, such as 22nd Street between 7th and 8th avenues. On the weekends, the now-famous **Chelsea Flea Market** dominates 6th Avenue between 24th and 27th streets, and its popularity has encouraged the birth of new restaurants and antiques shops to serve browsers. The **Chelsea Art & Antiques Building** (110 West 25th Street) houses a whole world of small dealers in everything from fine porcelains to Pez dispensers.

For music, there's a treasure trove hiding on the eighth floor of the office building at 236 West 26th Street, the **Jazz Record Center**, a mecca for the collector. For discount clothes, try your luck at **Loehmann's** (17th Street and 7th Avenue). If that doesn't work, there's bargains galore at **Daffy's** (34th Street and Broadway and 5th Avenue at 18th Street).

For cameras and electronics, try **B&H Photo-Video** (480 9th Avenue between 33rd and 34th streets).

New developments are brewing in the West 20s as galleries move in, bringing with them some designer boutiques and other shops.

# Where to...
# Be Entertained

## THEATER

### Astor Place Theater
The outlandish Blue Man Group performs the long-running show *Tubes*.
🚹 195 D3 ⊠ 434 Lafayette Street
☎ (212) 254-4370

### La Mama E.T.C.
This still vital East Village space birthed experimental theater in the 1960s.
🚹 195 E2 ⊠ 74a East 4th Street
☎ (212) 475-7710

### New York Theatre Workshop
Young directors cut their teeth at the venue where *Rent* was first performed.
🚹 195 E2 ⊠ 79 East 4th Street
☎ (212) 460-5475

### Public Theatre
Showcases contemporary plays.
🚹 195 E3 ⊠ 425 Lafayette Street
☎ (212) 260-2400

### Sullivan Street Playhouse
The world's longest-running show, *The Fantasticks*, plays here.
🚹 194 C2 ⊠ 181 Sullivan Street
☎ (212) 674-3838

## DANCE

### Joyce Theater
Dancers love this superb Chelsea showcase with great sight lines.
🚹 194 B4 ⊠ 175 8th Avenue
☎ (212) 242-0800

### Kitchen
Experimental dance and multimedia works are always cooking here.

🗺 194, off A4 🖂 512 West 19th Street ☎ (212) 255-5793

### P.S. 122
This great space hosts genre-busting performance art, dance and more.

## MUSIC

### Opera

### Amato Opera Theater
"Grand opera as good theater" is the goal at this house with about 100 seats.
🗺 195 E2 🖂 319 Bowery ☎ (212) 228-8200

### Contemporary

### Bitter End
Joni Mitchell, Tracy Chapman and others got started at this historic club.
🗺 194 C2 🖂 147 Bleecker Street ☎ (212) 673-7030

### Bottom Line
Blues artists and rockers like Lou Reed play this longtime showcase.
🗺 195 D2 🖂 15 West 4th Street ☎ (212) 228-6300

### CBGB
Punk stage, acoustic room, trip-hop lounge keep '70s legend current.
🗺 195 E2 🖂 315 Bowery ☎ (212) 982-4052

### The Cooler
Alternative and other music's on the bill at this renovated meat locker.
🗺 194 A4 🖂 416 West 14th Street ☎ (212) 229-0785

### Fez
Basement hosting jazz and new music.
🗺 195 D2 🖂 Time Cafe, 380 Lafayette Street ☎ (212) 533-2680

### Irving Plaza
Everyone from Cheap Trick to Tricky plays the midsize concert hall.
🗺 195 D4 🖂 17 Irving Place ☎ (212) 777-6800

### Joe's Pub
Acts like Joe Jackson play this sophisticated restaurant.
🗺 195 E3 🖂 Public Theatre, 425 Lafayette Street ☎ (212) 539-8770

### Jazz

### Blue Note
Jazz legends in intimate, pricey room.
🗺 194 C2 🖂 131 West 3rd Street ☎ (212) 475-8592

### Jazz Standard
Hip and hot, this Flatiron district club has a fine upstairs restaurant.
🗺 197 D1 🖂 116 East 27th Street ☎ (212) 576-2232

### Smalls
Great jams, all types of jazz and a low cover draw folks to tiny Smalls.
🗺 194 B3 🖂 183 West 10th Street ☎ (212) 929-7565

### Sweet Basil
Covers of albums recorded here line the walls of this important showcase.

### Village Vanguard
"Live at the Village Vanguard" still means the best in jazz.
🗺 194 B5 🖂 178 7th Avenue South ☎ (212) 255-4037

## COMEDY/CABARET

### Comedy Cellar
The feel is 1960s Greenwich Village at this subterranean showcase.
🗺 194 C2 🖂 117 MacDougal Street ☎ (212) 254-3480

### Judy's Chelsea
A gayish crowd hangs out at this cozy piano bar and cabaret.
🗺 194 B4 🖂 169 8th Avenue ☎ (212) 929-5410

### Rose's Turn
A laid-back and lively piano bar. Singers and revues play the cabaret.
🗺 194 B2 🖂 55 Grove Street ☎ (212) 366-5438

🗺 194 B4 🖂 88 7th Avenue South ☎ (212) 242-1785

# Lower Manhattan

# Getting Your Bearings

**Layers of history converge in Lower Manhattan. The Dutch settled on the island's southern tip in the early 1600s. The first U.S. capitol was established in 1789 near what became the New York Stock Exchange. The ancestors of millions of present-day Americans passed through Ellis Island from the 1890s to the 1920s. The area's most prominent modern landmark, the World Trade Center, was leveled in 2001.**

Despite the destruction, much of interest in Lower Manhattan remains accessible, though you may have to detour around reconstruction efforts. The absolute must-do is the excursion by ferry to the Statue of Liberty and Ellis Island. North of Manhattan's tip is Wall Street, the cradle of American commerce, and beyond that are the Civic Center and the delightfully overdone Woolworth Building. The historic ships and fine museum within the South Street Seaport Historic District compensate for that area's heavy commercialization. Just north of the seaport area the fabled Brooklyn Bridge, the engineering marvel of its day, catches the eye. North of the bridge lie Chinatown and SoHo.

Bleecker St

HOUSTON

STREET
Broadway-
Lafayette St

Prince St

WEST VARICK ST

HUDSON

AVE OF THE AMERICAS

BROADWAY

SoHo **16**

Spring St

Little Italy
**15**

Spring St

DE

BROADWAY

STREET

BOWERY

HOLLAND TUNNEL

CANAL STREET

GRAND

Canal St

Canal St

Canal St

STREET

Hudson River

WEST STREET

CHURCH ST

PARK ROW

**13**
TriBeCa

WEST ST

Chinatown **14**

ST JAMES PL

Hudson River Park

CHAMBERS ST

City Hall

Brooklyn Br-
City Hall

Park Place

**11** City Hall

BATTERY PARK CITY

Woolworth Building **10**

VESEY ST

Fulton St/
Broadway-Nassau

Ground Zero
(World Trade Center)

FULTON ST

South S
Sea

**4**
Western Waterfront

Trinity Church **6** **7**

Wall St

Wall Street Historic Dis
Area

**8** Wall St

BROADWAY

New York Stock Exchange

Broad St

WALL ST

WATER ST

SOUTH ST VIADUCT

Bowling Green

US Custom House /
National Museum of
the American Indian

Bowling Green

**5**

Whitehall St

Battery
Park

BROADWAY-BATTERY TUNNEL

**2** **3**
Statue of Liberty,
Ellis Island

**1** Staten Island Ferry

## ★ Don't Miss

## At Your Leisure

EAST HOUSTON ST

Lower East Side

PITT ST

East

Delancey St

Essex St

WILLIAMSBURG BRIDGE APPROACH

River

GRAND ST

Park

ver East Side
ement Museum

ST BROADWAY

FDR ROOSEVELT DRIVE (EAST RIVER DRIVE)

River

0   ½ mile

0   1 km

NKLIN

MANHATTAN BRIDGE

East

Brooklyn Bridge

**12**

BROOKLYN

BROOKLYN - QUEENS EXPWY

Page 135: The sculptor's mother was the model for Liberty's face

Iron staircases link the balconies on a typical brownstone apartment block in Little Italy

Your legs, a ferry, and a cab or the subway will convey you to Lower Manhattan's major attractions, a cross-section of which you can sample in a full but not too hectic day.

# Lower Manhattan in a Day

## 8:30 am

Beat the crowds by arriving as early as possible at round Castle Clinton (take the 4 or 5 subway train to Bowling Green), where you can buy tickets for the first (9 am; earlier in summer) ferry to the Statue of Liberty and Ellis Island, two of New York's stellar sights.

## 9:45 am

Stunning views of the harbor await you atop the pedestal of the **2 Statue of Liberty** (► 140–142). Tour the museum here and then reboard the ferry.

## 12:00 noon

The fascinating tour of the handsome buildings at **3 Ellis Island** (► 143–144), through which millions of America's immigrants passed, takes about 2 hours, after which you can board the ferry for the return trip to Manhattan.

# 3:30 pm

Departing the ferry, stroll north along the **western waterfront** (➤ 151),
to Robert F. Wagner Jr. Park, where you can rest a spell as you gaze eastward
at the Statue of Liberty and northern New Jersey.

# 4:00 pm

Hop on the uptown 4 or 5 subway train at Bowling Green station, transfer at
Brooklyn Bridge/City Hall to the uptown 6 train, and get off at Spring Street.
Meander through **16 SoHo** (➤ 147–150), with its shops and cast-iron architecture, and stop along the way for tea and a snack at Palacinka (➤ 150) or
the Dean & DeLuca (➤ 161) market. Alternatively, slip into a cab and head
to the **9 South Street Seaport Historic District** (below, ➤ 145–146).

# 7:00 pm

Stop for an early evening libation at Fanelli's (➤ 160), Bar 89 (➤ 180), or
one of the neighborhood's other watering holes. For a splurge, have dinner at
Savoy (70 Prince Street, tel: 212/219-8570; reservations essential, ➤ 159),
which serves innovative contemporary American cuisine in a Federal Revival-
style town house from the 1820s. For Continental and American cuisine in
an ever-so-New York establishment, head for TriBeCa's Odeon (145 West
Broadway, tel: 212/233-0507). If you're in the mood for Asian cuisine, head
to Chinatown and Joe's Shanghai (➤ 158) or Nha Trang (➤ 159).

# ❷ Statue of Liberty

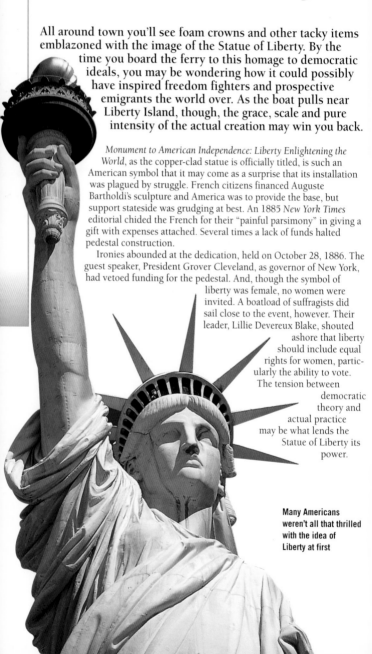

All around town you'll see foam crowns and other tacky items emblazoned with the image of the Statue of Liberty. By the time you board the ferry to this homage to democratic ideals, you may be wondering how it could possibly have inspired freedom fighters and prospective emigrants the world over. As the boat pulls near Liberty Island, though, the grace, scale and pure intensity of the actual creation may win you back.

*Monument to American Independence: Liberty Enlightening the World*, as the copper-clad statue is officially titled, is such an American symbol that it may come as a surprise that its installation was plagued by struggle. French citizens financed Auguste Bartholdi's sculpture and America was to provide the base, but support stateside was grudging at best. An 1885 *New York Times* editorial chided the French for their "painful parsimony" in giving a gift with expenses attached. Several times a lack of funds halted pedestal construction.

Ironies abounded at the dedication, held on October 28, 1886. The guest speaker, President Grover Cleveland, as governor of New York, had vetoed funding for the pedestal. And, though the symbol of liberty was female, no women were invited. A boatload of suffragists did sail close to the event, however. Their leader, Lillie Devereux Blake, shouted ashore that liberty should include equal rights for women, particularly the ability to vote. The tension between democratic theory and actual practice may be what lends the Statue of Liberty its power.

**Many Americans weren't all that thrilled with the idea of Liberty at first**

Its sponsors in France – which had reverted from a republic to an imperial regime when the statue was conceived (1865) – believed that the U.S. Constitution represented an exceptional framework for self-government. To reinforce the push for democracy in France (note that Liberty faces Europe) and elsewhere, they wanted to honor the American attempt.

Ferry tickets to the Statue and Ellis Island are sold in Battery Park at Castle Clinton, which opens at 8:30 am. The first ferry leaves at 9 (earlier in summer), and the last ferry leaves at 3:30. Security measures include the use of metal detectors and searches of persons and bags; closing hours may be earlier.

**Liberty shows the way in New York Harbor**

## Liberty's Hall of Fame
- **Auguste Bartholdi**: The sculptor devoted two decades to funding and creating the statue. In 1869 he proposed a similar statue for the entrance to the Suez Canal, but Egypt's leader didn't approve. Bartholdi's mother was the model for the face.
- **Gustave Eiffel**: The famed engineer and builder of the Eiffel Tower designed the statue's revolutionary support system of interlocking angle irons.
- **Richard Morris Hunt**: The New York architect designed the statue's 89-foot-high pedestal that lifts the statue 165 feet off the ground.
- **Eduoard Laboulaye**: The French politician and historian first suggested building the statue in 1865 and worked until his death in 1884 to make it happen.

---

🚇 192, off B1 ✉ Liberty Island ☎ (212) 363-3200 for statue; (212) 269-5755 for current ferry schedule 🕐 Daily 9–5 (morning and evening hours extended during summer); closed Dec 25 🚇 Bowling Green (4, 5) 🚌 M9, M15–South Ferry 💲 Moderate; includes ferry ride and Ellis Island admission

- **Emma Lazarus**: "I am not able to write to order," responded Emma Lazarus when asked to produce a fund-raising sonnet. Shortly thereafter she visited some quarantined immigrants. Shocked by their conditions and impressed by the talents they could offer America, she wrote the requested verse. "The New Colossus" includes the words "Give me your tired, your poor/Your huddled masses yearning to breathe free."

- **Joseph Pulitzer**: When the publisher of *The World* newspaper began printing the name of every contributor to the pedestal, money began to trickle in.

*The boat ride to Liberty Island is always a big attraction*

### TAKING A BREAK

The Statue's cafeteria serves standard fast food. You can dine indoors or out.

| VITAL STATISTICS | |
| --- | --- |
| *From ground to torch tip:* | **305 feet 1 inch** |
| *From ground to top of pedestal:* | **154 feet** |
| *Weight of copper in statue:* | **31 tons** |
| *Thickness of copper sheeting:* | **³⁄₃₂ inch** |

## STATUE OF LIBERTY: INSIDE INFO

**Top tips** For security reasons, no backpacks or bags (small purses are okay) are allowed, and touring inside the statue may be restricted; call ahead. Ferry hours may vary, and opening hours are subject to change.

- Arrive early in summer (the first boat leaves at 8:30) **to avoid long lines.**
- **Bring something to drink in summer** and **wear warm clothing in winter.**
- Save time by positioning yourself near the ferry gangway to exit first. Head to the line for the pedestal, whose observation deck has **superb harbor vistas.**

**One to miss** Forget visiting the crown (reservations may be required). You'll have to climb **354 steps,** and views are limited. No one is allowed in the torch.

# 3 Ellis Island

The second stop on the Statue of Liberty ferry loop may be the most foolproof of New York City's attractions. Few people fail to be fascinated by the evocative exhibits at Ellis Island, through which 12 million immigrants to the United States passed between 1892 and 1954.

If the Statue of Liberty (► 140–142) embodied the hopes and dreams of newcomers to the United States, Ellis Island represented the more sobering reality. Having scraped together the fee for third-class or steerage on an ocean liner, they would arrive in New York poor and often ill from the voyage.

Immigration officials processed first- and second-class passengers onboard and sent them directly to Manhattan, but the less well off headed to Ellis Island's redbrick Byzantine- and French Renaissance-style buildings. There they underwent medical, mental health, legal and other examinations to determine their fitness to enter the country.

For most immigrants, this was a nervous-making few hours, after which they, too, arrived in Manhattan. About one in six people, however, found themselves detained for days or even weeks, and two percent were deported. Among those regularly detained were unescorted single women. It was feared they would either become wards of

**Above: Millions of immigrants' first steps on American soil were on Ellis Island**

**Below: Luggage samples**

**The American Immigrant Wall of Honor stands behind the main building**

charity or be lured into prostitution. Rooms restored to the first two decades of the 20th century depict the immigration process step by step. You'll begin at the cavernous Spanish-tile Great Hall, where long lines wound toward overworked bureaucrats. Uniformed guards patrolled the hall, but anxiety would have been high in any case. The similarity to prison increased for detainees, who were held in jail-like quarters.

About three dozen galleries contain artifacts – photographs, costumes, luggage and posters – from the island's entire period as an immigration station (policy changes in the 1920s greatly reduced the flow of newcomers, who from then on were interviewed in their home countries before heading to the United States). The exhibits' designers added a few interactive touches but wisely let the words, culled from oral-history tapes, and the music of actual settlers tell the story. Other exhibits cover the island's history before and after immigration, and outdoors stands the American Immigrant Wall of Honor, with the names of more than half a million immigrants, famous and obscure.

### VITAL STATISTICS

❏ Between 1900 and 1915, as many as 5,000 people per day were processed through Ellis Island.

❏ About 40 percent of all Americans – more than 100 million people – are related to an immigrant processed at Ellis Island.

Ellis Island was originally 3.3 acres, but it was expanded to 27.5 acres.
Most of the landfill portion is in New Jersey, which successfully sued New York for co-ownership of the island.

### TAKING A BREAK

On a clear day, the harbor views make up for the standard fast-food fare served at the island's concession. Eating when you return to Manhattan is a better bet.

✚ 192, off B1 ☎ (212) 363-3200
🕐 Daily 9–5 (last ferry leaves New York at 3:30; morning and evening hours extended during summer). Closed Dec 25 🚇 Bowling Green (4, 5) 🚌 M9, M15–South Ferry
💵 Moderate; includes ferry ride and Statue of Liberty admission

### ELLIS ISLAND: INSIDE INFO

**Top tips** During the summer, the lines for the ferries grow longer as the afternoon wears on. **Try to finish up by 3 pm.**
• Even if you're the type who likes to experience sights on your own, consider renting the **enlightening two-hour audio tour**, which leads you in an orderly fashion through this large facility.

**One to miss** If you're pressed for time, skip the film presentations.

# ⑨ South Street Seaport Historic District

Indoor-outdoor museum? Shopping mall? Theme park? The muddle over what precisely South Street Seaport should be makes this potentially superb attraction a decidedly mixed bag.

The reasons to visit what was America's busiest port during the 18th and 19th centuries are the restored brick buildings and stone streets, the galleries surveying the history of ships and shipping, and some vessels you can board. Oh yes, and the splendid views of Brooklyn and the Brooklyn Bridge from the end of Pier 17 The distinctive odor that emanated for

**An old lightship provides artistic inspiration**

## South Street Seaport Museum

The museum's facilities are scattered throughout the district. You can buy a combination ticket to the galleries and ships at the visitor center. Below is a walking tour of the highlights:

• **207–213 Water Street**: A good first stop is the visitor center, at 209 Water Street. Also here is a splendid exhibit of ocean-liner models and memorabilia. Galleries display ship models and artifacts. At 211 Water is Bowne & Co., a re-created 19th-century print shop, where you can see how an old press worked. (New York was the center of America's printing industry during the 1800s.) Changing exhibits of ship-related art and artifacts are on display at 213 Water Street.

• **Schermerhorn Row**: This series of Federal-style brick buildings was erected in the early 1800s. The skewed supports of some upper-floor windows reveal how much these buildings have settled over time.

• **Pier 16**: The several ships available for boarding vary. They include the *Peking*, a four-masted barque built in 1911, and the *Ambrose*, a 1908 lightship that guided vessels into New York Harbor. An interesting stop is the *Wavertree*, one of the last wrought-iron ships ever built. The ship is undergoing a long-term restoration project, which the onboard exhibits explain. On weekends from May to October the ship often goes on short sailing excursions, which the public is invited to attend.

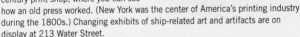

🔲 193 D3  ☎ (212) 748-8600  🕙 Daily 10–6 (also Thu 6–8 pm), Apr–Sep; Wed–Mon 10–5, Oct–Mar. Closed Thanksgiving, Dec 25  💲 Moderate

decades from the Fulton Fish Market has been replaced by the smells of area eateries.

## TAKING A BREAK

The **Bridge Café** (297 Water Street at Dover Street, tel: 212/227-3344) lies below the Brooklyn Bridge auto ramps in a building that's been used as a saloon since 1847 – the café is Manhattan's oldest continuously operating bar. The mood is casual, the food contemporary American. Lunch and dinner are served.

---

🖽 193 E2 ✉ South and Fulton streets
☎ (212) 732-7678 🍴 Bridge Café ($–$$);
Pier 17 restaurants ($) 🚇 Fulton Street/
Broadway-Nassau (A, C, J, M, 1, 2, 4, 5) 🚌 M15
💵 Inexpensive (museum/ships fee; free to Pier
17 and other dining and shopping areas)

---

**Left:** Preparing the day's catch
**Below:** Old ships and new buildings animate the South Street skyline

---

## SOUTH STREET SEAPORT: INSIDE INFO

**Top tip** If you've only got time for one gallery, head to **209 Water Street's** ship-model collection.

**One to miss** Avoid the Anywhere, U.S.A., shops at Pier 17. Even if you want their merchandise you'll find it **cheaper elsewhere**.

**Hidden gem** From the third level at the end of Pier 17, you'll get a head-on perspective of the **Brooklyn Bridge's suspension cables**.

# 16 SoHo

SoHo is the ultimate proof of a simple principle of Manhattan's real-estate physics: What goes up will come down, but will likely come roaring back up again. A center of light industry in the mid- to late 1800s, the area devolved into a commercial slum by the mid-20th century before rebounding in the 1970s.

In the mid-1800s, SoHo was brothel central. As with later neighborhoods like Chinatown and Harlem, slumming became faddish, and underground guides directed the curious to the houses of ill repute. The action in what was then known as Hell's Hundred Acres centered on Mercer, Greene and Wooster streets, which contained a good five dozen establishments.

In the mid- to late 19th century, the buildings so beloved today were made to house printing and other light industry. The facades were cast iron, in those days a cheaper construction material than stone. Architects mixed and matched from catalogs selling window frames, balustrades, columns and other components. Besides cost, a major selling point was that cast iron was supposedly fireproof. Technically it was. It didn't catch

Eclectic boutiques and galleries attract shoppers to SoHo

🚇 195 D1　🚉 Spring Street (C, E, 6); Prince Street (N, R); Broadway/Lafayette (F and downtown 6); Bleecker Street (6)　🚌 M5, M6

## Cast Iron or Limestone?

Most cast-iron facades were painted over to look like stone, so it can be hard to tell whether you're looking at metal or not. Cast-iron pillars are hollow, so if you bang on them, your ears may yield the answer. Foundries sometimes stamped their names on pilasters and pillars. If the building hasn't been freshly painted, you might detect rust spots. The foolproof method, though, is to slap a magnet (discreetly, of course) against the building.

**The mood is retro, but the food's au courant at Palacinka**

fire, but when the wood floors of a building burned, the cast iron melted.

The neighborhood went into a major decline after World War II, when businesses moved to more modern facilities elsewhere. In the 1960s, artists began settling and working in the deserted loft spaces. A change in the zoning laws in 1972 legitimized the artists' loft arrangements, at which point property values began to soar. Many of the original artists and even some of the galleries have been forced out by high rents. Some say SoHo has gotten too popular for its own good, but despite the arrival of chain stores and less highbrow art, it's still fun to stroll.

SoHo stands for South of Houston (as in How-stun) Street, the area's northern border; the southern border is Canal Street. The historic district's eastern boundary is Crosby Street, the western one is West Broadway.

## Museums and Galleries

### Museums

Broadway between Houston and Prince streets contains two art museums.

The **New Museum** (583 Broadway, tel: 212/219-1222), which is well worth stopping at, is one of the city's finest showcases for cutting-edge contemporary art. The permanent collection includes pivotal works by major New York artists of the past three decades.

The **Museum for African Art** (593 Broadway, tel: 212/966-1313) mounts impressive shows of works from Africa and the African diaspora.

### Galleries

Dozens of galleries do business here, some at street level, others in upstairs loft spaces.

Walter De Maria's conceptual work *The New York City Earth Room* has been intriguing viewers (from mid-September to mid-June) since 1977 at 141 Wooster Street. Other notable stops include **Howard Greenberg** (120 Wooster Street), **Tony Shafrazi** (119 Wooster Street) and **O.K. Harris** (393 West Broadway).

Museum and gallery hours vary, but most are closed on Monday and open at least from Wednesday to Saturday between 11 and 5. All the museums are open on Sunday, and the Museum for African Art and most of the galleries are open on Tuesday.

**Left: The Little Singer Building's facade is one of SoHo's most graceful**

**Opposite: Architects mixed and matched from catalog offerings to create cast-iron facades**

## Iron – and Steel – Maidens

Like the East Village, SoHo is a place you could easily enjoy fixated entirely on the here and now. But many of the buildings you'll be passing do have tales to tell. Here are a few of them:

- **Haughwout Building**, 488 Broadway at Broome Street. The owner of this 1857 structure wanted a Venetian palazzo at cast-iron prices, and his architect delivered one of SoHo's handsomest buildings. Elisha Graves Otis – the man behind Otis Elevator – installed his first steam-powered passenger safety elevator here.
- **St. Nicholas Hotel**, 499 and 521–523 Broadway. Two huge cast-iron buildings, themselves more than 100 years old, separate the remaining sections of New York's finest mid-1800s hotel, which has a limestone facade. Mark Twain met his future wife here (the night they met, they went to the old Steinway Hall to hear Charles Dickens read from his new novel, *David Copperfield*). For the best view, stand across the street at 504 Broadway, where Harry Houdini worked as a tie cutter before he became a famous escape artist.
- **Little Singer Building**, 561 Broadway at Prince Street. It looks like architect Ernest Flagg used fancier than usual cast-iron styling with this L-shaped building, which has a matching facade at 88 Prince Street. The 1904 structure is actually made of steel, making it something of a test run for Flagg's later stone, brick and steel skyscrapers, among them the Singer Tower (► 7).

## SOHO: INSIDE INFO

**Top tip** Bring your credit card – there's some **great merchandise** here.

**One to miss** SoHo is pretty much a mob scene on weekends, even in bad weather. Unless you like being jostled – on the street *and* in the stores – **come here on a weekday.** In general, the streets below Grand hold less of interest.

For a quick spin past galleries, of-the-moment shops, and some interesting architecture, head south from Houston Street on Broadway, make a right on Broome Street, right on Mercer Street, left on Prince Street, left on Greene Street, right on Grand Street, and right again on Wooster Street, which you can follow back up to Houston.

### TAKING A BREAK

Its sweet and savory crepes and circa-1930s ambience – travel posters, steamer trunks, pictures of Franklin Delano Roosevelt and other personalities – make **Palacinka** (28 Grand Street at Thompson Street, tel: 212/625-0362) worth the trek to SoHo's southwest quadrant. Sounds from Edith Piaf to Chris Isaak might warble through the old-fashioned wooden loudspeakers.

**Eat, drink, be merry and see a little art in SoHo**

# At Your Leisure

## 1 Staten Island Ferry

The cheapest thrill in New York (it's free) is the 25-minute ferry ride from Manhattan to Staten Island. Edna St. Vincent Millay immortalized the ferry's 24-hour schedule in her poem *Recuerdo*: "We were very tired, we were very merry/We had gone back and forth all night on the ferry…" On a clear day the views include the Statue of Liberty to the west and well beyond the Brooklyn Bridge to the northeast. When the boat lands at Staten Island (▶ 168), you can visit the Snug Harbor Cultural Center (originally known as Sailor's Snug Harbor, as it was created to provide homes for "decrepit and worn out sailors"), or other sights, or head right back to Manhattan.

➕ 193 D1 ✉ Foot of Whitehall Street east of Battery Park
☎ (718) 815-2628
🚇 Bowling Green (4, 5); Whitehall Street (N, R)
🚌 M9, M15–South Ferry
🎫 Free

## 4 Western Waterfront

New York was once America's premier commercial port, but following World War II union leaders and dock managers failed to embrace modern techniques like containerization (partly because on some piers there wasn't enough space), so business declined. Much of the Downtown port land has been developed as parks. From the shiplike, redbrick observation platform in Robert F. Wagner Jr. Park, just north of Battery Park, there are stunning views of New York Harbor and New Jersey to be had on a clear day. On the northern edge of Wagner Park is the Museum of Jewish Heritage (18 First Pl., tel: 212/509-6130), which documents the Jewish experience before and after the Holocaust.

➕ 192 A3 🚇 Bowling Green (4, 5) 🚌 M9, M15–South Ferry

## 5 U.S. Custom House and National Museum of the American Indian

Manhattan's port was still thriving in the early 1900s when architect Cass Gilbert designed this masterpiece. In the days before the income tax was

**Don't miss the Great Hall on the main floor**

instituted (in 1913), duties collected at the custom house provided much of the federal government's revenue. The sculptures along the roofline depict various maritime powers, from Greece and Rome on the left to France and England on the right. (During World War I the statue of Germany, third from the left, was altered to honor Belgium.) Daniel Chester French designed the ground-level sculptures of Asia, the Americas, Europe and Africa. The last one has generated controversy because it depicts a slumping Africa, yet to achieve its potential. On the ground floor is the entrance to a fine museum that documents the lives, cultures and histories of Native Americans. The Rotunda and former cashier's office on the second floor contain more of the museum's displays.

➕ 192 C1 ✉ 1 Bowling Green at the foot of Broadway ☎ (212) 514-3888 🕐 Daily 10–5 (also Thu 5–8); closed Dec 25 🚇 Bowling Green (4, 5) 🚌 M9, M15–South Ferry 🎫 Free

**Trinity Church's bronze doors**

## 6 Trinity Church

Statesman Alexander Hamilton was buried here after losing his 1804 duel with the then vice president of the United States, Aaron Burr (▶ 26). Nearby, also on the graveyard's Rector Street side, is a memorial to Robert Fulton, who built the first viable steamship. The huge cross in the graveyard north of the church is dedicated to Caroline Webster Schermerhorn Astor (▶ 26), who ruled New York society during the last part of the 19th century. Richard Morris Hunt, the designer of the Statue of Liberty's base, was responsible for the church's biblical-theme bronze front door.

➕ 192 C2 ✉ 74 Trinity Place at Broadway 🚇 Wall Street (4, 5) 🚌 M9

## 7 New York Stock Exchange

Two centuries ago, deals transpired under a tree near the 12 Broad Street building of the New York Stock Exchange, whose bulky Corinthian columns set a no-nonsense tone for the trading conducted inside. These days, the trading floor is filled with brightly jacketed people waving their arms around. A visit inside is worth your trouble only if the wait to get in is less than an hour. The Education Center will tell you more about traders working in an increasingly paperless environment. Tickets, on a first-come, first-served basis, are available at the stand at 20 Broad Street on weekdays, beginning at 9 am. In summer arrive by 12:30 pm or the day's allotment will be gone.

➕ 192 C2 ✉ Wall and Broad streets ☎ (212) 656-5168 🕐 Mon–Fri 9–4:30; closed most national holidays 🚇 Wall Street (2, 3, 4, 5); Broad Street (J, M) 🚌 M1–South Ferry, M6

## 8 Wall Street Area

The street synonymous with American commerce was named for a wall erected by the Dutch in 1653 as protection from hostile Native Americans and British intruders. The wall didn't do much good: The British conquered the city with little effort 11 years later. The main attraction here is the New York Stock Exchange (see above). If you're in the area on a weekday between 9 and 4, step into the art deco-style Red Room lobby of 1 Wall Street (at Broadway). Thousands of mosaic tiles cover the walls and ceiling. The subtle change in color from red to reddish-orange comes from the tiles, not the lighting. Even staff members admit that the

**George Washington's statue faces the Stock Exchange building**

public restroom in the basement is the big draw at the Federal Hall National Memorial (26 Wall Street at Nassau Street, tel: 212/825-6888), not the so-so historical exhibits inside the former custom house that replaced the first U.S. capitol. Admission is free; the hall is open on weekdays from 9 to 5.

➕ 192 C2 🚇 Wall Street (2, 3, 4, 5); Broad Street (J, M)
🚌 M9

the guard's desk, one sculpture shows Woolworth counting money and another depicts Gilbert holding a model of the building.

➕ 192 C3 ✉ 233 Broadway at Park Place 🚇 City Hall (N, R); Park Place (1, 2); Fulton Street/ Broadway-Nassau (A, C, J, M, 1, 2, 4, 5) 🚌 M1, M6, M22, M25

CHAMBERS ST
City Hall
Brooklyn Br-City Hall
PARK ROW
ST JAMES PL
Park Place
Woolworth Building **10**
VESEY ST
**11** City Hall
Fulton St/Broadway-Nassau
Brooklyn Bridge
**12**
BROOKLYN
TTERY
ARK
CITY
Ground Zero (World Trade Center)
BROADWAY
FULTON ST
South Street Seaport
Wall Street Area
South Street Historic District
**9**
**4** Western Waterfront
Trinity Church **6**
**8** Wall St
WALL ST
WATER ST
SOUTH ST VIADUCT
Wall St **7**
New York Stock Exchange
BROAD ST
Broad St
Bowling Green
US Custom House / National Museum of the American Indian **5**
Bowling Green
Whitehall St
SOUTH ST
Battery Park
BROOKLYN-BATTERY TUNNEL
**I** Staten Island Ferry
**2** **3**
↙ Statue of Liberty, Ellis Island

## 10 Woolworth Building
The headquarters of Frank W. Woolworth's variety-store chain started out modestly as a Gothic variation on Victoria Tower at the British Houses of Parliament. The designer, Cass Gilbert, tossed in accents inspired by the architecture of medieval Flanders, and the result is a playful skyscraper once known as the "Cathedral of Commerce." The quasi-religious motif continues in the lobby with its marble walls, stained-glass windows, Gothic flourishes and vaulted Romanesque ceilings. Underneath the balcony to the left of

## 11 City Hall
New York's City Hall sits daintily in a triangular park that marks the finish of Manhattan's famed ticker-tape parades for sports and other heroes. The three-story building's backside was originally faced in brownstone, because municipal leaders in 1802 couldn't imagine New York spreading farther north than Fulton Street. They may not have been prescient, but at least they were thrifty – they didn't want to waste money on marble no one would see. The whole building was refaced in limestone in the 1950s.

➕ 192 C3 ✉ Broadway and Park Row 🚇 Brooklyn Bridge/City Hall (4, 5, 6)
🚌 M1, M6, M22, M25

## 12 Brooklyn Bridge
The twin 272.5-foot Gothic towers of the Brooklyn Bridge lend a proper note of reverence to a very secular feat of 19th-century engineering: Upon its completion in 1883, this link between

Manhattan and the then independent city of Brooklyn was the world's longest suspension bridge. Hart Crane immortalized it in his epic-length poem, *The Bridge*. And John Augustus Roebling, the designer, died for it, following complications from a construction accident. His son, Washington, guided the project until an accident left him paralyzed, after which Washington's wife, Emily, took charge. The walk across takes a leisurely half hour, including time to snap an artsy photographs or two of the bridge's graceful cables, which contain 19 steel strands, each with 278 wires. To return to Manhattan via the subway, follow the directions in the Brooklyn Excursion (► 164–167) from the promenade's Brooklyn side to Cadman Plaza West and Middagh Street, where you'll see the High Street/Brooklyn Bridge station.

➕ 193 E3 ✉ Manhattan: near Chambers and Centre streets; Brooklyn: Cadman Plaza East (also Adams Street) 🚇 Manhattan: Brooklyn Bridge/City Hall (4, 5, 6); Brooklyn: High Street/Brooklyn Bridge (A, C) 🚌 M15

**A Chinatown fish seller at his stall**

## 🔟3 TriBeCa

TriBeCa stands for Triangle Below Canal (Street). The neighborhood was a center for food wholesalers well into the mid-20th century, but fell into major disrepair until the 1980s. By the time moviemakers like Harvey and Bob Weinstein of Miramax and Robert De Niro set up movie production facilities, the neighborhood was clearly on the way back. De Niro was an early pioneer on the culinary front with his Tribeca Grill. Clubsters and shopkeepers followed, and before long the place was almost as chic as SoHo. Almost, but not quite, which is fine with most residents. Though its cast-iron buildings are as historic as SoHo's, TriBeCa is less of a scene.

To take a quick spin through the area, proceed south from Canal Street on West Broadway, exploring any side streets or shops that catch your fancy. Walk west (right) on Reade Street and northwest (right) on Hudson Street. At one-block, Jay Street, head west and explore it and Staple Street, which bisects Jay. At the northern end of Staple, straight across Harrison Street, is the gabled former New York Mercantile Exchange (6 Harrison Street), where egg and other wholesalers did business. Walk east on Harrison to Hudson and head north. Laid-back Bubby's (120 Hudson Street at North Moore Street, tel: 212/219-0666) is known for its pies and busy weekend brunches (great pancakes). Walk east on North Moore Street to

Varick Street and make a left. You'll shortly be back at Canal Street.

➕ 192 B4 🚇 Canal Street (A, C, E, 1, 2) 🚌 M20

## ⓮ Chinatown

Mott, Pell and Doyers streets formed the heart of old Chinatown, which has expanded greatly since the termination in the 1960s of policies that restricted Asian immigration to the United States. For a quick overview, head south from Canal Street on Mott. Make a left at Pell, a right on Doyers, and at Chatham Square (where five streets intersect) another right, back on to Mott. Cecilia Tam sells yummy egg-puff cakes out of her Hong Kong Cake Co. shack at Mott and Mosco streets. Down Mosco at Mulberry Street is the modest but informative **Museum of Chinese in the Americas** (70 Mulberry Street, Second Floor, tel: 212/619-4785). Stop by the

Chinatown Ice Cream Factory (65 Bayard Street, tel: 212/608-4170) for a refreshing cone of lychee or green-tea ice cream. Markets here carry curious herbs and delicacies – in the window of Kam Man Market at 200 Canal Street, see if you can tell which are the braised pigs' ears and sliced noses.

➕ 193 D5 🚇 Canal Street (J, M, N, Q, R, W, 6) 🚌 M1, M103

## ⓯ Little Italy

What with the encroachment of Chinatown from the south and SoHo from the west, Little Italy – a century ago a dense and thriving enclave of Italian immigrants – gets littler and less Italian with each passing year. In shops and restaurants along Mott and Mulberry streets between Canal and Houston streets, you can still catch a glimpse of the old days and ways. The whole neighborhood comes alive during the 10-day Feast of San

**Bright colors and flavorful foods in Chinatown**

**Dining alfresco is popular in Little Italy**

fortune-cookie factory as a store selling bar mitzvah sets. Two interesting streets are Orchard, which on Sunday from Delancey Street to Houston Street becomes a pedestrian shopping mall, and Ludlow, one block east, where urban pioneers have opened some quirky new shops. Several of the food shops and restaurants mentioned in "Vintage Flavors" (▶ 31–32) are on the Lower East Side.

✚ 195 F1 🚇 Delancey Street (F); Essex Street (J, M) 🚌 M9, M14, M15

## 🔞 Lower East Side Tenement Museum

A must if you're a history buff, this museum is inside a tenement building erected in 1863. Well-informed guides conduct intriguing tours of one or more of four re-created apartments from the 1870s to the 1930s. For safety and other reasons only 15 people are permitted on each tour; reservations are advised on Saturday (you can't reserve on Sunday, so come early).

✚ 195 F1 ✉ 90 Orchard Street at Broome Street ☎ (212) 431-0233 🕐 Tours Tue–Fri 1–4, Sat–Sun 11–4:30 (also Mon 1–4, Jun–Aug, and Thu at 6 and 7, Apr–Oct); closed Jan 1, Thanksgiving, Dec 25 🚇 Delancey Street (F); Essex Street (J, M) 🚌 M15 💲 Moderate

Gennaro (the patron saint of Naples) in mid-September, and at a few smaller religious and secular fairs and festivals held at other times.

✚ 195 E1 🚇 Canal Street (J, M, N, Q, R, W, 6) 🚌 M1, M103

## 🔞 Lower East Side

Successive waves of Germans, Irish and Eastern European Jews inhabited the densely populated area south of Houston Street and east of the Bowery during the 1800s. At the dawn of the 20th century, 75 percent of New York's Jewish population lived here. The Jewish presence continues to this day, but now you're as likely to see a Chinese-run

# Where to...
# Eat and Drink

Prices The $ amounts indicate what you can expect to pay for an average, complete dinner for one person, including drinks, tax and tip.
$ = under $30     $$ = $30–60     $$$ = over $60

## RESTAURANTS

### Aquagrill $$

Expertly prepared seafood is served in a convivial contemporary setting. Lunch features some seven or eight types of fish sandwich platters. You can design your own meal by selecting the type of fish and cooking method, and then choosing from about 10 side dishes. Alternatively you can choose from the chef's specialties.

🚹 194 C1 ⊠ 210 Spring Street at 6th Avenue ☎ (212) 274-0505
🕐 Lunch Tue–Fri noon–3:30; dinner Tue–Thu 6–10:30, Fri–Sat 6–11:30, Sun 6–10:15. Closed Mon, Memorial Day

### Balthazar $$

You'll think you are in Paris when you spy the red awnings, the etched glass and mirrors, and the brass fixtures. The menu of this hip and popular restaurant is classic brasserie fare with a few contemporary twists. There are regular daily specials such as cassoulet, choucroute and bouillabaisse, and house specialties include a cold seafood platter and wonderful breads provided by the adjoining bakery. The service is smooth and pleasant, and the atmosphere cheery and bustling. Makes for a civilized breakfast option, though may be more interesting later in the day and night.

🚹 195 D1 ⊠ 80 Spring Street between Crosby Street and Broadway
☎ (212) 965-1414 🕐 Mon–Thu 7:30 am–1:30 am, Fri–Sat 7:30 am –2:30 am, Sun 7:30 am–midnight

### Bouley Bakery $$$

Notorious New York chef David Bouley is alive and well and said to be building an empire, and meanwhile he is still serving at this low-key but upscale little restaurant-off-a-bakery. The largely seasonal menu features specialty organic ingredients from various boutique producers.

🚹 192 B4 ⊠ 120 West Broadway between Duane and Reade streets
☎ (212) 964-2525 🕐 Lunch daily 11:30–3; dinner daily 5:30–11:30

### 🍷🍷🍷 Chanterelle $$$

The elegant dining room with pastel walls, antique armoires, private tables generously spaced and very high pressed-tin ceiling give visitors to this established TriBeCa destination a feeling of privilege and well-being. The menu by chef David Waltuck changes with the seasons, and you can choose the tasting menu or order a la carte. The food is contemporary French highlighting American ingredients, and the sommelier will help find the right wine to match. Save room for the cheese course.

🚹 192 B4 ⊠ 2 Harrison Street at Hudson Street ☎ (212) 966-6960
🕐 Lunch Tue–Sat noon–2:30; dinner Mon–Sat 5:30–11. Closed Sun, Memorial Day

### Honmura An $$

This is quintessential Japanese dining, with that unique ambience of meditation and ritualistic beauty. People come here for some of the finest buckwheat noodles, all hand-made on the premises. This is where you will learn to appreciate the soba (thin) and the udon (thick), have them hot or cold, and where you can bask in the peaceful mystique surrounding them. Try also the small tastings of edamame (fresh soybeans), Japanese pickles and marinated wild greens.

✚ 195 D2 ⊠ 170 Mercer Street
**between Houston and Prince streets**
☎ (212) 334-5253 ⏰ Lunch
noon–2:30; dinner Tue–Sun

## Jing Fong $

This is the best of the dim sum parlors, complete with an escalator to the main dining room with its red walls and dragons. Come here for a late brunch or lunch. On Sundays, many Chinese from out of town descend for a family meal. The tiny spare ribs are good, if tricky to negotiate, and the taro-wrapped packets of sticky rice with Chinese sausage are delicious. Steamed buns with pork or sweet bean paste can be a dessert. You could order a dish off the menu, but the dim sum is the thing here.

✚ 193 D5 ⊠ 20 Elizabeth Street
**between Bayard and Canal streets**
☎ (212) 964-5256 ⏰ Daily
10 am–3:30 am

## Joe's Shanghai $

Joe's unmatched, broth-filled crab or pork dumplings have become

the rage, and enthusiasts are happy to form a line to dine. You might heed the proper way to eat these just to be safe: Placing a dumpling in your spoon, bite a small hole into it and suck the hot broth carefully, whereupon you can safely eat the rest. Other excellent dishes include the turnip cakes, Shanghai rice cakes, braised pork shoulder, and the razor clams with a spicy black bean sauce (the latter two are usually listed as specials). Cash only. (Another branch has opened in Midtown, tel: 212/333-3868.)

✚ 193 D4 ⊠ 9 Pell Street between
**Bowery and Mott streets** ☎ (212)
233-8888 ⏰ Daily 11 am–11:15 pm

## Katz's Deli $

Come here for good deli fare – great pastrami, corned beef, pickles, hot dogs and matzoh ball soup eaten in a dining-hall atmosphere. You get a ticket when you walk in. Hand that to the counter staff as they present you with whatever has made you salivate the most. Or you can sit at a

"waiter-service only" table and let a waiter get it for you. Whatever you do, don't ask for "extra lean" meat in your sandwich, as the fattier stuff has the most flavor, and don't lose your ticket when they give it back to you with your food! You'll need it to be allowed to leave (pay as you exit). A classic accompaniment to your meal would be a Dr. Brown's soda.

✚ 195 F2 ⊠ 205 East Houston
**Street at Ludlow Street** ☎ (212) 254-
2246 ⏰ Daily 8 am–10 pm (also
Wed–Thu 10–11 pm, Fri–Sat 10–3 am)

## Lombardi's $

There's a long tradition of pizzas here; this is where New York City's very first pizza parlor used to be. It's an odd space, and the best seats may be the booths as you enter, or the table back by where they make the pizzas, if you enjoy the hustle-bustle. Regardless, you should certainly take a walk to the back to get a gander at the impressively deep, historic brick oven. All the pies are

good, and the toppings are of exceptional quality. You might want to try a white (tomatoless) pizza along with the regular type.

✚ 195 E1 ⊠ 32 Spring Street
**between Mott and Mulberry streets**
☎ (212) 941-7994 ⏰ Mon–Sat
11:30–11 (also Fri–Sat 11 pm
–midnight), Sun 11:30–10

## ▼▼▼ Montrachet $$$

A TriBeCa haven for new French cuisine and gracious service, this is a special destination. The decor is plain and unassuming, a fine backdrop for the true focus – the food and wine. Award-winning wine director Daniel Johnnes, his sommeliers, or the many wine-conversant waiters can find a wonderful match to complement your meal. Don't limit yourself – consider ordering the roasted chicken with truffles matched with an interesting red.

✚ 192 B5 ⊠ 239 West Broadway
**between Walker and White streets**
☎ (212) 219-2777 ⏰ Dinner daily
4–11; closed Jewish holidays

## Nha Trang $

Home of some of the best Vietnamese food in the city, this is a popular and lively spot with no-nonsense rooms and quick service. The hot and sour shrimp soup is recommended. There may be a line, but it moves quickly. Next door is Pho Pasteur, also good.

+ 193 D5 ⊠ 87 Baxter Street between Bayard and Canal streets ☎ (212) 233-5948 ⑥ Daily 10–10

### 🍷🍷🍷 Nobu $$$

The names behind this top-of-the-scale Japanese dining experience are Nobu Matsuhisa and Drew Nieporent. Even if you can get through on the phone, there will be few reservations available to enjoy inventive, modern Japanese cuisine as well as top sushi and sakes. Your senses begin to awaken when touched by the curved wall of Japanese river rocks and the beech trees. One specialty of the house is tiradito, a raw yellowtail dish garnished with tiny dots of a spicy Peruvian chile sauce. There is a new branch called Next Door Nobu a few doors up Hudson Street, or you can try for a spot at the Nobu sushi bar, also unreserved.

+ 192 B4 ⊠ 105 Hudson Street at Franklin Street ☎ (212) 219-0500 ⑥ Lunch Mon–Fri 11:45–2; dinner daily 5:45–10

### N.Y. Noodle Town $

There's nothing fancy about this place and there is often a line, but you'll find some of the best food in the city. Order one or several of the barbecued meats: duck, suckling pig, pork, soy chicken. Make sure you ask for the accompanying ginger sauce, which they often forget. It makes the dish. The waiters are quiet but competent. As with many restaurants in Chinatown, you may be seated at a big table with others, which can be both interesting and pleasant.

+ 193 D4 ⊠ 28½ Bowery at Bayard Street ☎ (212) 349-0923 ⑥ Daily 9 am–4 am

## Provence $$

A well-established and attractive French bistro with pretty windows, pastel walls and plenty of flowers, all serving as a comforting back-drop to robust Provençale dishes. Classic dishes to sample include the pissaladière (an onion and anchovy tart) or the bouillabaisse. The back garden is a pleasant place to sit if the weather's good.

+ 194 C1 ⊠ 38 MacDougal Street at Prince Street ☎ (212) 475-7500 ⑥ Lunch daily noon–3; dinner Mon–Thu 6–11:30, Fri–Sat 6–midnight, Sun 6–10. Closed Dec 25, Jan 1

## Sammy's Roumanian $$

You arrive at a rather down-and-out Lower East Side block and enter into a subterranean haven for some of the only remaining authentic Jewish cooking left in the city (the world?). Have things you'll remember for days, like the chopped liver and the brisket. Rendered chicken fat sits on the tables as a condiment, along with plenty of pickles and challah bread, and you can make your own egg creams with real seltzer. The "Jewish Rock and Roll" begins at 6:30, and everyone sings along, even you.

+ 195 E1 ⊠ 157 Chrystie Street at Delancey Street ☎ (212) 673-0330 ⑥ Daily 4–11 pm; closed some Jewish holidays

### 🍷🍷🍷 Savoy $$

This intimate corner restaurant is blessed with a charming and attractive storefront, as well as three fireplaces, one in the downstairs dining room, one upstairs in the lounge area, and one for the chef in the chef's dining room. Chef/owner Peter Hoffman uses local ingredients to present a lively, ever-changing menu reflecting the seasons and his eclectic gastronomic interests (which often lean toward the Mediterranean).

+ 195 D1 ⊠ 70 Prince Street at Crosby Street ☎ (212) 219-8570 ⑥ Lunch Mon–Sat noon–3; dinner Mon–Thu 6–10:30, Fri–Sat 6–11, Sun 6–10. Closed Jul 4, Dec 25

# Where to... Shop

In Lower Manhattan, the most well-established shopping area is SoHo, with some of the most impressive, high-priced boutiques in the city, providing the complete Downtown fashion statement and the furnishings that attend to the lifestyle.

## SoHo

The most recent trend here, however, has been a plethora of openings of the ubiquitous small chains (**Banana Republic, Williams Sonoma**, etc.), and the neighborhood is veering toward a certain middle ground, not quite as cutting edge as it used to be.

Art galleries line West Broadway from Houston to Canal. For

back home. (There is another branch in Times Square, tel: 212/333-4109.)

### Kavehaz

This is a hip coffee lounge with pastries and other snacks.

✚ 195 D1 ⊠ 123 Mercer Street between Prince and Spring streets ☎ (212) 343-0612 ◷ Daily noon–1 am (also Fri–Sat 1–2 am)

### Once Upon a Tart

A good spot for breakfast or a break, this cute storefront operation serves nice baked goods and fresh sandwiches.

✚ 194 C2 ⊠ 135 Sullivan Street between Houston and Prince streets ☎ (212) 387-7869 ◷ Mon–Fri 8–8, Sat 9–8, Sun 9–6

## BARS

### Bubble Lounge

At this TriBeCa hub they have 26 champagnes by the glass, and the foie gras, oysters and caviar to go with them.

✚ 192 B5 ⊠ 228 West Broadway at White Street ☎ (212) 431-3433 ◷ Mon–Sat 5 pm–2 am (also Sat 2–4 am)

### Fanelli's

This old watering hole is an oasis of real life floating in a stylish sea, with a beautiful wooden bar and classic decor, and regular, everyday food.

✚ 195 D1 ⊠ 94 Prince Street at Mercer Street ☎ (212) 226-9412 ◷ Daily 10:30 am–2 am

### Pravda

The still cool if no longer ultrachic Pravda, a suavely decorated subterranean lounge, specializes in martinis (the vodka selections number in the dozens).

✚ 195 D1 ⊠ 281 Lafayette Street at Prince Street ☎ (212) 226-4944 ◷ Daily 5 pm–1 am

## CAFÉS

### Caffe Roma

A nice choice, with the requisite hissing cappuccino and espresso machine, classic tiled floors and delicious-looking Italian sweets to tempt you.

✚ 195 E1 ⊠ 385 Broome Street at Mulberry Street ☎ (212) 226-8413 ◷ Daily 8 am–midnight

### Ceci-Cela

A low-key environment but fabulous almond croissants, among other pastries, make this an excellent choice, even worth a detour.

✚ 195 E1 ⊠ 55 Spring Street between Lafayette and Mulberry streets ☎ (212) 274-9179 ◷ Sun–Thu 8–7, Fri–Sat 7 am–10 pm

### Cybercafe

Munch on a pastry, sip an espresso and keep in touch with the folks

✚ 195 D1 ⊠ 273A Lafayette Street at Prince Street ☎ (212) 334-5140 ◷ Prince Street (N, R); Broadway/Lafayette, (F, S and downtown 6); Spring Street (6) ◷ Mon–Thu 11 am–10 pm, Fri–Sat 11–11 pm, Sun 11 am–10 pm

interesting housewares visit **Ad Hoc Softwares** (136 Wooster Street). Vintage tabletop can be found at **Mood Indigo** (181 Prince Street). For fun women's fashions try **Betsey Johnson** (138 Wooster Street). For more sedate attire try **Agnes b** (116 Prince Street). Less expensive new and old street clothes are at **Canal Jeans** (504 Broadway). Gently worn women's designer clothing is at **Ina** (101 Thompson Street). Italian retailer **Fiorucci** (622 Broadway, between Houston and Bleecker streets) has a department store full of men's and women's clothing. Gorgeous, well-made and expensive shoes are at **Varda** (149 Spring Street). **Peter Fox** (105 Thompson Street) is known for its lovely handmade women's shoes. **Kate Spade** (454 Broome Street) designs the chic handbags. Hip clothes with housewares are at **Anthropologie** (375 West Broadway).

Great bread is at the **Sullivan Street Bakery** (73 Sullivan Street),

and all manner of gourmet items are grandiosely displayed at **Dean & DeLuca** (560 Broadway). Things pertaining to photography, including books and objets d'art, are at **A Photographer's Place** (133 Mercer Street). Browse through a fabulous collection of old prints at **Pageant Book & Print Shop** (114 West Houston Street). **Enchanted Forest** (85 Mercer Street) is a fantasy toy shop for the young and young at heart. The fascinating and different **E. Buk** (151 Spring Street, upstairs) should be visited for a glimpse into one man's idea of collectible gadgets, and certainly for an interesting anecdote or two.

## NoLiTa

The sharper edge can now be found to the east of SoHo, in the unofficially named "NoLiTa" (north of Little Italy), particularly on Elizabeth, Mott and Mulberry streets between Houston and Broome streets. Here, vibrant, up-and-coming designers and

retailers in smaller spaces are able to take more risks due to lower rents. **Language** (238 Mulberry Street) specializes in clothing and accessories by small European designers. **Lucien Pellat-Finet** (226 Elizabeth Street) has fine cashmeres. **Resurrection** (217 Mott Street) has splashy antique and vintage designer clothing. At 263 Lafayette's **NY Firefighters Friend**, you can buy fireman paraphernalia, and a few doors down, there are NY Police Department items. Farther up on Lafayette are numerous stores specializing in vintage modern furniture and furnishings, and **Lost City Arts** (18 Cooper Square) has New York City architectural pieces and memorabilia.

## Lower East Side

On Orchard and Ludlow streets, young designers have opened fascinating clothing and accessory shops alongside the stalwarts of the old Jewish neighborhood, which have always provided discount

fabrics, clothing and luggage, and thrived on last-minute price negotiations. This area is a great destination on Sundays, because everything is open and bustling (having been closed Saturday for the Sabbath). In the old school, notable spots are **Beckenstein Fabrics, Home** (130 Orchard Street); **Beckenstein Fabrics, Men's** (133 Orchard Street); **Altman Luggage** (135 Orchard Street); **Fine & Klein** (119 Orchard Street) for handbags. Newcomers are hats by **Amy Downs** (103 Stanton Street); witty graphics on T-shirts at **Marcoart NYC** (186 Orchard Street); party dresses at **Mary Adams** (159 Ludlow).

Classic Jewish foods can be found at the take-outs **Gus's Pickles** (officially **Essex Street Pickles**, 35 Essex Street), where you can choose from barrels on the sidewalk, and **Kossar's Bialystoker** (367 Grand Street) for New York's best-kept bread secret, the bialy. A favorite bargain candy store is **Economy Candy** (108 Rivington Street).

## TriBeCa

TriBeCa has some interesting stores scattered about with an assortment of craftsy offerings, such as **TriBeCa Potters** (443 Greenwich Street, second floor), with studios of several ceramicists. Notable spots are **Urban Archaeology** (143 Franklin), with an amazing array of architectural elements, and the **Fountain Pen Hospital** (10 Warren Street between Church Street and Broadway), which has vintage and new pens. **Totem** (71 Franklin Street) sells high-style housewares, from small gadgets to furniture and decorations.

## Chinatown

Chinatown has a few treasures, such as the amazing **Pearl River Mart** (277 Canal Street) for all kinds of things Chinese, and **Kam Man** (200 Canal Street), with a good selection of tabletop items and Asian food ingredients. **Pearl Paint** (308 Canal Street) has five floors of well-priced art supplies.

# Where to...
## Be Entertained

### THEATER

### Performing Garage/Wooster Group

Willem Dafoe and other name actors are part of this experimental troupe.
**➕ 192 C5 ☒ 33 Wooster Street**
**☎ (212) 966-9796**

### MUSIC

#### Contemporary/Jazz

### Arlene Grocery

Indie bands play no-cover shows.
**➕ 195 F2 ☒ 95 Stanton Street**
**☎ (212) 358-1633**

### Bowery Ballroom

Emerging rockers and alternative cult faves play this Lower East Side venue.

**➕ 195 E1 ☒ 6 Delancey Street**
**☎ (212) 533-2111**

### Knitting Factory

This TriBeCa venue books avant jazz, experimental, rock and world music.
**➕ 192 C4 ☒ 74 Leonard Street**
**☎ (212) 219-3006**

### Meow Mix

Sapphic-centric hole-in-the-wall books gender-liberated music.
**➕ 195, off F2 ☒ 269 East Houston Street ☎ (212) 254-0688**

### Mercury Lounge

Here's the Lower East Side's best room for new rock and No Depression artists.
**➕ 195 F2 ☒ 217 East Houston Street ☎ (212) 260-4700**

## S.O.B.'s (Sounds of Brazil)

Always jumping, this club serves up world and Latin music and Caribbean food.
**➕ 194 C2 ☒ 204 Varick Street**
**☎ (212) 243-4940**

### Tonic

Offbeat jazz and other artists perform at this hot Lower East Side room.
**➕ 195 F1 ☒ 107 Norfolk Street**
**☎ (212) 358-7503**

### MOVIES

### Angelika Film Center

The specialty here is first-run American independent and international art films. There's an on-site café.
**➕ 195 D2 ☒ West Houston Street at Mercer Street ☎ (212) 995-2000**

### Film Forum

Classic-film series and indie and foreign pics screen here.
**➕ 194 C2 ☒ 209 West Houston Street ☎ (212) 727-8110**

# Excursions

For a taste of New York City life beyond Manhattan, slip away to one of the boroughs. You can walk – or take the subway – to Brooklyn or ride the ferry to Staten Island.

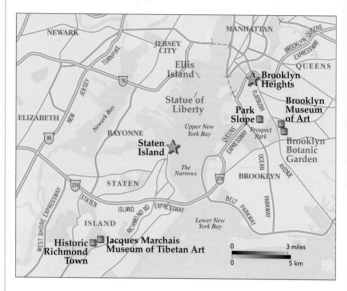

# Brooklyn

"Breuckelen" was one of a half-dozen towns established by the Dutch in the 17th century in what is now New York's most populous borough. In 1898, by a mere 300-vote margin, the electorate of the then thriving third-largest city in America agreed to join the Bronx, Queens, Manhattan and Staten Island to form New York City. Many residents later referred to the decision as "the great mistake," for in the process, Brooklyn lost part of its identity.

Walt Whitman edited the local paper (*The Brooklyn Eagle*) in the 19th century, by which time many captains of industry lived in Brooklyn Heights, along or near the waterfront. Since then, Brooklyn has produced many superstars, among them performers Mae West, Eddie Murphy, Jerry Seinfeld, Barbra Streisand and Woody Allen. This excursion involves a fair amount of walking, so it's best done in fine weather and from Wednesday to Sunday, when all the stops are open.

**1–2**
Begin by strolling across the **Brooklyn Bridge** (► 153–154). From Midtown, hop on a 4, 5 or 6 subway train heading Downtown to the City Hall/Brooklyn Bridge stop. Exit south, following the signs reading "Brooklyn Bridge." You'll exit into a small park with a view of the Brooklyn Bridge. Face away from the bridge and walk to the small triangle that begins the bridge promenade. (If you're taking a cab, the promenade is on the

east side of Centre Street south of Chambers Street.)

As you approach Brooklyn, stay to the left when the pathway forks (there's a stop sign for cyclists here). Walk down the stairs, make a right onto Cadman Plaza East, and veer right onto the first blacktop path. Cross Cadman Plaza West and you'll be on Middagh Street. (If you don't want to walk the bridge, you can reach this point by taking the A or C subway train from Manhattan to the High Street/Brooklyn Bridge stop. Follow the "Fulton Street" signs in the station, make a U-turn when you exit the station staircase, walk a half block, and take a left on Middagh.)

## 2–3

Make a left off Middagh at Henry Street. Walk two blocks south to Orange Street and make a right. Midblock is **Plymouth Church of the Pilgrims**, a major stop on the Underground Railroad, the path used by slaves from the South to reach freedom.

**A splash of color brightens the street in Brooklyn Heights**

## 3–4

Continue west to Willow Street, make a right, and walk north to Middagh. The three-story home at 24 Middagh is the oldest wood-frame house in Brooklyn.

## 4–5

Backtrack on Willow Street to Cranberry Street and turn right. A plaque describes the merits of the Mott Bedell House at 11 Cranberry.

## 5–6

Continue west on Cranberry until you come to a dead end at the Fruit Street Sitting Area, and make a left. A block farther along, the path veers to the right and merges with the Brooklyn Heights Promenade. A sign near the merge relates the history of Brooklyn Heights.

## 6–7

Along the promenade you can rest your feet as you enjoy the views across the East River to Lower Manhattan. A flagpole marks Montague Street, four blocks from where you entered the promenade. Make a left here.

## 7–8
Head east on Montague past some interesting shops and restaurants (the **Heights Café**, at 84 Montague, is a neighborhood favorite) to Montague and Clinton streets. From the intersection's southeast corner you can view four first-rate buildings in four architectural styles: Gothic Revival (the brownstone St. Ann's and the Holy Trinity Church, on the northwest corner), Italian palazzo (177 Montague); Roman Revival (183 Montague) and art deco (185 Montague).

## 8–9
Continue east on Montague to Court Street and make a right. Walk south on Court to Schermerhorn Street, make a left, and walk one block to the entrance of the diverting **New York Transit Museum**, which is full of vintage trains and memorabilia.

From any angle, this bridge is a looker

## 9–10
From the museum, backtrack on Schermerhorn to Court Street, walk south (left) two blocks to Atlantic Avenue, and head right. Amid the small enclave of Middle Eastern shops and restaurants here is **Damascus Bakery** (195 Atlantic Avenue), which sells inexpensive savory meat and spinach pies to go. More substantial fare can be had at **Tripoli Restaurant** (156 Atlantic Avenue), a Lebanese establishment.

## 10–11
You'll need to ride the subway or call a car service (easier than it sounds – ► 167) to get to the next stop, the **Brooklyn Botanic Garden**.

To take the subway, backtrack to Court, make a left, and walk five blocks north to the Borough Hall station. Take a 2 train heading to Flatbush Avenue or a 3 train headed toward New Lots Avenue (in either case, *not* toward Manhattan). Ride seven stops to the Eastern Parkway/Brooklyn Museum station. Follow the "Brooklyn Museum of Art" signs, and at the top of the exit staircase, turn around. The museum is to the left, the garden to the right. Head first to the garden, where the **azalea walk**, **Japanese Garden** and **Steinhardt Conservatory** are the must-sees.

In bloom at the Brooklyn Botanic

Cabs aren't as plentiful in Brooklyn as they are in Manhattan, so to get to the garden and museum it's better to call Atlantic Avenue Car Service (tel: 718/797-0666) or Montague Car Service (tel: 718/625-6666). (If you're going between 3:30 and 6:30 pm, call the service about a half hour before you want a car.) The ride should cost about $10.

The highlights at the top-notch **Brooklyn Museum of Art** include the Egyptian (third floor) and decorative-arts (fourth floor) collections. Local imagery in the sterling American painting wing (fifth floor) include Francis Guy's *Winter Scene in Brooklyn* (circa 1817) and Georgia O'Keeffe's *Brooklyn Bridge* (1948).

desk whether the free trolley to Park Slope is still running (service stops in the late afternoon). If it's not, call Brownstone Car Service (tel: 718/789-1536). The cost should be $6 or $7. If you stay for dinner, try **Cucina** (256 5th Avenue near Garfield Street, tel: 718/230-0711), which serves haute northern Italian cuisine, or the more informal and less expensive bistro **Max & Moritz** (426A 7th Avenue at 14th Street, tel: 718/499-5557). Ask at the restaurants how to catch the subway back to Manhattan, or call a car service. A ride to Midtown costs about $20.

### New York Transit Museum
✉ Boerum Place at Schermerhorn Street ☎ (718) 243-3060 🕐 Tue–Fri 10–4, Sat–Sun noon–5; closed Jan 1, Easter, Jul 4, Thanksgiving, Dec 25 💲 Inexpensive

### Brooklyn Museum of Art
✉ 200 Eastern Parkway ☎ (718) 638-5000 🕐 Wed–Fri 10–5, Sat–Sun 11–6 (also first Sat of month 6–11 pm); closed Jan 1, Thanksgiving, Dec 25 💲 Inexpensive

### Brooklyn Botanic Garden
✉ Eastern Parkway Gate north of Brooklyn Museum ☎ (718) 623-7200 🕐 Tue–Fri, 8–6, Sat–Sun and legal holidays 10–6, Apr–Sep; Tue–Fri, 8–4:30; Sat–Sun and legal holidays 10–4:30, Oct–Mar. Closed Jan 1, Labor Day, Thanksgiving, Dec 25 💲 Inexpensive

**11–12**
Return to Manhattan on the 2 or 3 subway train. If you want to explore trendy **Park Slope**, ask at the museum's admission

# Staten Island

A visit to marvelous, low-key Historic Richmond Town harks back a century or two, when learning took place in one-room schools and general stores stocked necessities like mole traps, sausage stuffers, eel spears and butter churns. According to the Dalai Lama, this excursion's bonus stop, the nearby Jacques Marchais Museum of Tibetan Art, contains superlative examples of his country's art.

You can picnic in the museum's garden (purchase food in Manhattan), which on clear days has views for miles. Richmond Town's snack bar sells soups, salads and sandwiches, and there's a pricey formal restaurant (reservations essential) with good American-Continental cuisine.

### 1–2

Hop aboard the Staten Island Ferry (▶ 151). On Staten Island, take the 30-minute ride on Bus S74. Ask the driver to call out the Historic Richmond Town stop, at Richmond Road and St. Patrick's Place.

Follow signs on St. Patrick's to the visitor center, which has site maps. The must-sees among Richmond Town's restored or reconstructed buildings include several homes and the tinsmith's and carpenter's shops.

### 2–3

Walk back down to Richmond Road and make a right. Walk three blocks,

make a left on Lighthouse Avenue, and follow it to No. 338, where you'll find the **Jacques Marchais Museum of Tibetan Art**. The last three minutes are up a steep grade.

### 3–4

Backtrack on Lighthouse Avenue to Richmond Road, where you'll see the stop for Bus 74.

**Historic Richmond Town**
✉ St. Patrick's Place off Richmond Road
☎ (718) 351-1611; (718) 351-7879 for restaurant ◷ Wed–Sun 1–5, Sep–Jun; Wed–Fri 10–5, Sat–Sun 1–5, Jul–Aug
💲 Inexpensive

**Jacques Marchais Museum of Tibetan Art**
✉ 338 Lighthouse Avenue ☎ (718) 987-3500 ◷ Wed–Sun 1–5, Apr–Nov; Wed–Fri 1–5, Dec–Mar (call first; winter hours sometimes vary) 💲 Inexpensive

**Staten Island Ferry: The best free ride in New York City**

# Walks

# 1 42nd STREET
*Walk*

**DISTANCE** 1.5 miles **TIME** 2 hours
**START POINT** 42nd Street/8th Avenue subway station (A, C, E) ✚ 196 B3
**END POINT** United Nations 46th Street and 1st Avenue (M15, M27, M42, M50 buses) ✚ 197 F4

The mood and architecture of 42nd Street fluctuate as it slices through Midtown. The pace is frenetic on the western end near Times Square, yet almost serene (for New York) near the East River. Along the way stand some of the city's finest Beaux Arts, art deco, modernist and postmodern buildings. One note of caution: As you cross back and forth on 42nd Street, resist the urge to jaywalk midblock. Traffic runs fast and in both directions; you're safer crossing at the traffic lights.

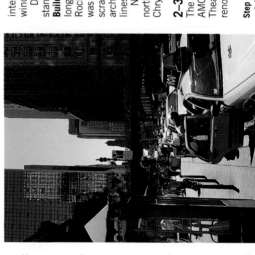

## 1–2

Exit the 42nd Street subway and proceed to the southeast corner of 42nd Street and 8th Avenue. Bright lights and high-tech amusements beckon to the east, but face west briefly for two views of the past. Midblock on the north side of 42nd between 8th and 9th avenues is the redbrick **Holy Cross Church**. Completed in 1867, it's one of the Times Square area's oldest buildings. Louis Comfort Tiffany designed the interior, though only one of his stained-glass windows remains.

Directly across 42nd Street from the church stands the blue-green terra-cotta **McGraw-Hill Building**, named for the publishing firm, its long-departed first tenant. Even more so than Rockefeller Center, for which Raymond Hood was also the chief architect, this 1931 skyscraper proclaimed the priorities of modern architecture, among them the love of soaring lines and disdain for ornamentation.

Now face east. Several blocks away on the north side of 42nd Street you'll notice the Chrysler Building. Walk east a few steps.

## 2–3

The present engulfs the past at the 25-screen AMC multiplex. The 3,700-ton former Empire Theatre, originally named for Julian Eltinge, a renowned early 20th-century female

**Step into the ebb and flow of Manhattan life on the celebrated 42nd Street**

impersonator, was moved 168 feet west and transformed into the multiplex's lobby. East of the theaters is an interactive version of **Madame Tussaud's Wax Museum**. Beyond that sits the **Candler Building**, a narrow skyscraper completed in 1913 and named for a founder of the Coca-Cola Co.

## 3–4

East of the Candler Building is the **New Amsterdam Theatre**, whose art nouveau lobby adornments merely hint at this showplace's splendor.

## 4–5

Across the street at the **New Victory Theater**, a grand double exterior staircase and windows of all shapes are among the pseudo-Venetian architectural details. Erected in 1900, the New Victory is the Broadway Theater district's oldest facility. Next door is the **Reuters Building**, at 3 Times Square, completed in 2001 with 34,000 square feet of exterior signage. Proceed east across 7th Avenue.

## 5–6

The triangle bounded by 42nd Street, 7th Avenue and Broadway is **Times Square** (▶ 63–64). The tower within the triangle is 1 Times Square, formerly the headquarters of

*The New York Times* and still the building from whose roof the lowering of an illuminated globe signals the New Year. Stop for a moment on 42nd underneath the tower's revolving news crawl and look east across Broadway.

On the southeast corner of 42nd and Broadway stands the former **Knickerbocker Hotel**. Now an office building, the redbrick structure was built by John Jacob Astor IV a decade before he perished aboard the RMS *Titanic*. With its wrought-iron balconies, terra-cotta detailing and ornate cornices, the natty Knickerbocker

UNITED NATIONS PLAZA

SECOND      AVE

THIRD      AVE

LEXINGTON      AVENUE

MADISON      AVE

FIFTH      AVENUE

SIXTH      AVE

SEVENTH      AVE

EIGHTH      AVENUE

NINTH      AVE

FIRST AVE

Tudor City

Daily News Building

Chrysler Building

Socony-Mobil Building

Chanin Building

Grand Central Terminal

New York Public Library

W R Grace Building

former American Radiator Building

Reuters Building

1 Times Square

4 Times Square

former Knickerbocker Hotel

New Amsterdam Theatre

AMC multiplex

Candler Building

New Victory Theater

McGraw-Hill Building

Holy Cross Church

42nd Street

United Nations Headquarters

East River

Ralph Bunche Park

TUDOR CITY PLACE

45TH STREET

EAST 43RD ST

EAST 42ND STREET

EAST

BROADWAY

TIMES SQUARE

Bryant Park

WEST

0    500 yards

0    500 metres

looks dressed up for a party that ended a century ago. The festivities these days happen on the northeast corner at the mirror-glass 4 Times Square skyscraper, with its huge cylindrical and other lighted signs.

Continue east on 42nd Street past 4 Times Square, crossing Broadway and then 6th Avenue (Avenue of the Americas). At 1114 6th Avenue is the **W. R. Grace Building**, a

white-travertine and tinted-glass modernist structure that looks like a ski jump.

### 6–7

The handsome **Bryant Park** (▶ 67–68) lies directly across 42nd Street from the Grace Building. On the park's 40th Street side stands the former **American Radiator Building**, strikingly decked out in black brick and gold and yellow trim.

### 7–8

The **New York Public Library** (▶ 68–69) abuts the park on its eastern side. Continue east to 5th Avenue and turn right. Two stone lions, dubbed Patience and Fortitude, flank the

**Bryant Park: A civilized patch of greenery along 42nd Street**

**New York Public Library Reading Room, below**

library's monumental staircase. If the library is open, enter via the middle door, catch a glimpse of the all-marble rotunda, Astor Hall, and then head up the stairs to the left to see the third-floor murals and reading room.

### 8–9

From the library, continue east two blocks on 42nd Street to **Grand Central Terminal** (▶ 52–55). If you need refreshment, head downstairs to the Dining Concourse, but view the ceiling mural in the Main Concourse before you depart.

## 9–10

A fantasy frieze depicting sea creatures decorates the **Chanin Building**, across from Grand Central at the southwest corner of 42nd Street and Lexington Avenue. The stark interior friezes and other appointments of the cathedral-like lobby vividly illustrate the German expressionist influences on 1920s American art-deco style.

## 10–11

Diagonally across the intersection of 42nd and Lexington stands the **Chrysler Building** (▶ 65), all done up like a 1929 Chrysler model. After viewing the outside, step into its cavernous lobby.

## 11–12

Remain on the same side of 42nd as the Chrysler Building for the best view of the stamped-aluminum **Socony-Mobil Building,** erected in 1955 on the south side of the street between Lexington and 3rd avenues. Then proceed to the entrance at 150 East 42nd Street. Its modernist lobby is brighter and airier than those of the Chanin and Chrysler buildings.

## 12–13

Continue east on 42nd Street to No. 220, the **Daily News Building** (another Raymond Hood

skyscraper), no longer occupied by the New York tabloid. Just inside the lobby, a huge sunken globe sits underneath a black-glass dome.

## 13–14

Cross 2nd Avenue. Halfway down the block a staircase leads up to the **Tudor City** apartment complex. The view from the overpass at the top of the steps includes the East River, the United Nations complex and the borough of Queens.

## 14–15

Head north (left) on Tudor City Place, make a right on 43rd Street, and descend the stairs to Ralph Bunche Park. Cross United Nations Plaza (1st Avenue) and make a left. At 46th Street you can enter the **United Nations Headquarters** (▶ 65). The angle on the U.N. buildings from the sweeping plaza accentuates the best elements of their modernist design.

**Don't miss**
Grand Central Terminal (▶ 52–55)
Chrysler Building (▶ 65)

**The Chrysler Building's peak is stunning, but don't forget to visit its distinguished art-deco lobby**

# 2 UPTOWN STROLL
### Walk

For a bucolic spin through a part of Manhattan far from the madding Midtown crowds, head to upper 5th Avenue. At 105th Street a three-story wrought-iron gate (don't miss the open-mouthed gargoyles over the doors) guards the entrance to the Conservatory Garden in Central Park (▶ 82–86). From here you'll pass through some of northern Central Park, visit the world's largest Gothic cathedral, and conclude on a ridge overlooking the Hudson River. A warm weekend day, when the locals are out and about, is the best time to take this stroll.

**DISTANCE** 2 miles **TIME** 1.5 to 2 hours
**START POINT** 5th Avenue and 105th Street (M4 bus to Madison Avenue and 104th Street; walk west one block to 5th Avenue) ✚ 200 B3
**END POINT** 122nd Street & Riverside Drive (M4/M104 from 122nd Street and Broadway) ✚ 200, off A5

## 1–2
Walk west one block from the M4 bus stop to the **Conservatory Garden**, which sits across 5th Avenue from **El Museo del**

**Barrio** (▶ 96). The garden's gate once protected Mr. and Mrs. Cornelius Vanderbilt II from any riff-raff who might have happened upon their mansion on 5th Avenue at 58th Street. Straight ahead across the lawn you'll see a fountain. Four manicured rows of hedges crowned by a wrought-iron trellis curve behind and above it. Tour the English garden to the south and the French garden to the north. You're entering in the center, so walk first to the left (south), and exit north from the Untermeyer Fountain, also known as *Three Dancing Maidens*.

## 2–3
Large boulders loom over the western side of Harlem Meer (*meer* is Dutch for "small sea"). As you approach the southern edge of the pond, turn right and follow the path – at this

Grant's Tomb ☐

Hudson River

[12] WEST 122ND STREET
Riverside Church
RIVER

Riverside Park

### Uptown perspective from Riverside Church

point parallel to and just steps from 5th Avenue – as it winds north and then west toward the Victorian-style **Charles A. Dana Discovery Center**.

## 3–4

Stop for a view of the water from the center's terrace. The next section of this walk passes through an isolated but generally safe area. If you're the cautious type, continue west to Frederick Douglass Circle along the path parallel to Central Park North (110th Street) and pick up the tour at steps 7–8, below. Otherwise, continue west and south around the pond, staying to the right (west) of the Loula D. Lasker pool/ice-skating rink when you get to the water's southern edge.

## 4–5

Just past the pool/rink you'll go down a few steps. At this point, two paths continue south through the type of rolling, rustic terrain that Frederick Law Olmsted and Calvert Vaux, Central Park's designers, liked best about their creation. Stay to the right and cross under the Huddlestone Arch.

## 5–6

When you come to the small wooden foot-bridge (a few hundred yards past Huddlestone), cross it and bear right. A few hundred feet ahead is the tall and narrow **Glenspan Arch**.

## 6–7

A waterfall past the arch feeds into the loch alongside the path you've been walking. Beyond the waterfall is the Pool. Willow trees droop languidly over the water's southern edge. Walk away from them around the northern edge, but before you have a chance to dip south, take the path that veers off to the northwest toward the 103rd Street and Central Park West entrance.

## 7–8

Walk north up Central Park West to Frederick Douglass Circle. Cross Central Park West at

## 8–9

Follow 110th Street, also known as Cathedral Parkway, two blocks, past Morningside Park to Amsterdam Avenue, and make a right. At 111th Street is the huge bronze **Peace Fountain**,

---

110th Street, following the curve of the circle west and then north to the stoplight. Cross north on 110th Street and make a left.

---

MADISON        AVENUE

FIFTH          AVENUE

Charles A Dana Discovery Center

Untermeyer Fountain

PARK NORTH

Harlem Meer

CENTRAL

Central Conservatory Garden

Loula D Lasker pool/rink

Huddlestone Arch

Central Park

The Loch

The Great Hill

Glenspan Arch

FREDERICK DOUGLASS CIRCLE

The Pool

CENTRAL      PARK      WEST

Morningside Park

Cathedral of St John the Divine

Peace Fountain

CATHEDRAL PARKWAY (110TH STREET)

AMSTERDAM AVE

Tom's Restaurant

WEST 112TH STREET

BROADWAY

400 metres

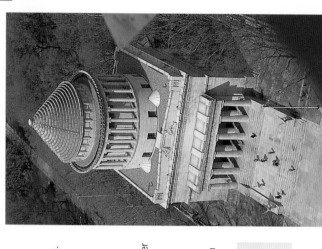

which portrays the Archangel Michael slaying the devil.

### 9–10

Towering over the fountain a few steps to the north is the **Cathedral of St. John the Divine** (▶ 99).

### 10–11

After you've explored the cathedral, head west one block on 112th to Broadway. Fans of the television show "Seinfeld" will recognize Tom's

Restaurant, the lead characters' favorite hangout, on the northeast corner. If you're ready to leave the area, on the west side of Broadway you can catch a Bus M4 heading south to Midtown East or a Bus M104 to Midtown West.

### 11–12

To continue the walk, head north on Broadway past Columbia University to 122nd Street and then west two blocks to Riverside Drive, which borders **Riverside Park** (▶ 99). To your left will be **Riverside Church**, to your right **Grant's Tomb**. On a clear day the view across the Hudson River from the church's tower is splendid.

### 12–13

If you're feeling intrepid, you can head toward Midtown along the Hudson through Riverside Park. Otherwise, catch the M4 or M104 bus on the west side of Broadway or hop in a cab.

### Don't miss

Conservatory Garden (▲ 84)
Cathedral of St. John the Divine (▶ 99)

Musical break in the park. View of Grant's Tomb from Riverside Church tower, right

## 3 WEST VILLAGE
*Walk*

DISTANCE 1.9 miles TIME 2 hours
START/END POINT West 4th Street/Washington Square subway station (A, C, E, F)
✚ 194 C2

Amble through the West Village's narrow lanes, peer into its secluded courtyards, and visit its quirky shops, and you'll quickly see what's charmed generations of artists and iconoclasts. Pay attention, though. The helter-skelter street layout can be confusing. Several sights mentioned below are described in greater detail in Greenwich Village (▶ 120–123). This walk is most enjoyable in the afternoon, when the shops are open.

### 1–2
Begin on the west side of 6th Avenue (Avenue of the Americas) at the Waverly Cinema. If you've exited the subway on the east side of 6th Avenue, walk across 6th at West 4th Street. As you face the theater, south is to your left. Head south on 6th Avenue to Carmine Street and make a right. On Carmine between Bleecker and Bedford streets are two great shops, the **Unoppressive, Non-Imperialist Bargain Books** store (real deals

on music, film, New Age and other genres) at No. 34, and the **House of Oldies Rare Records** shop, across the street at No. 35.

### 2–3
But you're here to walk, not shop (this tour ends back at Step 1, so you can return). Continue past the stores to 7th Avenue South, cross the avenue, and make a right. One block north at 7th Avenue and **St. Luke's Place** (▶121), also signed as Leroy Street, make a left. Seventh Avenue's traffic and tacky construction recede as you head into this tree-lined row of mid-19th-century homes.

### 3–4
Before it was paved over and turned into a playground, **Hudson Park**, across from St. Luke's Place to the south, was a graveyard. Village legends should be taken with a grain of salt, but a teaspoonful is required for the oft-told one about the burial here of the lost son of Louis XVI and Marie Antoinette.

### 4–5
Continue west on St. Luke's Place to Hudson Street and turn right, walking past cafés and shops until you get to Barrow Street, where you'll make a left. If you're lucky, the roses in the garden of the historic **Church of St. Luke-in-the-Fields** will be in bloom. The church, farther up Hudson Street, was built in 1822.

### 5–6
Backtrack east across Hudson on Barrow. A plaque at 81 Barrow Street gives the architectural lowdown on that 1850s Italianate. Near No. 79, Commerce Street angles into Barrow. Make a right onto Commerce, but immediately face left and stop. A garden with a purpose separates the three-story homes at 39 and 41 Commerce Street, reputedly built by a sea captain in 1831 for his two feuding daughters. Face right and continue along Commerce as it hooks left past the **Cherry Lane Theater**, at No. 38, where the works of Edward Albee, David Mamet and other playwrights have debuted.

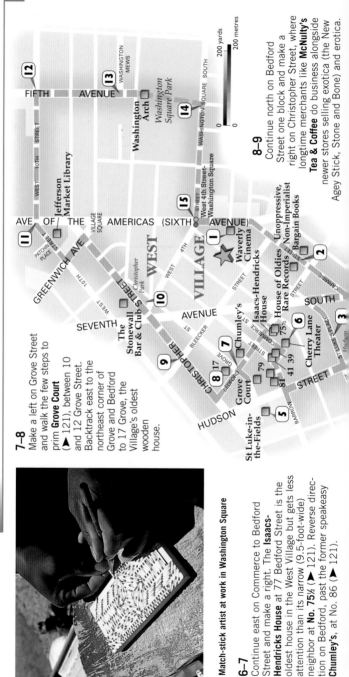

**Match-stick artist at work in Washington Square**

## 7–8

Make a left on Grove Street and walk the few steps to prim **Grove Court** (▲121), between 10 and 12 Grove Street. Backtrack east to the northeast corner of Grove and Bedford to 17 Grove, the Village's oldest wooden house.

## 6–7

Continue east on Commerce to Bedford Street and make a right. The **Isaacs-Hendricks House** at 77 Bedford Street is the oldest house in the West Village but gets less attention than its narrow (9.5-foot-wide) neighbor at **No. 75½** (▲121). Reverse direction on Bedford, past the former speakeasy **Chumley's**, at No. 86 (▶121).

## 8–9

Continue north on Bedford Street one block and make a right on Christopher Street, where longtime merchants like **McNulty's Tea & Coffee** do business alongside newer stores selling exotica (the New Agey Stick, Stone and Bone) and erotica.

**5th Avenue dead-ends at Washington Arch**

### 9–10

When you get to Bleecker Street you may be tempted to explore the shops in the blocks north of Christopher. By all means do so, but return to Christopher and continue east across 7th Avenue South, where you'll see **Christopher Park** (▶ 121).

### 10–11

Sit on the bench next to the two lesbians (don't be shy, they won't bite) in George Segal's *Gay Liberation* sculpture. The **Stonewall Bar & Club** is over your left shoulder at 53 Christopher Street (▶ 19). Cross to the Stonewall's side of Christopher and proceed east to Greenwich Avenue, where you'll make a left and then a quick right onto West 10th Street. To your left is Patchin Place, to the right stands the daffily Gothic **Jefferson Market Library** (▶ 121), which looks its most fetching from West 11th Street and 6th Avenue.

### 11–12

Cross 6th Avenue on West 10th Street and continue east toward 5th Avenue. The mostly mid-19th-century town houses on this block are among the Village's finest. Look south

(right) on 5th Avenue and you'll see the **Washington Arch.**

### 12–13

Just before the arch, on the east side of 5th Avenue, is **Washington Mews** (▶ 121).

### 13–14

From the mews walk south on 5th Avenue into **Washington Square Park** (▶ 121).

### 14–15

Exit the park heading west along Washington Square South, which becomes West 4th Street. The entrances to the subway are at 6th Avenue.

### Don't miss

**2 St. Luke's Place** (▶ 121).

**7 Christopher Street:** You can often distinguish 19th-century single-family homes from the later tenement apartments by looking at the exteriors. The homes usually have three sets of windows across and the doorway is to the left or right. The tenements usually have four windows, with the doorway in the center.

# 4 SOHO
Walk

For all its chic splendor, as a former industrial setting SoHo retains a down-to-earth feel. This walk takes you past historic cast-iron buildings, many of which contain of-the-moment shops, cafés or galleries.

**DISTANCE** 2 miles **TIME** 1.5 to 2 hours
**START POINT** Broadway/Lafayette subway station (F and downtown 6) ✚ 195 D2
**END POINT** Canal Street subway station (A, C, E) ✚ 192 B5

## 1–2
Start at the Broadway/Lafayette Street subway station, on the south side of East Houston Street. Walk east along Houston Street to Lafayette Street, where a gold-leaf statue of Puck adorns the German and Romanesque **Puck Building** at 295 Lafayette Street. The American edition of the *Puck* humor magazine was published in the building, where the character Grace of the TV show "Will & Grace" has her office. A plaque on the structure's north (Houston Street) side describes its history.

## 2–3
Walk south along Lafayette Street past art, design and clothing shops. Make a right at

the end of the block at Prince Street and a left at the next block, Broadway.

## 3–4
Its high-arched steel-and-glass front makes the **Little Singer Building** (➤ 149), on the west side of Broadway, one of this block's most distinctive sights. Designed by Ernest Flagg in 1903 for the Singer Manufacturing Company, the building has often been cited as a precursor to the 1950s style of skyscraper. The **Haughwout Building** (➤ 149), the oldest of SoHo's cast-iron structures, is to the south at the end of the next block. At Broome Street turn right, and at the next block, stone-lined Mercer Street, turn right again.

## 4–5
Walk north along Mercer Street. If you need refreshment, drop in at sleek **Bar 89**

**A golden statue of Puck stands watch over his ornate building of Lafayette Street**

(89 Mercer Street), which serves burgers and other comfort food to the groovy set. Up the stairs to the right, the unisex restroom is worth a look for its high-tech glass stall doors, which become opaque when you close them. A playful mood reigns at the **Enchanted Forest**, a fairy-tale-oriented gift shop at No. 85. Turn left into Prince Street, then left again into Greene Street. Don't miss the uninterrupted rows of cast-iron buildings here.

**5–6**
Embedded in the east sidewalk of Greene, in front of No. 104, is F. Schein's artwork, *Subway Map Floating on a NY Sidewalk.* The regal-looking building at No. 72–76 is known as the King of Greene Street, one of the most extravagant of cast-iron structures. The Queen of Greene Street is on the next block at No. 28–30.

**6–7**
Backtrack from the Queen of Greene to Grand Street. Make a left on Grand and a right on stone-lined Wooster Street. The upmarket **Tony Shafrazi Gallery** at

119 Wooster usually has a hot show mounted. If it's open, step into *The New York City Earth Room* (141 Wooster Street, ▶ 148), a conceptual environment.

**7–8**
At West Houston Street, turn left. When you get to West Broadway, make another left. Just before Canal Street is the **SoHo Grand Hotel**, whose first-floor lobby's postmodernist industrial decor merits investigation. If you're feeling fabulous, stop for a drink at the bar, unless the hotel's Caviarteria (exactly what the name implies) appeals to your palate.

**8–9**
Continue south along West Broadway from the SoHo Grand. At Canal Street, turn right. Two blocks west is the Canal Street station of the A, C and E subway. Two blocks beyond is another station, where you can catch a 1 or 2 train.

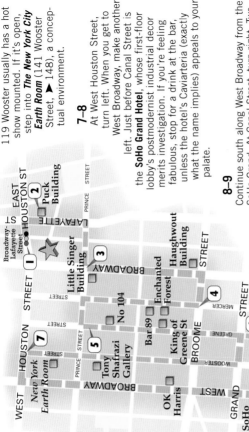

# 5 LOWER MANHATTAN

*Walk*

A terrorist attack destroyed key icons of recent Lower Manhattan history, but the area where New York City got its start remains eminently strollable.

## 1–2

Begin at Bowling Green station. As you exit the station you're heading south, already in Battery Park. Follow the path to the right, past benches and, often, people offering watches "for very good price." (Hot tip: Even stolen Rolexes cost more than $10 – these are fakes.) The path curves toward **Castle Clinton**, built in 1811.

## 2–3

Dioramas in a room just inside the east gate depict Castle Clinton's various incarnations as fort, entertainment center, immigration checkpoint and aquarium. These days it holds the ticket booth for trips to the Statue of Liberty and Ellis Island. Exit via the west gate, which frames the statue stunningly, and walk north past Gangway 6.

**DISTANCE** 2.5 miles **TIME** 1.5 to 2 hours
**START POINT** Bowling Green subway station (4, 5) ⊞ 192 C1
**END POINT** Fulton Street subway station (1, 2) ⊞ 193 D3

## 3–4

The sculptor Marisol created the evocative **American Merchant Mariners Memorial** from a photo of a sinking ship torpedoed during World War II. At high tide the water covers the head of the man overboard. Reverse direction and head south past the ferries to Gangway 3.

## 4–5

Walk up the steps to the left to view sculptor Albino Manca's

large bronze eagle clutching a funerary wreath. The bird is the centerpiece of the East Coast Memorial to

the seafaring ceiling reliefs of the former Cunard Line headquarters. Continue north up Broadway.

## 8–9

At **Trinity Church** (➤152), head east from the church to the **Wall Street area** (➤ 152–153). (Two blocks north of the church's rear is the World Trade Center site.)

## 9–10

Head north from Wall Street on William Street and make a left on Pine Street. Jean Dubuffet's large black-and-white *Group of Trees* sculpture dominates Chase Manhattan Plaza. Below the plaza's glass-walled circle is a sunken sculpture garden by Isamu Noguchi.

## 10–11

Stairs east of the *Group of Trees* sculpture lead back down to William Street. A left brings you to Louise Nevelson Plaza, which contains four large black metal works by the abstract sculptor. The somber-looking building across William Street from the largest Nevelson sculpture is the Federal Reserve Bank. Make a left on Maiden Lane and walk west behind the bank (smile, you're on its security cameras).

0  200 metres

Post Office **6**

Charging **Bull** **5**
Bowling
Green

US
Custom
House **5**
ST

STATE

Park **4**
East
Coast
Memorial

BATTERY PL.
Bowling Green **1**

*Battery*

Hope
Garden

Castle
Clinton **2**

American Merchant
Mariners
Memorial **3**

## 5–6

If the Custom House is open, ascend the stairs at the Great Hall and Rotunda.

As you head back down the stairs, the park you're facing is Bowling Green.

## 6–7

**Bowling Green** really was used for bowling. A statue of Britain's King George III stood here until American colonists toppled it in 1776. Walk north past Bowling Green up Broadway.

## 7–8

Arturo DiModica cast the huge bronze *Charging Bull* and installed it in the triangle across from 25 Broadway without permission. The city occasionally tries to remove it, but superstitious brokers intervene to keep this symbol of stock-market prosperity right where it is. If the post office at 25 Broadway is open, pop in to see

people lost in American coastal waters during World War II. As you stand in front of the eagle, to your left you'll see the path that leads you back to Castle Clinton. At the east gate, make a right and walk alongside the Hope Garden to the intersection of Battery Place, Broadway and State Street. Across State Street is the **U.S. Custom House** (➤ 151).

*Charging Bull,* unofficial mas-cot of the city's stockbrokers.

Engraved granite slabs lead to Albino Manca's giant bronze eagle at the East Coast Memorial

## 11–12

Modeled after a Florentine palazzo, the **Federal Reserve Bank of New York** holds approximately $100 billion worth of gold from several dozen countries. At Nassau Street make a right, and at John Street make another right.

## 12–13

The **United Methodist Church** (44 John Street) was built in 1841. Stand across the street to view the Palladian front window. The difference in scale between the church and its skyscraping neighbors is dramatic.

## 13–14

Continue east five blocks on John Street to Water Street. Make a left at Water which will bring you into the **South Street Seaport Historic District** (▶ 145–146). Continue to the end of Water where, in the shadow of the Brooklyn Bridge, you will find the **Bridge Café** (279 Water Street). The café is in a building that has been a saloon since 1847, making the café Manhattan's oldest continuously operating bar.

## 14–15

Make a right on Dover Street and another on Front Street. At the **Fulton Street Market** make a left, cross South Street, and walk to the end of Pier 17. Ascend the stairs at the east end of the pier for a great view of the **Brooklyn Bridge.**

## 15–16

Cross South Street and head west on Fulton Street past **Schermerhorn Row** (▶ 145). To catch the subway back, continue west on Fulton Street.

### Don't miss

**Battery Park:** This tour starts near the western waterfront in Battery Park, a former defense point that holds military and other memorials.

**U.S. Custom House** (▶ 151)

## GETTING ADVANCE INFORMATION

### Websites

- NYC & Company
  www.nycvisit.com
- Metropolitan Transit
  Authority
  www.mta.nyc.ny.us

- The Official New York
  City Web Site:
  www.ci.nyc.ny.us
- USA City Link Project:
  usacitylink.com

**In the U.S.A.**
NYC & Company
810 Seventh Avenue
New York
NY 10019
☎ 1-800 NYC-VISIT

---

## BEFORE YOU GO

### WHAT YOU NEED

- ● Required
- ○ Suggested
- ▲ Not required

| | UK | Germany | USA | Canada | Australia | Ireland | Netherlands | Spain |
|---|---|---|---|---|---|---|---|---|
| Passport/National Identity Card | ● | ● | ▲ | ○ | ● | ● | ● | ● |
| Visa | ▲ | ▲ | ▲ | ▲ | ▲ | ▲ | ▲ | ▲ |
| Onward or Round-Trip Ticket | ● | ● | ● | ● | ● | ● | ● | ● |
| Health Inoculations (tetanus and polio) | ▲ | ▲ | ▲ | ▲ | ▲ | ▲ | ▲ | ▲ |
| Health Documentation (▶ 190, Health) | ▲ | ▲ | ▲ | ▲ | ▲ | ▲ | ▲ | ▲ |
| Travel Insurance | ● | ● | ▲ | ○ | ● | ● | ● | ● |
| Driver's License (national) | ● | ● | ● | ● | ● | ● | ● | ● |
| Car Insurance Certificate | n/a | n/a | ● | ● | n/a | n/a | n/a | n/a |
| Car Registration Document | n/a | n/a | ● | ● | n/a | n/a | n/a | n/a |

### WHEN TO GO

Peak season          Off-season

| JAN | FEB | MAR | APR | MAY | JUN | JUL | AUG | SEP | OCT | NOV | DEC |
|---|---|---|---|---|---|---|---|---|---|---|---|
| 39°F | 41°F | 46°F | 61°F | 70°F | 81°F | 84°F | 82°F | 77°F | 66°F | 54°F | 39°F |

Very wet   Wet   Cloud   Sun   Sun/Showers

Temperatures are the **average daily maximum** for each month. Average daily minimum temperatures are approximately 14 to 18°F lower.

The best times of the year for **good weather** are May, early June, September and early to mid-October. In July and August the temperature can rise to more than 86°F (35°C), sometimes reaching 104°F (40°C), and the **humidity** can rise as high as 90 percent.

Every few years or so the city has **blizzards** during the winter months, but generally the annual **snowfall** is less than 2 feet. When snow does fall in quantity, however, life in the city is rarely disrupted, particularly over the Christmas period.

## GETTING THERE

**By Air** New York has three main **airports**, John F. Kennedy (JFK), Newark and La Guardia. Most major international carriers and U.S. domestic carriers serve JFK and Newark, while La Guardia receives a few international flights.

There are **direct flights** from London (Heathrow, Gatwick and Stansted), Birmingham, Manchester, Glasgow, Dublin, Montreal, Toronto and Vancouver. Flights from Auckland and Sydney generally stop en route in Los Angeles. There are some direct flights from mainland Europe, although some may stop at another European airport.

**Ticket prices** tend to be highest in summer and at Easter and Christmas, although Christmas Shopping **packages** can be reasonably priced. Check with the airlines, travel agents, flight brokers, travel sections in newspapers and the Internet for the best deals and special offers. Airlines operating **nondirect** flights may offer substantial savings on standard fares. Tickets for **short stays** are generally expensive unless a Saturday night is included. **City Break** packages include flights, accommodations and sightseeing discounts. Approximate **flying times** to New York: east coast of Australia (22 hours), New Zealand (20 hours), Berlin (9 hours), London and Dublin (7 hours), Vancouver (6 hours), Montreal (1 hour), Toronto (1.5 hours).

All **airport taxes** are usually included in the price of the ticket.

**By Rail and Bus** Alternative options for travelers from Canada or elsewhere in the United States are **Amtrak trains** (tel: 800/872-7245), which stop at Pennsylvania Station (33rd Street at 7th Avenue, tel: 212/630-6400), and **long-distance buses**, which terminate at the Port Authority Bus Terminal (8th Avenue at 42nd Street, tel: 212/564-8484).

## TIME

 New York is on Eastern Standard Time, which is one hour ahead of Central Time, two hours ahead of Mountain Time and three hours ahead of Pacific Time.

## CURRENCY AND FOREIGN EXCHANGE

**Currency** The basic unit of currency in the United States is the dollar ($1). One dollar is 100 cents. **Notes** (bills) come in denominations of $1, $5, $10, $20, $50 and $100. All bills are green and are the same size, so look carefully at the dollar amount on them. **Coins** are: 1 cent (penny), 5 cents (nickel), 10 cents (dime), 25 cents (quarter) and 50 cents (half-dollar). There are also one-dollar coins, but these are comparatively rare. An unlimited amount of U.S. dollars can be imported or exported.

U.S. dollar **traveler's checks** are the best way to carry money, and they are accepted as cash in most places (not taxis), as are **credit cards** (Amex, VISA, MasterCard, Diners Card).

**Exchange** The best place to exchange non-U.S. currency in New York is at a bank. There is an automated currency exchange machine at the Times Square Visitor Center (1560 Broadway at 46th Street). Automated teller cards can be used to withdraw money from your bank account in U.S. currency. Your bank will provide you with details of where your cards will be accepted in New York.

## TIME DIFFERENCES

| GMT | New York | U.K. | U.S.A. West Coast | Australia | Germany |
|---|---|---|---|---|---|
| 12 noon | ← 7 am | 12 noon | ← 4 am | → 10 pm | → 1 pm |

## WHEN YOU ARE THERE

## CLOTHING SIZES

| U.K. | U.S.A. | |
|---|---|---|
| 36 | 36 | |
| 38 | 38 | |
| 40 | 40 | |
| 42 | 42 | Suits |
| 44 | 44 | |
| 46 | 46 | |
| 7 | 8 | |
| 7.5 | 8.5 | |
| 8.5 | 9.5 | |
| 9.5 | 10.5 | Shoes |
| 10.5 | 11.5 | |
| 11 | 12 | |
| 14.5 | 14.5 | |
| 15 | 15 | |
| 15.5 | 15.5 | |
| 16 | 16 | Shirts |
| 16.5 | 16.5 | |
| 17 | 17 | |
| 8 | 6 | |
| 10 | 8 | |
| 12 | 10 | |
| 14 | 12 | Dresses |
| 16 | 14 | |
| 18 | 16 | |
| 4.5 | 6 | |
| 5 | 6.5 | |
| 5.5 | 7 | |
| 6 | 7.5 | Shoes |
| 6.5 | 8 | |
| 7 | 8.5 | |

## NATIONAL HOLIDAYS

| Jan 1 | New Year's Day |
|---|---|
| Third Mon Jan | Martin Luther King Day |
| Third Mon Feb | President's Day |
| Mar/Apr | Easter (half day Good Friday, whole day Easter Monday) |
| Last Mon May | Memorial Day |
| Jul 4 | Independence Day |
| First Mon Sep | Labor Day |
| Second Mon Oct | Columbus Day |
| Nov 11 | Veterans' Day |
| Fourth Thu Nov | Thanksgiving |
| Dec 25 | Christmas Day |

Some stores are open for business on national holidays.

## OPENING HOURS

○ Stores
● Offices
● Banks
● Post Offices
● Museums/Monuments
● Pharmacies

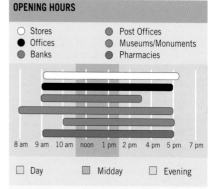

8 am  9 am  10 am  noon  1 pm  2 pm  4 pm  5 pm  7 pm

☐ Day          ☐ Midday          ☐ Evening

**Stores** Hours vary greatly, but most open till 9 pm on one day. Some open Sun noon–5.
**Banks** Some open till 4 pm, or Fri 6 pm. Most are closed Sat, all are closed Sun.
**Post Offices** Open till 1 pm Sat. Smaller offices keep shorter hours.
**Museums** Hours vary. Most open 9:30 or 10 am to 5 or 6 pm. Some keep longer hours Thu, Fri, or Sat. Many are closed Mon.
**Places of Worship** See the Yellow Pages.

**POLICE 911**

**FIRE 911**

**AMBULANCE 911**

**DENTAL EMERGENCY (1-800) 439-9299**

## PERSONAL SAFETY

Crime levels in New York have fallen sharply over recent years, but it is still wise to take sensible precautions:

- At night on the subway stand in the after-hours waiting areas and ride in the center car where the conductor sits.
- Don't walk alone in quiet streets or Central Park after dark.
- Carry only the cash you need; leave other cash and valuables in the hotel safe.
- Report theft or mugging to the police to provide a reference for an insurance claim.

Police assistance:
☎ **911 from any phone**

## TELEPHONES

There are pay-phones on many street corners and most are coin oper-ated. From public phones dial 0 for the operator and give the name of the country, city and number you are calling. You will need at least $5.50 in quarters for an overseas call. Some phones take prepaid phone cards, available at drug-stores and newsstands, and some take credit cards. Dial 1 plus the area code for numbers within the U.S. and Canada. Dial 411 to find U.S. and Canadian numbers.

**International Dialing Codes**
**Dial 011 followed by**
| | |
|---|---|
| **U.K.:** | **44** |
| **Ireland:** | **353** |
| **Australia:** | **61** |
| **Germany:** | **49** |
| **Netherlands:** | **31** |
| **Spain:** | **34** |

## POST OFFICES

The main post office is at 421 8th Avenue/33rd Street. Open 24 hours. Other post offices can be found in the Yellow Pages. Larger branches open Mon–Fri 8–6, Sat 8–1. Mail-boxes are on street corners, often next to litter baskets.

## ELECTRICITY

The power supply is 110/120 volts AC (60 cycles). Sockets take two-prong, flat-

pin plugs. An adaptor is needed for appliances with two-round-pin and three-pin plugs. European appliances also need a voltage transformer.

## TIPS/GRATUITIES

Tipping is expected for all services. As a general guide:

| | |
|---|---|
| Restaurants (service not included) | 15–20% |
| Bar service | 15% |
| Tour guides | discretion |
| Hairdressers | 15% |
| Taxis | 15% |
| Chambermaids | $1 per day |
| Porters | $1 per bag |

## CONSULATES

**U.K.**
(212) 745-0200

**Ireland**
(212) 319-2555

**Canada**
(212) 596-1628

**Australia**
(212) 351-6500

**New Zealand**
(212) 832-4038

## HEALTH

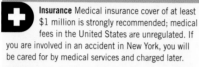

**Insurance** Medical insurance cover of at least $1 million is strongly recommended; medical fees in the United States are unregulated. If you are involved in an accident in New York, you will be cared for by medical services and charged later.

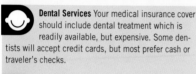

**Dental Services** Your medical insurance cover should include dental treatment which is readily available, but expensive. Some dentists will accept credit cards, but most prefer cash or traveler's checks.

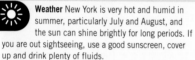

**Weather** New York is very hot and humid in summer, particularly July and August, and the sun can shine brightly for long periods. If you are out sightseeing, use a good sunscreen, cover up and drink plenty of fluids.

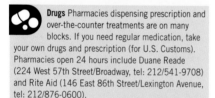

**Drugs** Pharmacies dispensing prescription and over-the-counter treatments are on many blocks. If you need regular medication, take your own drugs and prescription (for U.S. Customs). Pharmacies open 24 hours include Duane Reade (224 West 57th Street/Broadway, tel: 212/541-9708) and Rite Aid (146 East 86th Street/Lexington Avenue, tel: 212/876-0600).

**Safe Water** Drinking unboiled tap water is safe. Mineral water is cheap and readily available.

## CONCESSIONS

**Students** Holders of an International Student Identity Card are entitled to discounts on many attractions.

**Senior Citizens** Seniors will find discounts on many services and attractions. Qualifying age varies from 55 to 65. You need to request a discount up front and may be asked to show proof of age.

**Citypass** A Citypass will save about 50 percent of the cost of full-price admission to attractions like the Empire State Building, and you'll avoid ticket lines. Citypasses, valid for nine days, are available at participating attractions and NYC & Company (▶ 36 and 46).

## TRAVELING WITH A DISABILITY

Since the Americans with Disabilities Act (1990) mandated that public facilities should be accessible to people with disabilities, most of New York has become accessible. Some of the main subway stations in Manhattan are equipped with ramps and elevators, but most are not, however, and some elevators are accessible only with the help of station staff. Public buses, all with lifts and wheelchair spaces, are more reliable.

## CHILDREN

New York is child friendly. Baby-changing facilities are provided in many restrooms in hotels, restaurants and public spaces. Children's events are listed in the Weekend section of the *New York Times*.

## RESTROOMS

Cleanest and safest restrooms are in large hotels, chain bookstores and department stores.

## WILDLIFE SOUVENIRS

Importing wildlife souvenirs sourced from rare or endangered species may be illegal or require a special permit. Before purchase you should check your home country's customs regulations.

# Streetplan

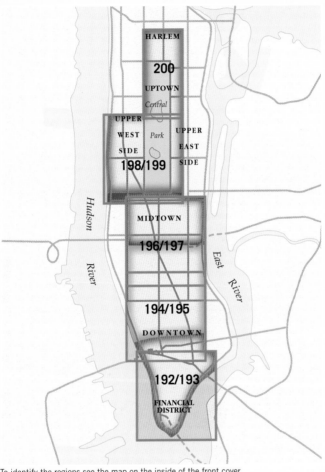

To identify the regions see the map on the inside of the front cover

## Key to Streetplan

- Main road
- Other road
- Park

- Place of interest
- Featured place of interest
- Subway station
  (Station status may be subject
  to change in Lower Manhattan)

| 0 | 100 | 200 | 300 | 400 | 500 yards |
| 0 | 100 | 200 | 300 | 400 | 500 metres |

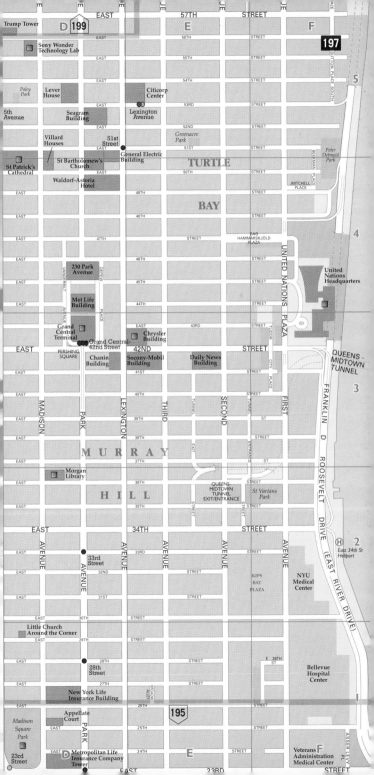

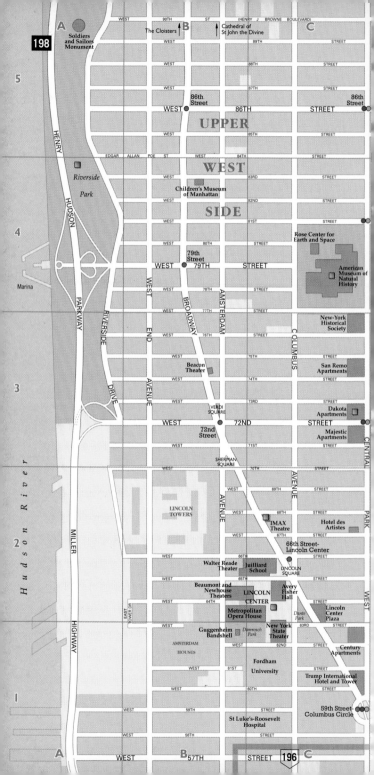

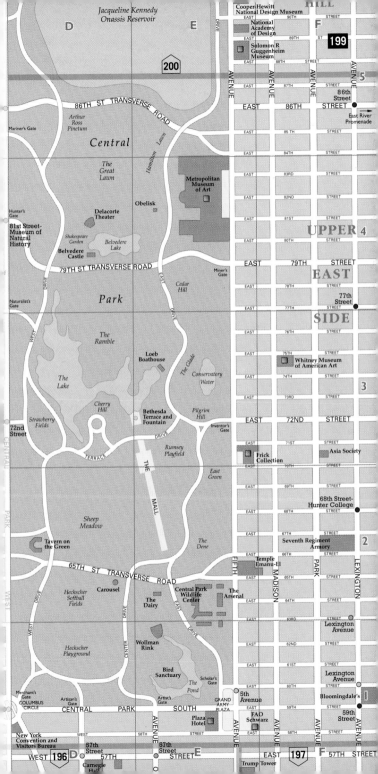

Jacqueline Kennedy
Onassis Reservoir

D    E

DRIVE

Cooper-Hewitt
National Design Museum
National
Academy
of Design

Solomon R
Guggenheim
Museum

90TH    STREET

F    HILL

STREET

199

89TH    STREET

AVENUE

AVENUE

AVENUE

EAST    88TH    STREET

AVENUE

5

EAST    87TH    STREET

86th
Street

86TH    ST    TRANSVERSE    ROAD

EAST    86TH    STREET

Arthur
Ross
Pinetum

East River
Promenade

Central

EAST    85    STREET

Mariner's Gate

EAST    84TH    STREET

The
Great
Lawn

EAST    83RD    STREET

Metropolitan
Museum
of Art

EAST    82ND    STREET

Hamilton Lawn

Obelisk

EAST    81ST    STREET

Hunter's
Gate

Delacorte
Theater

UPPER    4

81st Street-
Museum of
Natural
History

Shakespeare
Garden

Belvedere
Lake

EAST    80TH    STREET

Belvedere
Castle

EAST    EAST

79TH    STREET

79TH ST TRANSVERSE ROAD

EAST    78TH    STREET

Naturalist's
Gate

DRIVE

Cedar
Hill

Miner's
Gate

77th
Street

Park

EAST    77TH    STREET

SIDE

EAST    76TH    STREET

The
Ramble

EAST    75TH    STREET

Whitney Museum
of American Art

DRIVE

Loeb
Boathouse

EAST    74TH    STREET

The
Lake

The Glade

Conservatory
Water

EAST    73RD    STREET

3

Cherry
Hill

Strawberry
Fields

Bethesda
Terrace and
Fountain

Pilgrim
Hill

EAST    72ND    STREET

72nd
Street

Inventor's
Gate

EAST    71ST    STREET

TERRACE

DRIVE

Rumsey
Playfield

Frick
Collection

Asia Society

East
Green

EAST    70TH    STREET

THE MALL

EAST    69TH    STREET

Sheep
Meadow

EAST    68TH    STREET

68th Street-
Hunter College

The
Dene

EAST    67TH    STREET

Seventh Regiment
Armory

2

Tavern on
the Green

EAST    66TH    STREET

FIFTH

Temple
Emanu-El

MADISON

PARK

LEXINGTON

65TH    ST    TRANSVERSE    ROAD

EAST    65TH    STREET

Heckscher
Softball
Fields

Carousel

Central Park
Wildlife Center

The
Arsenal

EAST    64TH    STREET

The
Dairy

DRIVE

EAST    63RD    STREET

Lexington
Avenue

Heckscher
Playground

Wollman
Rink

EAST    62ND    STREET

WEST

DRIVE

CENTER

EAST    61ST    STREET

Lexington
Avenue

Bird
Sanctuary

Scholar's
Gate

EAST    60TH    STREET

Bloomingdale's

1

Merchant's
Gate

COLUMBUS
CIRCLE

Artisan's
Gate

The
Pond

Artist's
Gate

GRAND
ARMY
PLAZA

5th
Avenue

EAST    59TH    STREET

59th
Street

CENTRAL    PARK    SOUTH

Plaza
Hotel

FAO
Schwarz

AVENUE

AVENUE

AVENUE

New York
Convention and
Visitors Bureau

WEST    58TH    STREET    EAST    58TH    STREET

196    D    57th
Street    57TH    STREET

E    EAST

F    57TH    STREET

WEST    57TH    STREET

197

Carnegie
Hall

Trump Tower

200

# STREETPLAN INDEX

## Picture credits

Key for terms appearing below: (t) top; (b) bottom; (l) left; (r) right; (c) center.

Front & back covers (t): Tony Stone Images, (ct): AA Photo Library/Richard G. Elliott, (cb): AA Photo Library/Paul Kenward, (b): AA Photo Library/Ellen Rooney.

The Automobile Association wishes to thank the following photographers and libraries for their assistance in the preparation of this book:

Aquarius Picture Library 14, 114/5; Capital Pictures 17; Corbis 8 (Bettmann), 12 (Craig Lovell), 19, 20/1, 26, 29 (Bettmann); Ronald Grant Archive 15t, 15b; Robert Harding Picture Library 59b; Hulton Getty 26/7, 27, 28, 28/9; Images Colour Library 30; Kelly/Mooney Photography 2ct, 2cb, 2b, 3t, 3b, 11t, 11b, 16, 33, 47, 48, 49, 50t, 51, 52, 53t, 54t, 54b, 55, 56t, 56b, 58, 59t, 60, 64, 65, 68t, 68b, 77, 80, 81t, 81b, 82, 83, 84t, 84b, 85, 86, 87, 89b, 90, 92, 93, 94, 95, 100, 107, 109, 110t, 110b, 111, 113, 114t, 114b, 116t, 116b, 117, 118, 119, 120, 121, 122, 123, 124, 125, 127, 138t, 138b, 140b, 143, 145, 146t, 146b, 148t, 148b, 149, 150t, 150b, 151, 152t, 156, 166b, 169, 172l, 173, 174, 176l, 176r, 178, 180, 183, 184, 185, 189t, 189bl; Chris Orr & Associates 7; Pictures Colour Library 32, 53b; Tony Stone Images 2t, 5; Vintage Magazine Co. Ltd. 13tr; World Pictures 22, 62.

All remaining pictures are held in the Association's own library (AA Photo Library) with contributions from the following photographers: 9, 50b, 88, 89t, 91, 97, 141, 154, 165, 172r, 184 (Richard G Elliott); 9, 57, 99, 139, 142, 144, 168, 179 (Paul Kenward); 10, 61, 63, 108, 166t, 170 (Simon McBride); 126 (David Pollack); 112, 163 (Ellen Rooney); 3c, 135, 137, 140t, 147, 152b, 155 (Clive Sawyer); 189br James Tims.

# Questionnaire

## Dear Traveler

Your comments, opinions and recommendations are very important to us. So please help us to improve our travel guides by taking a few minutes to complete this simple questionnaire.

*Send to:* Spiral Guides, MailStop 66, 1000 AAA Drive, Heathrow, FL 32746–5063

## Your recommendations...

We always encourage readers' recommendations for restaurants, nightlife or shopping – if your recommendation is added to the next edition of the guide, we will send you a FREE AAA Spiral Guide of your choice. Please state below the establishment name, location and your reasons for recommending it.

_____

_____

_____

_____

_____

**Please send me AAA Spiral**_____

(see list of titles inside the back cover)

## About this guide...

**Which title did you buy?**

_____ **AAA Spiral**

**Where did you buy it?** _____

**When?** m m / y y

**Why did you choose a AAA Spiral Guide?** _____

_____

_____

_____

**Did this guide meet your expectations?**

Exceeded ☐   Met all ☐   Met most ☐   Fell below ☐

**Please give your reasons** _____

_____

_____

_____

continued on next page...

**Were there any aspects of this guide that you particularly liked?**

_____

_____

_____

_____

_____

**Is there anything we could have done better?**

_____

_____

_____

_____

_____

## About you...

**Name (Mr/Mrs/Ms)** _____

**Address** _____

_____

_____ **Zip** _____

**Daytime tel nos.** _____

**Which age group are you in?**

Under 25 ☐  25–34 ☐  35–44 ☐  45–54 ☐  55–64 ☐  65+ ☐

**How many trips do you make a year?**

Less than one ☐  One ☐  Two ☐  Three or more ☐

**Are you a AAA member? Yes** ☐  **No** ☐

**Name of AAA club** _____

### About your trip...

When did you book? m m / y y     When did you travel? m m / y y

How long did you stay? _____

Was it for business or leisure? _____

Did you buy any other travel guides for your trip? ☐ Yes  ☐ No

If yes, which ones? _____

_____

**Thank you for taking the time to complete this questionnaire.**